BREAKING

BREAKING

How the Media Works, *when it doesn't* And Why it Matters

MIC WRIGHT

bl!nk

First published in the UK in 2025 by Blink Publishing
An imprint of Bonnier Books UK
5th Floor, HYLO, 105 Bunhill Row,
London, EC1Y 8LZ

Copyright © Mic Wright, 2025

All rights reserved.

No part of this publication may be reproduced, stored or transmitted in any form or by any means, electronic, mechanical, photocopying or otherwise, without the prior written permission of the publisher.

The right of Mic Wright to be identified as Author of this work has been asserted by him in accordance with the Copyright, Designs and Patents Act, 1988.

A CIP catalogue record for this book is available from the British Library.

Hardback ISBN: 9781785121364

Also available as an ebook and an audiobook

1 3 5 7 9 10 8 6 4 2

Design and Typeset by Envy Design Ltd
Printed and bound in Great Britain by Clays Ltd, Elcograf S.p.A.

Every reasonable effort has been made to trace copyright holders of material reproduced in this book, but if any have been inadvertently overlooked the publishers would be glad to hear from them.

The authorised representative in the EEA is
Bonnier Books UK (Ireland) Limited.
Registered office address: Floor 3, Block 3, Miesian Plaza, Dublin 2, D02 Y754, Ireland compliance@bonnierbooks.ie

www.bonnierbooks.co.uk

For Kate, Rosie and Lyra

Contents

Introduction ix
1. **Becoming a Journalist** 1
2. **Who Owns The News?** 23
3. **What's The Story?** 55
4. **An Anatomy of The News** 85
5. **A Matter of Opinions** 113
6. **Political Theatre** 137
7. **The Impractical Question of Impartiality** 161
8. **Interviews and The Art of War** 191
9. **Ethics Isn't a County in England** 213
10. **The Cock-up/Conspiracy Interface** 245
11. **When You Become The Story** 267
12. **The Future of The News** 285
Epilogue 309
Acknowledgements 311
Endnotes 313

Introduction

It was 19 April 2019. I woke up in the early hours and picked up my phone. I opened Twitter and almost immediately I saw the news: my friend, the journalist Lyra McKee, had been shot and killed the night before in Derry. She was 29. She had gone to witness the disturbances in the Creggan area of the city that night because she was a journalist to her core. She wanted to see the events firsthand and explain them to the world. It was the same desire that had led her to start a school newspaper aged 14 and win the Sky News Young Journalist of the Year award at 16. It was this commitment that led her to tell the stories of her ceasefire generation and those of others who died before the fragile peace was achieved.

This book is not about good journalists like Lyra. Nor is it about journalists who risk their lives to report from the world's most dangerous places and those who, like Lyra, are killed in the process. This is a book about the bad news of bad news. I come not to praise journalism nor to bury it, but to look at where and why the media fails us. It's not just about the spread of misinformation, the demand to pump out more content more cheaply, or the temptation to let AI regurgitation take the place of real reporting and insight. It's about those media figures that squander what little trust in journalism remains and the executives who exploit the high hopes of young reporters and put them to work pumping out lowest common denominator slop.

To truly understand the news you consume, you have to understand the processes and people behind it. The sheer volume of information that crashes over us daily means that we need tools to identify the bad faith actors and where misinformation and disinformation twist stories out of shape. We need good journalism. And to know what deserves to be seen as good, you need to be able to identify where journalism is going wrong and, crucially, *why* it's going wrong. That's what I aim to do with this book – to take you on a tour of the terrible so you can focus your attention on the news that really matters.

If you want a book where journalists are the heroes, *All the President's Men* is still in print. This one focuses on the worst aspects of the media in the hope of inspiring those who want to do better. I'm no saint and am very aware of the glass house in which I'm typing these words. It's often said it's easy to criticise but it's not really. To be a media critic is to put yourself into a piñata for an industry that's extremely good at character assassination. So before we get started, let me say it again: if you're one of the good ones, this book isn't about you. Then again, villains never think they're villains, do they?

1.

Becoming a Journalist

How to Get Into It and Why You Probably Shouldn't

'You're miserable, edgy and tired. You're in the perfect mood for journalism.'
– Transmetropolitan, Warren Ellis and ...
Darick Robertson (1997)

'As far as I can remember I always wanted to be a journalist ...' Imagine that narration in a Ray Liotta voice, stick on Tony Bennett's 'Rags to Riches' and smash cut to a montage of footage from films where reporters are the heroes. Leave out the clips of Rupert Murdoch pulling a rubbery face of contrition in front of a parliamentary committee, of Paul Dacre's sneer, of Evgeny Lebedev's desperately unfunny elevation to the House of Lords, of hacks doorstepping the relatives of the recently dead, of cruelty, callousness and cant. Instead, make it look *cool*.

As an industry, journalism is very pleased with itself. Even as circulation figures nosedive, the number of awards ceremonies balloons. The Backslappers Union is bursting at the seams with people whose mantra is that careworn canard about 'speaking truth to power' – an ancient notion that was pinned down by Euripides in the fifth century as *parrhesia* ('to speak boldly'). In fact, journalists generally *love* power; they love to be near it and to feel the indulgent glow of its approval. And people whose fortunes have been built up in other spheres love owning newspapers – they're no longer money-making machines but they remain a means of projecting power and influence.

I spend a lot of my time writing a newsletter about the worst aspects of journalism but I also still love it. As a teenager, I read music magazines voraciously and I was often as much of a fan of the people writing about the bands as the bands themselves. That's why so much of the garbage that is produced under the banner of journalism makes me so angry and anxious. There are many brilliant journalists out there: the ones who shine light into corners of the world that the Establishment's Eye of Sauron would rather remain in darkness; the investigators who pull at knots and loose threads, untangling secrets that the mad, bad and dangerous don't want us to know; and the writers whose knack of turning and re-turning a phrase reveals things about ourselves and the world around us which we'd never thought about before. But those examples can be drowned out by the marketers, the mean and the mendacious. When I was interviewing a senior broadcast journalist for this book, they told me: 'There's a general feeling that has persisted for a good few years now that journalism is worthy of scorn and contempt. That now permeates everything. I don't know how we get that trust back.'

BECOMING A JOURNALIST

That's a damning picture and presents a difficult challenge for a media critic.

I want to subject the industry I've worked in for the past 20 years to a level of scrutiny that it rightly wants to apply to other areas of public life. When Sir Alec Guinness was preparing to play John le Carré's deceptively ordinary spy, George Smiley, in the 1979 TV adaptation of *Tinker Tailor Soldier Spy*, he and the author had lunch with Sir Maurice Oldfield, the former head of the UK's Secret Intelligence Service (a.k.a. MI6). The 'retired' spook was blunt, according to le Carré, who claimed in his autobiography, *The Pigeon Tunnel* (2016), that Oldfield told the actor that the spy novels 'made it that much harder for the Service to recruit decent officers and sources'. Another MI6 officer approached le Carré at a party and snarled that he was 'an utter bastard'. Being considered a traitor to your trade is a tricky position to be in, though it was softened substantially for le Carré by his undeniable talent and the huge sales that came with it. I don't have either of those comforts but, if I get it right, this book should reveal some of the media's secrets and make recruitment to the worst parts of it that bit harder. I'm hoping to be called worse things than 'bastard'.

The British press has a very strong immune response to criticism. Journalists, columnists and their editors circle the wagons faster than a bunch of a cowboys in a cheap Western. Though hacks are fond of posturing as tough types with a relationship to criticism like the one between water and ducks' backs, most – and I don't exempt myself from this – are thin-skinned name-searchers with eggshell egos and a need for attention that would provoke a blush from even the most narcissistic toddler.

BREAKING

So having written all of that, who'd want to be a journalist anyway? And how do you become one?

> Journalism is, as it always has been, one of the freest of all trades . . . No apprenticeship is needed for entering it, and no preliminaries are required for participation in its highest rewards. As a matter of fact, indeed, those rewards are often assigned to men sufficiently qualified for them by native wit or training in other ways, without any previous newspaper drudgery . . . A smart member of parliament, a successful barrister, a versatile clergyman, a retired schoolmaster, a popular novelist, or anyone else with enough influence or intellect, or with a name likely to prove useful, may slip into an editorship or be made a principal lead writer in preference to men of long standing in the office, who perhaps have to teach him his duties and correct his blunders.[1]

The journalist, essayist and historian H.R. Fox Bourne wrote that summary of how people slipped into the trade of journalism in 1887. It could easily be applied to the modern industry where lords and former MPs litter the opinion pages alongside wayward vicars, jobbing novelists, minor celebrities and the offspring of other well-known journalists. For a brief spread of decades in the mid- and late-twentieth century, it was a lot easier for people with no useful family connections, fame or independent wealth to inveigle their way into print and broadcast media. But as local newspapers have fallen into decline, taking much of the on-the-job training with them, and the number of national outlets has contracted, journalism has snapped back to being a trade in which nepotism and dilettantism are rampant.

I'm part of the problem. I'm the first journalist in the history of my family and the first to go to university. But I *did* go to university – and not just any university but one of the two whose graduates are grotesquely over-represented in the ranks of British journalism. Neither Cambridge – where I went – nor Oxford have undergraduate journalism courses but their student newspapers produce a steady stream of people who go on to be writers, reporters, columnists and editors at a national level. Those alumni then tend to repeat the process by hiring in their own image, despite lots of loud public pronouncements on diversity and equality of opportunity. In 2019, *Elitist Britain*, a report produced by the education charity the Sutton Trust and the Social Mobility Commission, found that 44 per cent of Britain's top newspaper columnists had been to Oxford or Cambridge, part of the 72 per cent who attended a Russell Group University, the self-declared gang of Britain's 'most prestigious'. Just 11 per cent of journalists hadn't been to university at all.

It wasn't always like that. While the posh, the pretending to be posh and the desperate to be posh have always been well represented in British journalism – which has always been whiter than a Bing Crosby movie – there did used to be more routes for working-class people to get in at the ground floor and make it to the top. In 1970, the proportion of graduates to non-graduates in journalism was 30:70; by the year 2000, that ratio was reversed. It's shifted from a world where a degree was a bonus to one where it's usually a requirement. That's a big change. For most of the history of journalism in Britain, you had no choice but to learn on the job.

BREAKING

In the United States, universities began offering journalism programmes in 1908. The UK failed to follow suit in any kind of reliable or widespread fashion for the next 60 years. London University's diploma for journalism started in 1919 with no lecturers and no specific teaching on journalism skills, sending its students – including the future novelists Elizabeth Bowen and Penelope Mortimer – to lectures for its existing courses instead. Dr Fred Hunter, in his study of the first journalism courses at London University,[2] writes that there were no journalism exams until 1927, when the papers were set by *Times* journalist F. J. Mansfield, who lectured the students twice weekly.

Mansfield's lectures were compiled into two books, both of which remained in print for more than 30 years. The first, *Sub-Editing: A Book Mainly for Young Journalists*, was published in 1932 and was a textbook on the sub-editor's art – fact-checking, editing, fixing, tweaking, rewriting and restructuring copy, as well as writing intros, subheadings and headlines – but also includes many of its writer's theories and digressions about his trade. *The Complete Journalist* (1936) was intended as a more extensive survey of the industry at the time. Its foreword was written by that famous bastion of ethics David Lloyd George, who made a fortune from flogging honours in his latter years as prime minister and boosted his wealth by investing in newspapers. Sidney Jacobson, who later became Baron Jacobson after a long career as an editor and newspaper executive, studied under Mansfield before starting his career as a reporter on the *Daily Sketch*. He recalled that Mansfield's syllabus covered subbing, reporting, proofreading and newspaper organisation, and that he encouraged his students to produce their own publications once a term.

BECOMING A JOURNALIST

However, *The Complete Journalist* shows that the main source of training for young journalists at the time was through gaining a foothold in the newsroom of one of the many local newspapers. Mansfield wrote that 'the provinces are the natural training ground for all-round journalism. They give the range and variety of experience and the practical touch that is invaluable'.

In 1935, King's College London appointed a full-time director of practical journalism, *News Chronicle* editor Tom Clarke, who developed a course that focused on teaching students how to do the job. This was in line with how journalism education was evolving in the United States but the inconvenient arrival of the Second World War got in the way. University journalism courses in Britain slipped off the agenda until 1970 when the University of Wales in Cardiff began to offer postgraduate diplomas, first in print and then broadcast journalism.

From 1951 onwards, the bulk of professional journalism education was provided by the National Council for Training Journalists (NCTJ), which was founded in response to the 1949 Royal Commission on the Press, which was set up due to public concerns that the small number of media proprietors was leading to limits on free expression, factual inaccuracies (a polite term for barefaced lies) and advertisers influencing editorial content (Boy! Imagine having to worry about all of that . . .) The commission concluded:

> The problem of recruiting the right people into journalism, whether from school or from university, and ensuring that they achieve and maintain the necessary level of education and technical efficiency, is one of the most important facing

BREAKING

the Press, because the quality of the individual journalist depends not only on the status of the whole profession of journalism but the possibility of bridging the gap between what society needs from the Press and what the Press is at present giving it. The problem is the common interest and the common responsibility of proprietors, editors, and other journalists ...

NCTJ trainees worked in newsrooms and were sent out, like a strange category of convicts, to attend day-release classes at local further education colleges. After three years, they took the General Proficiency Test – an appropriately low bar of a name. Then, as now, the grand title of the NCTJ was somewhat deceptive – there was and remains no requirement for journalists to have an NCTJ qualification. In 1965, the NCTJ began to introduce 'pre-entry' courses for students to learn journalism skills *before* securing a job as well as postgraduate qualifications. Later, it began accrediting undergraduate degree programmes with vocational elements, in-company training schemes, and courses developed by other companies. The NCTJ is still the most prominent journalism training programme in the UK.

I didn't do NCTJ training. I learned on the job.

Some jobs just sound cooler than others. Despite usually ranking somewhere between estate agents and cartoon bad guys twirling sinister moustaches in public surveys on trustworthiness, journalists benefit from having an occupation that people assume is quite cool and relatively interesting. Movies and TV shows help enormously by creating a sense that it's all about meeting shadowy

BECOMING A JOURNALIST

sources in dark parking garages and monologuing to corrupt politicians and unhinged industrialists about the meaning of truth. That's partly because showing someone struggling to cut the TV listings to fit or explaining, with fast evaporating patience, to a pushy PR person that their email about a company that sells 'the world's best lug-nuts' will not prompt a big piece in a national newspaper would make for far less engaging dramas.

Fresh out of university, I got my first job in journalism. I found that telling people what I did started well ('Oh, you're a journalist . . . !') but deflated quickly when I said where (' . . . for *Pensions World* magazine.') Pensions?! World?! I was proud of my job (and lucky to get it) but the title sounded instantly comic to anyone expecting me to say something in line with a typical 21-year-old's interests. (No, I *still* don't have a decent pension, even though my two years at *Pensions World* taught me I needed one.) After spending my teenage years obsessed by music magazines and glossy American titles like *Vanity Fair* and *GQ*, why did I end up on a trade magazine based in a monstrosity of an office building opposite East Croydon station? Money. They were willing to give me a salary when other publications, puffed up on prestige, offered only internships and exposure – the thing that kills mountain climbers.

I'd been offered 'jobs' at lots of places with big names but seemingly small wallets when it came to paying for entry-level positions. Internships suited graduates with parents who could bankroll them for six months or more in London or who lived there already. In the absence of rich parents or a booming publishing industry near to me in Norfolk, I had to find a role that paid from day one. My editor at *Pensions World*

BREAKING

was a veteran finance journalist called Stephanie Hawthorne. She'd been at the magazine for quite a few years by the time my CV landed on her desk and had an instinct for avoiding the usual student waffle. Luckily, I stood out to her and I was hired as a staff writer (definition: a person who will be asked to do literally any and all tasks that occur to the editor up to and including the humiliation).

The team was small – the editor, the deputy editor and me – and we shared a design department with other magazines. I quickly got used to tramping upstairs to negotiate a layout with one of several designers whose patience was more worn than the ageing carpets in our singularly unloved office block. Designers often see hacks as a pain in the arse, littering their beautiful creations with lots of ugly and inconvenient copy, while editors tend to expect the moon on a stick, delivered yesterday, with every one of their precious words uncut rather than sacrificed to small gods of style and limited space.

The upside of trade titles is that you learn skills far more quickly than you might at a better resourced and more glamorous title. Responsibility comes quickly. After about six months at *Pensions World*, the deputy editor headed off to a job on a newspaper's money section and I was promoted. I wrote features and edited copy, learning proofing marks that littered the margins like very limited hieroglyphs, and picked up a few rudimentary management skills when a new staff writer was hired to fill the spot I'd vacated. All the time, *Pensions World*'s most famous graduate loomed over us: Madeline Wickham, who'd been a staff writer just like me and had regenerated as Sophie Kinsella, the chart-busting romantic fiction superstar. I could see why a life talking to pensions

BECOMING A JOURNALIST

managers and actuaries might lead someone to fantasising about a world of shoes, sex and shopping.

Pensions World gave me the chance to interview my first politician – the cracker-dry Philip Hammond, then an opposition pensions spokesperson, a long way from his future role as Chancellor – and write my first long-form features. On trade titles, you've got to make your own fun, however tenuous, which is why a feature on flexible benefits went out under the headline 'The Joy of Flex' and a picture of the then-Chancellor was nonsensically captioned 'Gordon Brown: Texture Like Sun' in tribute to The Stranglers' 'Golden Brown', a song about smack rather than the thwack of firm fiscal policy. I could have stayed at *Pensions World* for a few years – my editor was kind, I had lots more to learn, the job was getting easier all the time and the salary was creeping up – but in the end, I only spent 18 months there. I was 22, in possession of ambition almost as big as my unjustified ego, and then ... the iPhone happened.

Stuff magazine was already established as the top title for tech-obsessed people – mostly men, to be honest, as the years of *Loaded* and *FHM*'s market dominance had convinced the publishers that covers with a woman holding the latest hot gadget were essential. When the job of front section editor at the mag was advertised, I applied the same day with a hyperactively written 'review' of the iPhone, a device I had neither seen nor could afford. I was invited to an interview with the editor, an amiable Scot called Fraser MacDonald, and the Apple super fan editor-in-chief, Tom Dunmore, both of whom seemed very cool to me, the accidental finance journalist. After passing the 'is this person going to be bearable in the pub?' portion of the recruitment process, I got the job.

BREAKING

I spent my two years at *Stuff* in charge of the first 20 or so pages of the magazine. My days were filled with seeking out the hundreds of gadgets I needed to fill the space and my nights going to press events promoting those gadgets. It was a riot. We got new toys in the office almost daily and the storeroom was an Aladdin's Cave of samples. I learned how to present videos and make podcasts there as well as a lot more about how to construct a compelling magazine. My deskmate was a very even-tempered guy called Will Findlater – a man with a name that sounds like a distracted sentence from someone who has lost their wallet. Will was very tolerant of my over-energised demeanour and tendency to go from calm to livid in about 30 seconds. The other big influence on me while I was there was Simon Osborne-Walker, the deputy editor, who would oversee me constructing my flat plan (a paper representation of what would go where in the finished magazine), which stretched over several desks and was not to be moved by anyone. Describing it now makes it sound unbelievably archaic.

Stuff was a team and the secret ingredient was that we all got along. The game was to make a magazine that readers would love and which we could, in our monthly post-mortems, convince ourselves was better than our direct rival, the 'hated' *T3*, to which *Stuff*'s beloved former editor had defected not long before. In truth, our 'hatred' for *T3* was more of a professional wrestling-style rivalry.

My problem was I remained ambitious to a fault, still chasing something else even though I loved my job at *Stuff*. The promise of music journalism remained in my peripheral vision. I heard that the music magazine *Q* was planning a redesign and when an ad for a new front section editor there

BECOMING A JOURNALIST

appeared, I *had* to apply. This was destiny, this was a shaft of sunlight breaking through the clouds and hitting a golden typewriter on a pedestal. This was my chance to be in the same world as the names I'd studied in *NME*, *Melody Maker*, *Select*, *Smash Hits* and *Kerrang!* bylines as a teenager: David 'Mr Agreeable' Stubbs, the incomparable Neil Kulkarni, Simon Price (whose Manic Street Preachers' book *Everything* had been a kind of Holy Bible to me as a 15-year-old), the hilarious Sylvia Patterson, endlessly acerbic Steven 'Swells' Wells, Johnny 'Cigarettes' Sharp, David Quantick, Everett True, Ian Penman, Simon Reynolds, the elegant Jon Savage . . . you get the idea.

I did well at the interview, turning up to talk to the publisher, Stuart Williams, and the editor, Paul Rees, with hand-drawn flat plan and a head overflowing with ideas. I think I got the job in the room and spent my two weeks' notice at *Stuff* fizzing with excitement that was close to mania by the time I reached the music floor of Mappin House, just off Oxford Street, where the *Q*, *Kerrang!* and *Mojo* logos were etched into the glass door. Finally, I was a music journalist . . . I thought.

Within the first few hours, it became clear that the *Q* office was not a very happy place and that my arrival was not welcomed. I thought I was going to rock and roll all night and party every day – just one of many occasions that relying on Kiss lyrics has let me down – but it looked more like I was going to stress all day and worry every night. This was not the dream. In fact, it was shaping up to be a complete nightmare. It was only years after I left *Q* that I realised what I'd got wrong: I had wanted to be a music journalist in 1968 or 1978, or, at a push, 1988. But I became one in 2008, at a magazine in crisis, coming from another

BREAKING

sector that no one else on the *Q* staff even remotely respected. An unwise combination of hope and ego had made me think they might be glad to see me. I was living in a dream world. I thought I was joining a pirate ship but I was setting myself up to, at best, walk the plank and more likely be keel-hauled.

The problem with *Q* was the same most music magazines were having at the time: it no longer knew what it was for or who it was trying to please. For several years, it had been addicted to lists and chasing the kind of editorial ideas that had led men's magazines into a death spiral around the U-bend ('The Sex Issue!!!!!!'). Constant redesigns are a sign of a diseased magazine. When I arrived at *Q*, yet another redesign and rebrand was in progress, and the well-respected but extremely taciturn deputy editor was being 'managed out' – he went to the *Observer*, where he's much happier – and a talented but wayward designer who'd been a big hit at the movie mag *Empire* had been recruited. He spent money like a horny sailor on shore leave, usually with the same sort of underwhelming returns.

My job was to fill the front section of the magazine just as I had at *Stuff*, but where I'd been trusted and valued there, at *Q* I felt undermined and actively disliked. Looking back at the situation as a 40-year-old rather than as the over-emotional, over-enthusiastic 24-year-old that I was then, I completely understand. There had been other candidates for the role who the other section editors knew and liked. And there I was, looking by any measure like a clueless cuckoo in the nest, a little shit who was surely only hired because the editor assumed he could rely on him to do what he was told and so would, no doubt, be utterly untrustworthy.

I could feel my enthusiasm draining from me day by day. I was expected to plan and commission the section, but any

BECOMING A JOURNALIST

writing beyond filler and captions was to be farmed out to one of a huge list of commissioned writers, among them many of the people I had admired so much as a teenage music magazine fanatic. Sometimes that could be fun – I got to send David Quantick out dressed as Angus Young from AC/DC, complete with schoolboy outfit – but it was often frustrating. I would have a good idea for a feature or interview and then be presented with half-arsed and half-written copy from a jaded hack which I would then have to smash into shape before it was further tenderised by the subs desk.

I managed nine months at *Q*. My resignation was hastened by incidents such as being bollocked after I explained to the Dandy Warhols' PR that it was the boss rather than me who had spiked a feature where they were going to play cricket at Lord's, and the interminable inquest into why Razorlight's Johnny Borrell – a frontman so irritating the magazine should have come with a free packet of antihistamines – featured on the front cover of a disastrously low-selling issue even though all three section editors had vehemently argued against it. I hated my job and it's particularly grim to hate your job when you'd stumbled into it thinking you'd achieved your dream.

In Ted Kessler's excellent book, *Paper Cuts*,[3] about his long career as a music journalist, my short stint at *Q* is rightly covered as a total disaster. While I appear by name in the acknowledgements, in the narrative itself I'm just one of 'a raft of fresh editors hired for the new dawn specifically from non-music titles from film, lads' and tech magazines'. That I was (and remain) fanatical about music didn't and doesn't matter because I never got a chance to show it; I arrived when the magazine was being forced in an insane direction, totally diluting anything that made it interesting.

BREAKING

Out of *Q*, aged 25, and not certain that I could hack it as a journalist at all, I was lucky enough to be invited for a meeting by David Rowan, the launch editor of the newly rebooted UK edition of *Wired*. I pitched the idea of a story on the Impossible Project, an ultimately successful attempt to reboot the production of Polaroid-style instant film, and found myself dispatched to the Netherlands on a reporting job that restored my faith in my ability to talk to people and line up words in vaguely appealing ways. That assignment went well enough that I was then commissioned to write about Kodak's attempt at a revival. I flew out to Rochester, New York, to meet the executive team and wander around the snowy city. The third in that trilogy of *Wired* pieces was a feature on Stuxnet, a computer virus designed to destroy Iranian nuclear reactors that was absolutely covered in the virtual fingerprints of the US and Israeli intelligence services.

Feature writing for American publications is an entirely different beast to the somewhat looser approach of the UK industry: there is less space for jokes and far more of a focus on fact-checking. *Wired* features – in common with pieces in the magazine's Condé Nast stablemate *The New Yorker* – are subjected to line editing and fact-checking that produces long lists of queries and requests for clarification, some for the writer and others for the subjects of the piece.

Freelancing for *Wired* was as close to perfect as the job gets; I now knew I was capable of writing 5,000 words and telling a complex story with no problem. Those trips – snowbound in a motel in upstate New York and wandering around the post-industrial landscape of a strange Dutch city – made me feel like a real reporter, even without the trilby with a piece of card sticking out of the brim

BECOMING A JOURNALIST

reading PRESS. Writing long features is fun because you start with a lot of space and only a rough idea of how you're going to fill it. The challenge isn't just to get hold of the facts – that's the relatively easy part – but to find the 'colour', the details that will elevate it into something truly entertaining and carry the reader with you. For great colour, you need to watch and listen intently, taking account of the small details that fill in the scene.

I was just finding my feet as a freelancer when I was offered the chance to go back to *Stuff* as the news editor of its website. The temptation to be back with my friends again was too much to resist – but I should have. I lasted two months. I had work for *Wired* that hadn't been published yet. One day, I was called from my desk by the publisher and told in portentous terms that I was being suspended for moonlighting for a competitor. I hadn't been, and the fact that I was marched off the premises set me off: I resigned the same day with the kind of self-righteous and self-dramatising high dudgeon that only someone in their mid-twenties can manage.

Freelancers are mercenaries but without the potential for glory or the pay packet. The term 'freelancer' is derived from an old word for a soldier of fortune – literally someone whose lance had not been sworn to any particular master – but the modern version tends to earn far fewer medals. It's a similar kind of sad decline as ancient wolves becoming modern lap dogs. I've been freelance on and off since I left *Stuff* for the second time. The freelancer's curse is that a large percentage of your time is spent chasing payments as invoices disappear into the publishers' accounting departments and then have to be pursued like so many white rabbits. One wheeze particularly beloved by the bigger companies is to introduce a new

BREAKING

payments system that requires you to fill in an ever more byzantine range of forms, as well as supplying a blood sample and a full set of fingerprints. These new 'efficient' systems never result in faster payment despite the same reassurances every time.

Another truism of the British media is that right-wing outfits pay more and faster than their supposedly more egalitarian centre-left rivals. Publications like the *Guardian* and the *New Statesman* tend to take the position that you should feel rather grateful for gracing their pages and that payment is very much at their discretion. Some more moneyed editors at those titles seem to consider it an appalling oversight to be born without some form of independent wealth. As in many areas of British society, the media's posh kids go out of their way to pretend they're (lower) middle class or even drag up entirely as what they imagine a working-class person may be like. However, you'll soon discover who they really are when they buy a home in their early twenties or coyly reveal that their 'housemates' serve double-duty as tenants.

Deprived of a rich but ailing distant relative with a haunted house that I need only live in for one night to inherit, I was reduced to bumbling around looking for work again. This time, I found myself as a contracted writer for the *Daily Telegraph*'s 'Blogs' section, a long-since erased project which was edited at the time by Damian Thompson, a somewhat Mephistophelian figure who styles himself as 'Holy Smoke' on Twitter. Damian – whose book *The Fix: How Addiction Is Invading Our Lives and Taking Over Your World* prompted the writer Tanya Gold to accuse him of writing 'a poison pen letter to Alcoholics Anonymous' – was an enthusiastic promoter of young writers but also more than mildly terrifying. He would occasionally burst into editorial meetings or

BECOMING A JOURNALIST

leader conferences to offer a furious denunciation of someone or something, and was somewhat capricious when it came to who was up and down among his office favourites.

For £1,000 a month, I was meant to write one piece a week for *Telegraph* Blogs, but I wrote far more, addicted to the bylines and the controversy that came with them, and utterly blind to how I was dragging down my own rate. The name of the game was to respond at speed to the news lines of the day, finding the most enervating angle possible, something to make the comment section froth. If your pieces could provoke a social media storm and a multi-day scrap, well, that was all the better.

After the *Telegraph*, I spent some time writing for the tech news site The Next Web before a failed attempt at starting my own publication – The Malcontent – which taught me how quickly you can run out of budget when you're trying to pay all your contributors and drum up advertising. I went back to freelancing and since 2020 have run a media criticism newsletter called Conquest of the Useless, its title borrowed from Werner Herzog's account of the chaotic process of filming *Fitzcarraldo*. That film's story of dragging a steamship over the Andes seemed like a good analogy for the experience of working in the British media.

I've shared my own path through journalism to show you that I've experienced the industry from many different perspectives, seeing the patterns and pitfalls along the way. I don't criticise journalism because I hate it but because I love what it can be.

I like newsrooms. They are edgy places that once revolved around getting the next print edition 'off stone' but are now round-the-clock machines for pumping out content. The word 'content'

BREAKING

used to really wind me up but it's a bit like being a butcher and objecting to how sausages get made. You can spend ages on some copy or toss it off with casual contempt, but it all becomes 'content' in the end. And online it's often – despite the claims of various vendors of expensive analytics software – hard to predict what will be a hit. A piece you've laboured over for weeks and feel deeply proud of may languish unloved and largely unread while a quick news hit, gimmick or juvenile observation might rack up hundreds of thousands of views in a couple of hours. It pays not to get precious about the things you write, especially as you'll meet plenty of editors who'll rip your copy apart or furnish it with a headline that entirely misrepresents your point.

Young writers are often lured into mining their personal lives and, more importantly, personal problems when they really shouldn't. In my twenties, I would write about pretty much anything, up to and including the time when I was violently assaulted outside a pub. That means pictures of my red eyes and swollen jaw are available online for anyone to 'enjoy' via Google, as well as many, many half-arsed, quarter-thought-out opinions that I had when I was 25, which can be dug out and presented to me with the now classic online riposte, 'This you?' Editors have a duty of care to young writers but they also have targets to hit, and if they've got some kid who can type straight and is willing to say controversial things and expose aspects of their life that the comment section and social media will descend upon like hungry, hypocritical vultures, they will exploit them.

The other thing that is almost unavoidable in the British media – if you decide to work in the mainstream – is that you will work for and with an almost comically appalling rogues gallery

BECOMING A JOURNALIST

of bastards, charlatans and outright monsters, who, like all great villains, will not remotely recognise themselves as such. High on the list of the notorious ones I've worked alongside is Milo Yiannopoulos, a man who'd done his time at the *Daily Telegraph* as one of Damian's proteges but who was running his own publication – *The Kernel* – by the time I came into his orbit. It was a chaotic outfit – cruel, recklessly uninterested in legal concerns and glacial in paying its invoices. My brief association with Milo – a man who worked very hard to turn his name into a mononym and succeeded for a while – was like seeing kerosene tossed around on a daily basis. He postured as a journalist, acted like a troll and ached to be a celebrity. After we had splintered apart due to his ongoing unwillingness to pay his bills (and my invoices), I hugely regretted ever being connected to him. I've been explaining ever since that I knew him in his 'regional troll' phase rather than his 'international alt-right influencer' incarnation, but it's not a great excuse. I should have stayed very far away from him.

Apologising or admitting to any kind of regret is basically a professional disadvantage in the British media; columnists simply pretend their minds are wiped on a regular basis, allowing them to totally disavow previous opinions that now look idiotic or cruel. One of the best examples of this is when the commentariat went from denouncing Princess Diana as a harlot, a hussy and a bad mother on the day before her sudden death in Paris to heralding her as a saint, more sinned against than sinning, once the news broke. They experienced no shame about this; shame is for people who don't have media jobs.

Some journalists see journalism as a trade, others see it as a profession; I prefer to think of it as an affliction. I've tried to stop

BREAKING

being a journalist several times in my career so far and abjectly failed to make it stick, bouncing back into the world of bylines and gossip with a grim inevitability. On the odd occasion when I'm asked to talk about the job in schools and colleges, I try to strip it of any sense of glamour. At its most basic – and most journalism is basic – a journalist's role is to notice things, ask questions about them, write down what they find out and double-check that they're right. In the world of political journalism, you need to add an extra layer based on the question popularised by Jeremy Paxman but originally formulated by legendary *Times* foreign correspondent Louis Herren: 'Why is this lying bastard lying to me?'

While the routes into Establishment journalism are narrower now than they were in the mid- and late-twentieth century, there are many more ways of doing the job without asking for permission. The golden age of blogs may be over and the newsletter boom may not last much longer, but new platforms mean new ways of reaching audiences and reporting on stories. You don't need to be employed by a media proprietor to tell stories and their power is receding. It's also possible to make money producing journalism solo but you have to build and maintain a personal audience in a way writers, columnists and reporters in the past simply didn't need to do. They could rely on the amplifying power of the masthead – and those people lucky enough to still be employed by news organisations still do. I make a large part of my income now as an independent media critic with a newsletter I built up from nothing, but I still write columns and do original reporting for other publications. As much as the industry frustrates and angers me, I can't help myself. You can always spot a journalist by their penchant for running towards disaster.

2.

Who Owns The News?

Who Pays the Piper and Who Sets the Tune?

'What the proprietorship of these papers is aiming at is power, and power without responsibility – the prerogative of the harlot throughout the ages.'
– Stanley Baldwin in a speech to his supporters at the Queen's Hall, London (17 March 1931)

To get to the root of how and why 'news' and the wider media works in Britain, you need to understand two men – one long dead and one stubbornly still alive (at the time of writing): Alfred Harmsworth (a.k.a. Lord Northcliffe) and Rupert Murdoch (unlikely to ever be Lord Anything). The former created the modern tabloid sensibility and the latter rebooted it for the late twentieth century, changing the role and reach of the newspaper proprietor forever.

Harmsworth was a genius. Not a genius for *good* but a genius

BREAKING

nonetheless. The Dublin-born son of an English barrister and well-to-do amateur opera singer Irish mother, he became a freelance journalist after his teacher, J. V. Milne – father of *Winnie the Pooh* creator A. A. Milne – encouraged him to start a school magazine. By 1888, when he was just 23, Harmsworth had devised *Answers to Correspondents*, a magazine that did exactly what the title promised – readers submitted questions and it published answers, padding out its pages with jokes, short articles and fiction. A slim publication – just 12 pages long – priced at an affordable penny, it was published on Saturdays, when Harmsworth's target audience of literate clerks and shop workers generally had a day off and money to spend.

Using a business strategy of which his descendants remain fond, Harmsworth's concept was 'inspired' – a word I'm using here as it's more polite than 'shamelessly ripped off from' – by *Tit-Bits*, a weekly magazine founded in 1881 which collected interesting bits of information and mixed them with dramatic human interest stories and fiction. In fact, *Answers to Correspondents* was so 'inspired' by *Tit-Bits* that its name was lifted whole cloth from a regular section in the older magazine called . . . 'Answers to Correspondents'.

While *Tit-Bits* published early stories from authors including H. Rider Haggard (author of *King Solomon's Mines*), Isaac Asimov and P. G. Wodehouse, Harmsworth either wrote *Answers* himself or plagiarised material from American publications that his readers were unlikely to have seen. The questions included hypochondria-stoking health concerns ('How can you cure freckles?', 'Should men shave?'), speculative gossip ('What does the Queen eat?') as well as the bizarre and outright racist ('Can monkeys smoke?', 'Why don't Jews ride bicycles?'). When Harmsworth published

WHO OWNS THE NEWS?

fiction written by other people, he often rewrote the stories to add his own 'to be continued . . .' cliffhanger.

With his brother, Harold, handling the finances, Harmsworth began to build an empire, using his instinct for hyperbole, tricks, distortion and deception. At first, *Answers* wasn't profitable but the brothers rapidly increased the readership with gimmicks and competitions. Long before newspaper and magazine executives began talking about 'brand extensions', the Harmsworths produced puzzles, fountain pens, pipes, 'health cures' and even a line of coffee as a means of pushing the magazine. Their competitions included giving away a £100 note and offering £1 a week for life to the reader who could most accurately guess how much gold and silver was stored in the Bank of England.

In 1894, the Harmsworths acquired London's *Evening News* and the *Edinburgh Daily Record*, before Alfred founded his first original newspaper, the *Daily Mail*, in 1896. His stable also included a wide range of halfpenny periodicals – undercutting the salacious, thrill-packed Victorian penny dreadfuls – that stretched from true crime to children's titles like *Comic Cuts* ('Amusing without being vulgar!') and a women's magazine, *Forget-Me-Not* ('A pictorial journal for the home'). Harmsworth's original title, *Answers to Correspondents*, was ultimately so successful that it ran as a standalone publication until 1956 and lives on as a page in the *Daily Mail* to this day.

Shortly after they launched the *Daily Mail*, Alfred and Harold incorporated Harmsworth Brothers Limited; their publications were selling more than one million copies combined by that point. Five years later, in 1849, they brought together their many ventures as Amalgamated Press and began launching and acquiring more

BREAKING

newspapers. Alfred founded the *Daily Mirror* in 1903, swooped in to take over the *Observer* – the world's oldest Sunday newspaper, founded in 1791 – in 1905 and *The Times* (founded 1785) in 1908 after both teetered on the edge of closure. He also snatched the *Sunday Times* – which had first been published under that name in 1822 but wasn't then connected to *The Times* – in 1908. The game of Monopoly wasn't invented until 1935 but in 1900s Britain, Harmsworth was already playing it and winning.

The *Daily Mail* fundamentally changed how newspapers worked. As he did with his magazines, Harmsworth ruthlessly undercut his rivals; they sold for a penny so his *Daily Mail* went for a halfpenny. With its populist tone and news values that always privileged entertainment over facts, the *Mail* was an instant success. The Harmsworths had planned a print run of 100,000 copies on day one, but it rose to almost 400,000 and the company quickly had to secure more printing capacity as readership swelled to 500,000.

Politicians and other grandees rushed to congratulate Harmsworth on his success. They included the Prime Minister, Lord Salisbury, who sent an enthusiastic telegram. Harmsworth replied with (faux) modesty that the rising circulation figures were 'sudden and unexpected'. The suggestion that Salisbury was rather less kind in private has been a resilient one. The quote attributed to him – 'It is a newspaper produced by office boys for office boys' – echoes a line from Thackeray's novel *The History of Pendennis*, in which the fictional *Pall Mall Gazette* is described by the titular character as 'written by gentlemen for gentlemen'. There's no solid proof that Salisbury delivered that Thackerayian sneer but plenty of others made similar remarks on the record.

WHO OWNS THE NEWS?

The historian G. M. Trevelyan snobbishly wrote: 'The printing press following the law of supply and demand, now appeals to the uneducated mass of all classes.'[4] Harmsworth simply saw the business opportunity offered by an increasingly literate population in the wake of the Education Act of 1870, which gave every child the chance to attend school.

The *Mail* also recognised that women were a profitable market and dedicated a section to 'female interests' from the very beginning. Of course, Harmsworth announced the innovation in the most patronising and of-the-time manner possible: 'Movements in a woman's world – that is to say, changes in dress, toilet manners, cookery, and home matters generally – are as much entitled to receive attention as nine out of ten of the matters which are treated of in the ordinary daily paper. Therefore, two columns are set aside exclusively for ladies.'

Harmsworth warned his newsroom that he consulted 'fifty women of all classes' for their opinions about the paper's features and that they would not 'be bluffed by journalists with only a men's outlook', so the *Mail*'s staff should 'read the woman's page every day'. In 1899, Harmsworth hired Winston Churchill's aunt, Lady Sarah Wilson, to become one of the world's first war correspondents, tasking her to send dispatches from the Siege of Mafeking, where she was living with her husband, Captain Gordon Chesney Wilson, the aide-de-camp to Colonel Robert Baden-Powell, the future founder of the Scouts and then-commanding officer of the British forces fighting the Boers.

This feature not only welcomed women into the fold, but also introduced a key facet of the paper: the *Mail* relied heavily on having an 'enemy' for its readers to fear. The Second Boer War

BREAKING

allowed it to adopt a jingoistic and aggressively patriotic tone, and the paper went on to exploit Chinese immigration to Britain in the early twentieth century with a barrage of 'Yellow Peril' stories. Those only died down when the growing threat from Germany gave Harmsworth and his editors a more immediate 'terrifying' story. When the First World War began in 1914, Harmsworth – who was made Lord Northcliffe in 1903 then bumped up to Baron Northcliffe in 1905, after handing over a huge amount of cash for the privilege – published the sarcastically titled *Scaremongerings from the Daily Mail 1896–1914* to hammer home how long he'd been prophesying war with Germany. The *Star*, a rival newspaper, sneered: 'Next to the Kaiser, Lord Northcliffe has done more than any other living man to bring about war.'

Lord Northcliffe's fellow press baron Lord Beaverbrook, who himself had started out as plain old William Maxwell Aitken, wrote of him:

> [Northcliffe was] a man of brilliant creative talents, touched by the hand of genius. He was on the whole democratic in opinion and was never carried away by royalty or aristocracy, yet he liked his titles ... His power was so considerable that it was of the utmost importance to secure his assistance or at any rate his neutrality.[5]

The two men were both heavily involved in the production of government propaganda during the First World War; Northcliffe as director of propaganda in enemy countries and Beaverbrook as minister of information.

Tom Clarke, who you met in the previous chapter kicking off

WHO OWNS THE NEWS?

journalism education at King's College London, wrote a book about his time as the *Daily Mail's* news editor. *My Northcliffe Diary*[6] is a unique insight into the proprietor's thinking, though it comes garnished with an unhealthy portion of sycophancy: Clarke often refers to Northcliffe by his nickname 'The Chief' and seems rather bedazzled by his boss. Early in the book, he writes:

> Working for Northcliffe, one got four compelling impressions:
> 1. His ambition for power through his newspapers, though not necessarily for money;
> 2. His 'Britishness' which did not prevent his working always of closer amity between the English-speaking peoples;
> 3. His volcanic intolerance of slipshod work of any sort, whether in his own business or elsewhere;
> 4. His uncanny instinct, which he called his 'sixth sense'.

Clarke's analysis of his boss's strengths was astute. Northcliffe did have an innate understanding of what interested the public. His perception of stories and how they sell a newspaper is as valid now as it was in the early twentieth century when he was lecturing Clarke on his vision. He separated news stories into two categories – actualities ('reports of happenings') and talking points ('getting topics people are discussing and developing them or stimulating a topic oneself'). Northcliffe's instinct was that triggering debates was the way to hold onto a reader.

He was right. By 1914, Northcliffe controlled 40 per cent of Britain's morning newspaper market, 45 per cent of the evening newspaper audience and 15 per cent of Sunday sales.

BREAKING

He dominated the industry in a way that no other proprietor had done before or since. The *Daily Mail*'s model of short news stories with lashings of emotion and sensationalism shared a lot with the sex-, crime- and fear-drenched 'yellow journalism' practised by William Randolph Hearst and his rival Joseph Pulitzer across the Atlantic. There was something of a mutual appreciation society. In 1900, Pulitzer invited Northcliffe to come to New York and edit an edition of his newspaper, *The World*.

On 31 December 1900, Northcliffe took charge of Pulitzer's newsroom; he demanded that no story be longer than 250 words. News was to be boiled down to the bone with plenty of space for the advertising to shine. The special edition sold out and the print run was extended by 100,000 copies. In his editorial, Harmsworth laid out his vision for a 'twentieth-century newspaper': 'I am profoundly hopeful of the future. I am convinced that the Press has its best days to come ... Already, it is casting off the domination of party and the serfdom of tradition, and has set its face steadfastly toward the light.'

Northcliffe's definition of 'the light' differed greatly from the generally accepted notion. The historian Piers Brendon, in a book that placed the press baron alongside Arthur Balfour, Emmeline Pankhurst and Robert Baden-Powell as one of 'four figures who defined their age', wrote:

> [His] methods made the *Mail* the most successful newspaper hitherto seen in the history of journalism. But by confusing gewgaws with pearls, by selecting the paltry at the expense of the significant, by confirming atavistic prejudices, by oversimplifying the complex, by dramatising the humdrum,

by presenting stories as entertainment, and by blurring the difference between news and views, Northcliffe titillated, if he did not debouch, the public mind; he polluted, if he did not poison, the wells of knowledge.[7]

Every part of Brendon's criticisms about Northcliffe could be applied to certain elements of the modern British media. It is as easily distracted as a toddler in a toy shop, drawn to novelty over depth and addicted to boiling every issue down to a soap opera of personalities. Northcliffe taught the press the true power of titillation and it's an addiction it has happily maintained ever since.

On 24 March 1921, as recorded in Tom Clarke's *My Northcliffe Diary*, the real-life equivalent of a crossover episode in a long-running TV series took place on the French Riviera. Clarke writes that he met 'a big, hefty Australian, as jolly and mischievous as a schoolboy'. That big character was Keith Murdoch, who was running the Australian United Cable Service in London from *The Times* office, where he came into frequent and friendly contact with Northcliffe.

Before the war, Murdoch had started his journalism career at the *Pall Mall Gazette* in London – a job he lost because of his stammer – before returning to his native Australia, where he worked as a parliamentary reporter and political correspondent. When war broke out, he attempted to become Australia's official war correspondent but lost out to the more experienced Charles Bean. He was instead appointed managing editor for the London cable service run by the Australian *Sun* and *Melbourne Herald*. However, he ended up getting one of the biggest scoops of the war through circuitous means.

BREAKING

In January 1915, Murdoch headed to New Zealand to cover talks between the country's Prime Minister, William Massey, and Australia's Prime Minister, Andrew Fisher. While there, he was asked by the Australian Defence Minister, George Pearce, to break his return journey to London and visit Egypt to check on some issues with supplies and mail destined for Australian troops. Murdoch, suspecting all was not well, then took a chance and got permission from Sir Ian Hamilton, the commander of the Australian campaign in Turkey, to visit Australian troops in Gallipoli and write his impressions for various newspapers, subject to the usual military censorship.

Upon arrival, it was clear that the Gallipoli campaign was an ongoing disaster. Not only this, but Murdoch was persuaded by Ellis Ashmead-Bartlett, the *Daily Telegraph*'s correspondent in the region, that censorship was being used to suppress criticism of the failing leadership and fatal tactics. Carrying a letter from Ashmead-Barlett to the British Prime Minister, Herbert Asquith, Murdoch was arrested by British military police as he passed through Marseille. Hamilton had got wind of the letter's existence and it was confiscated. That didn't stop Murdoch who, after arriving in London, wrote his own account – 8,000 words made up of his own impressions, second-hand accounts and what he remembered from Bartlett's letter. He sent it to Prime Minister Fisher and it was excoriating: 'Along the line of communications ... are countless high officers and conceited young cubs who are plainly only playing at war ... appointments to the general staff are made from motives of friendship and social influence.'

Fisher passed the letter to Asquith and the British war cabinet, then to the editor of *The Times*, triggering a huge splash.

WHO OWNS THE NEWS?

That, in turn, brought Murdoch into Northcliffe's orbit. With no children that he publicly acknowledged – he actually had four: a son conceived with a 16-year-old maid when he was 17 and two further sons and a daughter with his mistress, Kathleen Wrohan – Northcliffe became a mentor and sort of surrogate father to Murdoch, easing his progress in London society and the press.

Leveraging those new connections and pushing for his byline to be featured prominently on his reports, Murdoch gained a level of fame in Australia. When he returned after the war, he was appointed editor-in-chief of the *Melbourne Herald* and began investing in other newspapers. He also encouraged the *Herald* to explore the new and burgeoning field of radio – leading to stakes in 11 stations – and, presaging his son's true antipathy for the BBC and public-service broadcasters, worked hard to prevent the Australian Broadcasting Commission (later the Australian Broadcasting Company) from starting its own news service.

While his father began building his empire, Rupert – the second of his four children with Elisabeth Murdoch née Greene – attended the private Geelong Grammar School, where he edited the school newspaper (the *Corian*) and a student magazine (*If Revived*), as well as working part-time for his father at the *Herald*. Like his father, Rupert was drawn to the UK and headed to Worcester College, Oxford, aged 18, to study philosophy, politics and economics (PPE), the degree most beloved by politicos and hacks. An unnamed contemporary of the student Murdoch, quoted by William Shawcross in *Murdoch: Ringmaster of the Information Circus* (1992), remembered him as being 'mainly known to be richer than the rest of us in the sense that where everyone else went on foot or on a clapped-out bicycle, he was the only person one

BREAKING

knew who had a car'. Another little birdie – perhaps a red-breasted one – told Steve Hewlett that, as well as having a bust of Lenin in his rooms, the young Murdoch had connections with the Oxford Communist Party.[8] On one occasion, having travelled down to London for a demonstration organised by the *Daily Worker* (the party paper which later became the *Morning Star*), Murdoch got back late and found himself locked out of college. He told his friend not to worry and produced the key to the Communist Party office, where the pair then slept on the floor. In the morning – or so the pal claimed – the man delivering that day's pile of the *Worker* greeted Murdoch with a cheery, 'Morning, comrade!'

This student leftism was not well received by Sir Keith – the elder Murdoch had been knighted in 1933 – who wrote in a letter to Hugh Cudlipp, the *Daily Mirror*'s famous editor-turned-editorial-director, that his son was '[developing the] most alarming left-wing views'.[9] Despite an unsuccessful run to become Oxford Labour Club treasurer – he was expelled after throwing a party to bribe people to vote for him – and earning the nickname Red Rupert, Murdoch's politics weren't taken all that seriously by other students. The university newspaper, *Cherwell*, described him as 'Rupert Murdoch, cataclysmic chauffeur from the outback' and 'a brilliant betting man'. On another occasion, Murdoch was featured in an article headlined 'Australians at Worcester', which saw him pictured alongside the college's only other prominent antipodeans: a pair of wallabies which had been purchased for the grounds as a novelty.

After he graduated from Oxford, Murdoch worked as a sub-editor at the *Daily Express*, having been set up in the job by his father, who of course knew its proprietor, Lord Beaverbrook.

WHO OWNS THE NEWS?

He was just 21 when, in October 1952, Sir Keith died suddenly. Murdoch flew back to Australia to take control of his father's company, News Ltd, and discovered that, as a result of tax bills and corporate manoeuvring, he was left with one small newspaper – *The News* in Adelaide. Summoned decades later to give evidence to a UK parliamentary committee that was examining the phone hacking scandal which engulfed his British newspaper empire, Murdoch said: 'I was brought up by a father who was not rich but who was a great journalist, and he, just before he died, bought a small paper, specifically in his will saying that he was giving me the chance to do good.'

Did Murdoch take that 'chance to do good'? I don't think so. But what he did do was move quickly and ruthlessly to acquire other titles in Australia. Once he achieved almost total domination of that media market – including making shrewd use of airfreight to found the country's first national newspaper, *The Australian*, in 1964 – the company spread to New Zealand. And then, in 1968, Murdoch arrived in the UK, securing a stake in the *News of the World*, a scandal sheet that had survived and occasionally thrived since 1843 by serving up a sensational soup of crime, sleaze and titillation. The *News of the World*'s reputation was set early in its existence. J. W. Robertson Scott's institutional biography of the *Pall Mall Gazette*[10] describes how the paper's editor Frederick Greenwood is given a copy of the *News of the World* by its then owner Lord Riddell, looks at it, throws it in the wastepaper basket then retrieves it and decides to burn it for fear that 'the cook may read it'. When Murdoch originally arrived on the scene in 1968, he presented himself to the paper's owners, the Carr family, as a saviour, protecting them from a takeover bid by the rival publisher

BREAKING

Robert Maxwell, the future owner of the *Daily Mirror*. By June 1969, Murdoch had manoeuvred himself to gain total control of the *News of the World* and replaced Sir William Carr, who had been in poor health, as chairman of the company.

The concept of the 'kiss and tell' – dumping a truckload of cash on a celebrity or celebrity-adjacent person's doorstop in return for 'sordid' revelations – began with the *News of the World*. In 1960, with circulation falling, the paper paid the enormous sum of £35,000 (roughly £675,000 in today's money) for a series of interviews with British actress and 'blonde bombshell' Diana Dors. She desperately needed money after the breakdown of her marriage and, to borrow the language of the tabloids, 'revealed all' about the sex parties she and her husband held at their home with celebrity guest lists.

Murdoch's *News of the World* continued this tradition from day one. He promoted the paper's relaunch under his ownership by serialising the memoirs of Christine Keeler, the model, showgirl and chair-bestriding innovator, whose brief affairs with the Minister for War, John Profumo, *and* the Soviet naval attaché Yevgeny Ivanov, were the catalyst for the ultimate collapse of Harold Macmillan's government. The scandal was both well-known and five years in the past by the time Murdoch decided to drop his 'scoop'; Profumo was out of politics and working for an anti-poverty charity in search of some measure of redemption. However, while Sir William Carr had reassured his wife that Murdoch was 'a gentleman', there was Establishment uproar over the reheating of the Keeler story and a growing consensus that he was nothing of the sort. With no shortage of bias, Profumo's friend Lord Longford accused Murdoch of 'journalistic exhumation' and

WHO OWNS THE NEWS?

'cashing in on pornography'.[11] Adverts promoting the story were banned by the Independent Television Authority for 'offending public feeling', which was an interesting notion given how copies of the *News of the World* were flying off the shelves.

Murdoch paid £20,000 (roughly £277,000 today) for the serialisation rights and claimed that he and his then-wife Anna had read the manuscript of the memoir and concluded that it was 'a good lesson to all politicians'.[12] The *News of the World*'s front page – acting as a megaphone for Murdoch – screamed that 'an ex-King of England' and four past prime ministers had penned memoirs and claimed, 'what is good for those out of the top drawer is also good for others who made a contribution to contemporary history'. Murdoch and his papers have a particular knack for sounding high-handed while engaged in lowdown and dirty tricks. However, the big boss tends to avoid interviews and interviewers who'll probe his tactics too closely.

There's a good reason for that: on Friday 3 October 1969, Murdoch appeared as a guest on David Frost's London Weekend Television (LWT) show, *Frost on Friday*. He'd been persuaded that the angle would be positive and focused on his business success. Quite why a man of Murdoch's towering cynicism would have been fooled by that I don't know, but he was a mere 38 years old at the time so perhaps some traces of youthful naivety remained. If they did, the sanctimonious and prosecutorial Frost was about to obliterate them for good. Accompanied by an entourage made up of his wife Anna, newspaper executive right-hand man Bert Hardy and PR guru John Addey, Murdoch stumbled into Frost's trap immediately, boasting about the Keeler scoop: 'I certainly sub-edited a tremendous amount of the book.'[13]

BREAKING

The host pounced immediately: 'You have done that yourself? Since we talked on the phone this afternoon, I spent four dismal hours reading through the [Keeler] manuscript ... What is your argument of positive merit?' Murdoch tried to argue that it was 'the first time the whole story [had been] told' but Frost quickly got him to admit that other books had already covered the same territory. Murdoch tried a different tack – 'There is nothing wrong in telling a story twice' – but Frost countered: 'If you admit that the story has been told twice, then we are making progress. But I mean, you started off by saying there were new things. I went through this. I combed this through very carefully and I could not find any new facts in it at all, except a couple of minor personalities.'

Frost went on to point to Addey, who had been sitting in and cheering on his boss's answers with ludicrous enthusiasm: 'Your PR man's going mad again. Your PR man is the only person who's applauded – you must give him a raise.' Agitated, Murdoch fell back on one of his key beliefs about Britain, declaring that the controversy over the Keeler story was stirred up 'by members of the sort of Establishment'. Frost dismissed Murdoch's riposte as 'an Australian view of England', saying that the press baron mistakenly believed the Establishment was more organised than it actually was.[14]

If he'd been less rattled, Murdoch could have replied that Frost himself, for all his posturing, was rather keen on being part of the Establishment. Instead, he grumbled, 'You reckon?'

Storming out after the interview, Murdoch turned to Bert Hardy and snarled: 'I will buy this company.' He did. Just over a year later, in November 1970, he became an LWT shareholder after buying a 7.5 per cent stake from the General Electric

WHO OWNS THE NEWS?

Company. The following month, Murdoch became a part-time LWT executive, invested a further £500,000 in the company – equivalent to roughly £6 million today – and increased his share to 30 per cent. His first major demand? Frost and his production company, Paradine, should be terminated immediately. Despite having taken revenge so swiftly, Murdoch didn't feel vindicated. In his 2008 biography, *The Man Who Owns the News*, Michael Woolf claims Murdoch told him 'almost forty years later that he [hadn't] spoken to Frost since' and that he '[felt] like saying, "I'll get the bastard one day, but he'll die before I get him."' The prediction was spot on. David Frost died of a heart attack in 2013, aged 74.

The row over the Keeler memoirs reveals a lot about how Murdoch goes about business and how this, in turn, impacts the wider media landscape. He is cold and calculating when it comes to his business interests and other people's feelings but becomes emotional and vindictive when under attack himself. The man who has funded so many stings, set-ups and paparazzi packs is distinctly uncomfortable with scrutiny of his life and actions. No matter how rich he has become – and he is a multi-billionaire – he will continue to believe that he is an outsider and an enemy of 'the Establishment', whoever and wherever they might be.

Murdoch brought that attitude in concentrated form to the *Sun* – a paper written in the voice of an imaginary working-class white man trapped permanently in a cartoon 1970s. It holds a special place in his heart because it is his first original creation. The first version of the *Sun* was launched in 1964 by the International Publishing Corporation (IPC), owner of the *Daily Mirror*, as a replacement for one of its other papers, the *Daily Herald*, which was in terminal decline. The *Herald* was a Labour-supporting paper which – ironically, given Murdoch's later war on the trade unions – started life in 1910 as a daily strike bulletin issued by the London Society of Compositors, a printers' union.

Prior to the *Sun*'s launch, IPC had been told by Mark Abrams – a market researcher who also worked as a private pollster for Labour leaders Hugh Gaitskell and Harold Wilson – that the *Herald*'s readership of 'political radicals' could grow to include an emerging 1960s class he called 'social radicals'. In his study, *The Newspaper Reading Public of Tomorrow* (1964), Abrams painted a picture of a sophisticated, politically engaged middle class that was aching for its own newspaper and felt unserved by the existing titles. That vision persuaded the leadership at IPC – chairman Cecil Harmsworth King (Northcliffe's nephew) and *Mirror* editor Hugh Cudlipp – to create a new broadsheet newspaper with a striking design, a £40,000 advertising budget (roughly £635,000 today) and an initial print run of 3.5 million.

A combination of novelty and an advertising blitz meant the *Sun* sold well at first, but it quickly dropped back down to the same 1.2 million circulation that *the Daily Herald* had been achieving. In today's era of terminal print decline that would be a huge success, but it was a crushing disappointment in the 1960s when newspapers were still on the rise. Despite having made agreements with the unions that they would invest in the *Sun* for at least five years, printers and journalists alike suspected Cudlipp and King were secretly planning to fold the *Herald*'s circulation into the *Daily Mirror*, which was booming. The *Sun* became a financial blackhole, an ongoing disaster. By 1969, it was losing £2 million a year and sales had dipped below 800,000. It was mortally wounded and two familiar vultures were circling.

WHO OWNS THE NEWS?

Murdoch and Robert Maxwell, then a war hero turned publisher turned Labour MP, both wanted the *Sun*. Commentary in the *Spectator* suggested that the unions were suspicious of Maxwell. Union leaders worried he'd run the Labour-supporting paper for 18 months until the next general election, secure a spot in the House of Lords 'for his devotion to the cause of socialism' then drop the enterprise, leaving staff 'out on the streets, a couple of years older, and that much less employable'.[15] Maxwell would eventually go on to become a media mogul in his own right but with a far less prosperous conclusion. After securing control of the Mirror Group in 1984, he raided its pension fund to keep his empire afloat, a scheme that was only revealed after he fell from his yacht and drowned in the Atlantic Ocean in 1991.

In the battle for control of the *Sun*, Murdoch outflanked Maxwell by promising unions there would be fewer redundancies if he took over and assuring the IPC that he would publish a 'straightforward, honest newspaper' which would continue to back Labour. But in an interview with the *Sunday Times*, which Murdoch would later acquire (but was then owned by the Thomson family), he expressed his intentions far more bluntly. The journalist Godfrey Hodgson asked Murdoch if there was anything he admired about the rival *Daily Mirror*, saying he personally liked the pull-out news feature section, Mirrorscope. Murdoch picked up the supplement with his finger and thumb and dropped it in the bin: 'If you think we're going to have any of that upmarket shit in our paper, you're very much mistaken.'[16] And, to this very day, the *Sun* isn't upmarket, but it *is* shit; the kind of shit that fills rivers, poisons seas and swamps entire ecosystems; the kind of shit that can choke a country.

BREAKING

So Murdoch took control and, with the new *Sun*'s first editor Larry Lamb – a former *Mirror* man who Murdoch poached from the *Mail* – worked on a radical tabloid reinvention. They stole liberally and shamelessly from the *Mirror* while dialling up the sex and sensationalism, and ditching Cudlipp's notions of 'improving' content. I have a copy of the first edition of Murdoch's *Sun* and it doesn't differ that much from the paper that is still being published in the twenty-first century: the front page has a screaming headline – HORSE DOPE SENSATION – combined with a picture of an attractive woman, Lady Leonora Grosvenor, who by dint of her status as Prince Charles' suspected love interest of the moment kicked off the paper's obsession with royal stories. The rest of the page is taken up by trails for stories inside the paper – politics! (an exclusive interview with Prime Minister Harold Wilson), sex! ('The Love Machine'), football! ('the most brilliant, most controversial star of them all – George Best') and tits! ('a remarkable series of interviews with some of the most beautiful women of our time'). And inside? The first Page 3 girl – 'tall, lithe Ulla Lindstrom' – albeit fully dressed for the time being.

The template was set from the start and has remained largely unchanged since, but among the editors who've worked within it, one stands out. Beyond Murdoch, the *Sun*'s animating daemon is Kelvin MacKenzie, who edited the paper from 1981 until 1994. MacKenzie took his boss's growling irritation at the Establishment and amoral thirst for a story and ran with it, indulging the paper's most sociopathic tendencies and formulating its argot – a vocabulary splattered with 'romps', 'love rats', 'tragic tots', 'crims', 'compo', 'stunners', 'kiddies' and 'cops'. In Peter Chippindale and Chris Horrie's *Stick It Up Your Punter: the Rise and Fall*

WHO OWNS THE NEWS?

of the Sun, MacKenzie responds to a feature editor's suggestion that the paper run a piece on the pros and cons of legalising marijuana by screaming: 'You must be fucking joking! You just don't understand the readers, do you, eh? He's the bloke you see in the pub – a right old fascist, wants to send the wogs back, buy his poxy council house, he's afraid of the unions, afraid of the Russians, hates the queers and the weirdos and drug dealers...'[17]

MacKenzie was the man described frequently as 'Murdoch's favourite editor' and, like his boss, he indulged in two self-serving fictions: one that the 'right old fascist' developed those fears and hatreds of his own accord without the encouragement of the *Sun*, and two, that – in the words of the infamous 1992 post-election splash – It Was The Sun Wot Won It; if the paper backed a party, so too would its readers. Neither theory is entirely correct. Yes, through relentless attacks, chivvying and bullying the *Sun* could, at its height, shift public opinion, but it has also shifted its allegiance when it knows the wind is already changing. Murdoch backs winners and then claims credit for their wins.

MacKenzie's *Sun* was virulently homophobic, in line with his own bigoted views and Murdoch's distaste for 'poofters'.[18] In 1987, it splashed a story that falsely claimed Elton John had been with underage male sex workers. Despite a warning from his own legal department and the paper's only source being a man known as 'American Barry', MacKenzie ran with it under the headline ELTON IN VICE BOYS SCANDAL with a trail promising details of the 'star's lust for bondage on pages 4 and 5'. One detail omitted from the salacious story was that 'Barry' had been promised a job at the paper once the uproar was over and had been paid £2,000 plus a £250 weekly retainer.

BREAKING

A libel writ from Elton John's lawyer, Frank Presland, arrived the next day as the paper's second spurious front page on the singer was being pulled together. It appeared under the headline ELTON'S KINKY KINKS with a double-page spread (ELTON'S DRUG CAPERS) on the inside pages. A second writ duly arrived. MacKenzie doubled down with a howling headline YOU'RE A LIAR, ELTON and a strapline touting it as 'the story they're all suing over'. Other papers quickly pulled apart the *Sun*'s fiction and things reached a stalemate.

The *Sun* – which had seen huge sales dips with every Elton John story – should have stopped there but MacKenzie couldn't help himself. Five months after its last front page about the singer (publishing old and consensually taken nude photos under the headline ELTON'S PORNO SHAME), it returned to the issue with an even more outrageous invention. On 28 September 1987, the paper's splash read MYSTERY OF ELTON'S SILENT DOGS and claimed that the singer had ensured 'his vicious Rottweiler dogs [were] silenced by a horrific operation' and were now 'silent assassins'. MacKenzie and his executives *knew* this wasn't true, especially after they sent a photographer to snap pictures of the beastly mute bastards and discovered that they were Alsatians, still in full possession of their barks.

Elton's legal team quickly showed that their bite was equal to their bark. They issued another writ and were helped by a *Mirror* splash featuring 'American Barry' confessing that he'd never met Elton John and had made up the whole story in return for the *Sun*'s money. Rather than face a High Court case in which MacKenzie or even Murdoch might be called to give evidence, the *Sun* settled. Elton demanded – and got – an apology to match the smear, printed in plain language and detailing the exact amount of money News Corp was forced to hand over rather than hiding it behind the usual euphemism 'substantial damages' – £1 million. The grovelling apology was printed under the headline SORRY ELTON! and MacKenzie was subjected to 'the bollocking of a lifetime'[19] from Murdoch.

MacKenzie was in no way repentant. Asked about the case by *Press Gazette* in 2006, he said: 'I think the *Sun* should have its million quid back. It hasn't damaged him at all, has it? Libel can only have a value if there has been some kind of damage, right? Where is the damage? Where? There's nothing wrong with him. So no, I don't feel bad about him, not at all.'[20]

The battle with Elton John may have been over but the campaign of homophobia continued. It was an obsession that went far beyond a single celebrity. An attack on gay vicars was headlined PULPIT POOFS, while a sequel, penned by the *Sun*'s showbiz editor, an egotistical non-entity called Piers Morgan who was never heard of again, appeared under the headline THE POOFS OF POP. And when *EastEnders* featured its first gay kiss, in the ancient year of 1989, the *Sun* called it EASTBENDERS and followed the headline with a story laden with faux 'won't somebody think of the children?' concern: '[It was] . . . a homosexual love scene between yuppie poofs . . . when millions of children were watching.'

MacKenzie also sent photographers to break into a psychiatric hospital where the actor Jeremy Brett was being treated for manic depression and heart disease, then wondered if he was 'dying of AIDS' in print. It was also under MacKenzie's tenure that the *Sun* printed the headline STRAIGHT SEX CANNOT

BREAKING

GIVE YOU AIDS – OFFICIAL. His attitude to the truth was summed up in his demand to staff for more stories on the royals: 'Don't worry if it's not true – so long as there's not too much fuss about it afterwards.'

But MacKenzie inevitably couldn't even follow his own advice. Six months before the abysmal AIDS story, he was responsible for one of the most notorious crimes against journalism and human decency in the *Sun*'s sordid history. On 15 April 1989, a deadly crush during the FA Cup semi-final at the Hillsborough stadium in Sheffield caused the deaths of 97 Liverpool fans. Three days later, the *Sun* ran a leader column that claimed people were 'scapegoating' the police and blame should rest on 'thousands of fans, many without tickets [trying] to get into the ground just before kick-off – either by forcing their way in or by blackmailing the police into opening the gates'.

The following day, the *Sun* went much further with a front page headlined THE TRUTH. It accused Liverpool fans of stealing from the dead and attacking and urinating on the police and emergency services. The person MacKenzie had assigned to pull together the story, Harry Arnold, who was usually a royal reporter, warned him that they were dealing with allegations rather than proven facts. MacKenzie assured him that he would say 'some fans' rather than producing a blanket attack on all Liverpool supporters. And then, having toyed with the idea of splashing with YOU SCUM, he personally sketched out THE TRUTH front page. Truth had seemingly never been of much interest to him and it appeared to be the same here...

The 'some fans' caveat MacKenzie had promised Arnold was included but it was a chocolate fireguard in front of a raging inferno. Those two words – THE TRUTH – were followed by a volley of lies, each prefaced with the phrase 'some fans' – 'Some fans picked pockets of victims'; 'Some fans urinated on the brave cops'; 'Some fans beat up PC giving the kiss of life'. In September 2012, the independent panel investigating the disaster confirmed in its report that 'the source of these despicable untruths was a Sheffield news agency reporting conversations with South Yorkshire Police and Irvine Patnick, the then MP for Sheffield Hallam'. Patnick was knighted five years later and it took him until 2012 to apologise for the lies he spread.

In the immediate aftermath of the front page, Murdoch dispatched MacKenzie to apologise on BBC Radio 4's *The World This Weekend*. It was an empty gesture and, in 2007, MacKenzie told attendees at a private lunch held by a Newcastle law firm that he only made the BBC appearance 'because Rupert Murdoch told me to. I wasn't sorry then and I'm not sorry now because we told the truth'.[21] He continued clinging to the 'T' word after the *Sun* published a front-page *mea culpa* in 2004 – with the sales boycott by the people of Liverpool still holding firm – and finally offered a weak apology in 2012, which still claimed that he 'published in good faith'. The Hillsborough Families Support Group rightly dismissed it as 'too little, too late'.

That MacKenzie was Murdoch's favourite editor and continued to work for him after his tenure at the *Sun* tells you as much about the boss as his subordinate. Murdoch appreciates brutality and rewards it. Winning counts above all and he will tolerate practically any tactics to ensure that. When the tabloid *Sun* first launched, Murdoch and Lamb composed an editorial that promised a newspaper which would care 'about the quality of life; about the kind of world we live in; and about people'. This flatpack utopianism reflects the *Sun* far less than a quote from Lenin, the man whose bust stood in the young Murdoch's student rooms: 'A newspaper is not only a collective propagandist and a collective agitator, it is also a collective organiser.'[22]

In its pomp, selling 5 million copies a day, the *Sun* was a huge moneymaker for Murdoch and bankrolled his expansion into the US, but it was also (and continues to be) a tool of undoubted influence on politicians, who fear a megaphone for the Murdoch mindset that's guaranteed instant attention from the broadcast media.

Though in 2011, it looked as though Murdoch's political power might be coming to an abrupt end – to the painfully optimistic, at least. Back in 2007, the *News of the World's* oleaginous royal editor, Clive Goodman, and a private investigator called Glenn Mulcaire were convicted of illegally intercepting phone messages. The paper claimed that it was an isolated incident ('one rogue reporter') about which its editors and executives were blissfully and conveniently unaware. But Nick Davies of the *Guardian* discovered that wasn't true, after being approached by an anonymous source ('Mr Apollo'), who knew what the tabloids had been doing.[23]

The whistleblower told Davies that the *News of the World* had been hacking phones with impunity, sourcing a huge number of its stories from intercepted voicemails and then getting photographs and quotes to create a false impression that the information had been uncovered through legitimate reporting. Mr Apollo told Davies that Goodman had not been 'one rogue reporter' as News UK had claimed, but one of many who had used the

WHO OWNS THE NEWS?

'one simple trick' of exploiting voicemail accounts where the owner hadn't changed the PIN from the factory setting or had opted for something easily guessable like their birth year.

In an avalanche of stories that began in July 2009 and continued through to 2011, the *Guardian* revealed that reporters at the *News of the World* and private investigators employed by it hacked the phones of politicians, celebrities, relatives of dead soldiers, victims of terror attacks and, most disturbingly, 13-year-old Milly Dowler – who was later found murdered – at a time when her family was still holding out hope that she might be alive. They briefly thought her messages being picked up was a sign she *was* alive. After News UK shuttered the *News of the World* in the hope of containing the fallout, Murdoch and his obsequious son James were brought before a UK parliamentary select committee. In a seemingly rehearsed 'bit', the elder man said, 'This is the most humble day of my life,' before throwing James, then CEO of News UK, under the bus, claiming to have known nothing about illegality at the company.

Meanwhile, the Prime Minister, David Cameron – who'd hired ex-*News of the World* editor and future ex-con Andy Coulson as his director of communications – was cornered and announced an investigation into 'the culture, practices and ethics of the British press' to be led by Lord Justice Leveson. One of the iron-clad rules of British politics is this: if you want to look like you're doing something but ensure that nothing actually changes, order an inquiry and, if possible, a 'judge-led' one (it just *sounds* firmer). Leveson heard from hundreds of witnesses – top politicians, normally camera-shy editors and proprietors, and victims, both famous and 'civilians', between November 2011 and March 2012.

BREAKING

The result was a 2,000-page report published in November 2012. It was largely ignored or rejected by press and politicians alike, aside from the creation of two new regulators – the Independent Press Standards Organisation (IPSO), which 'regulates' the majority of the larger publishers but is neither independent nor inclined to do much upholding of standards, and IMPRESS, an alternative that handles a ragtag collection of generally smaller outlets.

With Murdoch's 'most humble day' behind him, he quickly returned to a position of whispering influence over British politicians. The *News of the World* was swiftly replaced by the *Sun on Sunday* – the *News of the World* in barely more respectable drag – and News Corp's British arm, News UK, expanded further into radio and TV, with Talk TV and Times Radio added to Talk Radio, Talk Sport and Virgin, to create a broadcasting division.

After stepping down as chairman of News Corp and Fox in September 2023, aged 92, Murdoch made it clear he was *not* retiring. Instead, he awarded himself the title of chairman emeritus and put the fear of god – in this case, a god with a gravelly Australian accent – into his employees. He wrote that he would remain 'involved every day in the contest of ideas' and that staff could 'expect to see [him] in the office late on a Friday afternoon'.

The prospect of Rupert Murdoch looming up from behind the water cooler on a Friday afternoon carries more than a little of the menace Marlon Brando injected into the line, 'I'm going to make him an offer he can't refuse.' While his oldest son Lachlan is his named successor, the *capomandamento* – the boss of bosses – retains the real power in the business. And while his era, like Northcliffe's before it, will come to an end soon, Murdoch's impact will be as long-lasting. His father learned

WHO OWNS THE NEWS?

from Northcliffe; he learned from his father and the whole of the British media has learned from him, no matter how much it protests otherwise.

In fiction, the most blandly named companies are the ones you can be sure are the most demonic (Soylent; LexCorp; Globex – Hank Scorpio's employee-focused evil empire in *The Simpsons*). News Corp fits with that pattern; it's a name that makes it sound like a neutral purveyor of current affairs content. Fox, Murdoch's other baby, sounds bright-eyed and bushy-tailed, but takes more from the vulpine tendency to rootle through your bins, snarl at you in the street and shag in your garden. The Murdoch companies are like chimeric crosses between an axolotl and a parasitic wasp: capable of regenerating when injured and when they take root in a country, apt to consume their host until their desires come to dominate and define culture and politics.

While I'm sure they all consider themselves beautiful and unique snowflakes, the other proprietors in British media are all variations on the templates established by Northcliffe and Murdoch. The current owner of the *Daily Mail*, *Mail on Sunday*, *Metro* and *MailOnline* among other properties is Jonathan Harmsworth, the 4th Viscount Rothermere. He's Northcliffe's great-great-nephew, and follows his great-grandfather, grandfather and father in the family business of poisonous newspaper production. While he outsources most of the unpleasantness to editors such as the infamous Paul Dacre, Rothermere preserves the *Mail* as the outraged voice of middle England, albeit without his great-grandfather's explicit taste for fascism. In January 1934, the first Viscount Rothermere put his name to an editorial cheering

BREAKING

Sir Oswald Mosley's British Union of Fascists, 'Hurrah for the Blackshirts'. His ancestor is a lot more careful.

And so, what of the others?

At the *Evening Standard* and the *Independent*, Evgeny Lebedev, a.k.a. Baron Lebedev of Hampton in the London Borough of Richmond upon Thames and of Siberia in the Russian Federation, combines Northcliffe's taste for publicity and love of titles with Murdoch's penchant for unconvincingly claiming that he doesn't exert influence on his editors. Having acquired the newspapers with his father, Alexander, a 'former' KGB agent, Lebedev has been inserting himself into their pages since he was in his early twenties, tarting about with stars so much that he co-owns an east London pub with Sir Ian 'Gandalf' McKellen. Is Lebedev more than a 'conjuror of cheap tricks'? No. He's a man of almost endless bad taste, who purchases status and influence, and postures as an intellectual while displaying a Chapman Brothers dick-faced child statue in his office. It's a great metaphor for Lebedev: crassness elevated to the highest levels at ludicrous expense. Murdoch showed how much influence a foreign newspaper proprietor could have. Lebedev has followed that pattern with far less subtlety.

Until very recently, the *Daily Telegraph*, *Sunday Telegraph* and *Spectator* were owned by the Barclay brothers. Now one of the pair – David – is dead (and not just for tax reasons) and the other – Frederick – has lost control of the media empire after the banks grew tired of debts going unserved. The titles were briefly owned by Redbird IMI, a consortium that included investment from the rulers of the United Arab Emirates, but the Middle East money led to the deal being blocked by the UK government. Paul Marshall, a hedge fund manager who founded the right-wing commentary site UnHerd, purchased the *Spectator* for £100 million in September 2024 while the *Telegraph* titles remained in limbo as an auction process dragged on. What the *Telegraph* brand will become is unclear. Under the Barclays, the titles moved further and further to the right, from tweedy Tory reading matter for retired colonels in the Home Counties to the house journals of calliper owners, eugenicists, cranks and conspiracy theorists.

The company Reach is the latest regeneration that began when Northcliffe launched the *Daily Mirror* ('for gentlewomen') in 1903 and was once Robert Maxwell's Mirror Group. Listed on the Stock Exchange, it hasn't had a singular proprietor since Maxwell's death in 1994 but it's no more free of the curse of the British press than its rivals. On a national level, it owns both the *Daily Mirror*, which is a travesty of the paper it once was, purporting to be on the left but often as reactionary as its natural enemy, the *Sun*, and the *Daily Express*, which remains almost as toxically right wing as it was under the stewardship of former porn baron Richard Desmond. As a company, Reach has become notorious for slashing journalist numbers while demanding that the remaining staff produce more.[24]

The other outlier is the Scott Trust, which owns the *Guardian*. It was established in 1936 by John Russell Scott, then owner of the *Manchester Guardian* and *Manchester Evening News*, for two reasons – one principled and one practical. The *Guardian* tends to focus on the first – protecting the paper from the individual whims of a future proprietor and maintaining a liberal editorial line. But there were financial reasons too. Scott also wanted to avoid future death duties, having seen his father, C. P. Scott, and brother

BREAKING

Edward die in quick succession. The Trust has been reconstituted several times since – it's now a limited company – but its aim of ensuring the future of the *Guardian* remains unchanged. That commitment did not extend to the *Observer*, the Sunday paper which it bought in 1993 and sold to the news startup Tortoise in late-2024, despite strike action from staff over concerns about the younger company's plans and potential for investment.

In 1977, the report of the Royal Commission on the Press concluded:

> Newspapers and periodicals serve society in diverse ways. They inform their readers about the world and interpret it to them. They act as both watchdogs for citizens, by scrutinising concentrations of power, and as a means of communication among groups within the community, thus promoting social cohesion and social change.

Not even the most deranged advocate for the newspapers would make that argument now. The remaining newspaper barons *are* a 'concentration of power' and they make sure to avoid scrutinising each other. A very small group of people own the news and for all the talk of democratisation that pinged about in the early days of the consumer internet, they've worked very hard to keep it that way.

3.

What's The Story?

What Makes Something News? And What Responsibility do *we* Have for That?

> *'News is what a chap who doesn't care much about anything wants to read. And it's only news until he's read it. After that it's dead ... If someone else has sent a story before us, our story isn't news.'*
> – *Scoop*, Evelyn Waugh (1938)

The underlying realities of the news business, as explained to the naive (and accidental) foreign correspondent William Boot by the hard-bitten news agency hack Corker in *Scoop*, haven't really changed in the nearly nine decades since Waugh turned his real-life experiences as a foreign correspondent in Ethiopia into a fictional farce. For something to be deemed as actual 'news', it has to be interesting, not generally known and, despite the best efforts of the industry's worst, feature facts that you can prove. Finding that proof, otherwise known as 'standing the story up', should require multiple sources. Gossip can be the catalyst for a story, and is enough for certain newspapers, but it's not *news* if you can't stand it up and feel confident you could defend it in a court of law.

One of the classic definitions of what makes something a news story is the terrifically glib line: 'When a dog bites a man that's not news, but when a man bites a dog? That's news.' The credit for this quote has slipped and shifted over time. While it's often attributed to John B. Bogart, the city editor at the *New York Sun* in 1812, Joseph Pulitzer or Viscount Northcliffe, it was in fact coined for a fictional reporter in Jesse Lynch Williams' 1899 book, *The Stolen Story and Other Newspaper Stories*. The most regularly wheeled-out quote defining what makes something news is fictional. It feels all too appropriate.

Multi-award-winning journalist Gary Younge, delivering the inaugural Rosemary Hollis Memorial Lecture at City University in 2024, argued that the aphorism needs a footnote because some phenomena have news value precisely because they happen so often. He went on to suggest that 'there is value in asking, "Why do dogs keep biting people?", "Who owns those dogs?" and "Why do the same people keep getting bitten?"'

Younge raised the US Justice Department's report into policing in Ferguson, Missouri, produced following the 2014 killing of Michael Brown by a police officer. The investigators found that every time a police dog bit someone in the city, the victim was black. Younge concluded: 'That suggests sometimes "Dog Bites Man" really is the story. The trouble is, journalists keep missing it.'

The definition of what constitutes 'news' has been convoluted and chaotic for as long as the modern concept of 'the news' has existed. In *The Anatomy of Melancholy*, Robert Burton's sprawling treatise on depression, first published in 1621, he writes of

WHAT'S THE STORY?

hearing 'new news every day' before listing topics that include local concerns – 'fires, thefts, murders' – and foreign stories – 'wars . . . battles fought . . . leagues, stratagems, and fresh alarms'. Burton's description of news as 'a vast confusion of vows, wishes, actions, edicts . . . complaints [and] grievances [that] are daily brought to our ears' sounds very similar to modern complaints about news fatigue.

News value is subjective, not objective. There are topics that some journalists believe are vital and urgent while others think they're barely worth thinking about. Outside of natural disasters, horrendous crimes and wars, the value of most stories is up for debate, dependant on one's own set of values and situation. The intricate analysis of the internal politics at Premier League football clubs that fills the back pages of British newspapers is vital information for many but to others is as irrelevant as a soap opera they've never watched. For some people, the goings-on at the 'highest level' of the British Establishment are of paramount importance and worthy of inclusion in every news bulletin. I happen to believe that the pack of hounds who chase after the British royal family – or any royal family, for that matter – should no more be called 'reporters' than a watch you buy from a bloke in a pub car park should be considered a genuine Rolex. 'Reporting' on the royals is less about seeking stories and more like being a baby bird waiting for pre-chewed worms to be dropped straight into your beak by PR handlers. Real reporting on the British royal family – investigations into their finances or revelations about their actual personal conduct – is rare and rarely comes from royal reporters, but rather general news reporters who aren't reliant on access. But, back to what *is* news . . .

BREAKING

Aside from personal persuasion and 'specialties' of certain journalists, a more formulaic definition of the news does exist – in principle, anyway. Often quoted on journalism courses, there's a list of 12 common factors that contribute to newsworthiness: negativity, proximity, recency, currency, continuity, uniqueness, simplicity, personality, predictability, elite concerns, exclusivity and size. This list is used to help budding young journalists assess what stories make the news. It comes from a paper written in 1965 by the Norwegian academics Johan Galtung and Mari Holmboe Ruge, which considered the presentation of stories about Cuba, Congo and Cyprus in Norwegian newspapers.[25] The problem is that the pair intended the list to serve as a warning to journalists rather than a guide to be consulted when producing news.

The Reuters Institute for the Study of Journalism at Oxford University has called the paper 'the most cited work on news value' and claimed that almost all research into news and its origin carried out since has used it as a starting point.[26] That the researchers observed what was happening rather than saying what *should* be happening was almost entirely missed. Galtung and Holmboe Ruge's paper concluded that journalists were creating 'an image of the world that gives little autonomy to the periphery but sees it mainly existing for the sake of the centre. Conflict will be emphasised, conciliation not.' In 2019, Galtung told the *Guardian* that the consequence of the warning being misinterpreted was that 'news media give a total biased picture of reality. The perception of reality in the public becomes overly negative'.[27] By focusing on negative events, the news presented the world as far darker than it ever really was.

That original list, while having its limits, certainly reflected

WHAT'S THE STORY?

large swathes of written journalism in the years following its publication. As the media has evolved, so too have the factors which the authors have noted as worthy of inclusion. A key factor that has joined the 12 identified by Galtung and Holmboe Ruge in the years since is shareability. In the media environment of the 1960s, stories moved more slowly via newspapers and limited TV and radio news bulletins. Now news has to be framed in a way that will lead to it being shared online and the incentives created by chasing traffic mean events that might never have been covered in the past are picked up because of their potential for a quick hit. A dire example of that tendency is the genre of news features that focus on young people who've bought houses, with headlines promising they achieved it by sheer graft and self-abnegation before revealing in the copy that their parents gave them the deposit or they stumbled into a sizeable inheritance when an elderly relative died.[28]

In 2016, two journalism academics at the University of Huddersfield, Tony Harcup and Deirdre O'Neill, put together an updated set of news values based on an analysis of new stories in the British press.[29] They listed exclusivity, negativity, conflict, surprise, striking audio or visuals, shareability, entertainment, drama, following up on previous stories, a focus on powerful individuals, relevance, magnitude, celebrity, positivity and whether the story fitted with a news organisation's existing agenda.

This list is useful, and you can see many of these aspects reflected in our daily news, but we could reformulate taxonomies of news values forever – it's a great way to keep media theorists busy – and ultimately what makes the news cannot always be boiled down to lists. As the news has become something to

BREAKING

be shared by more than just journalists and news anchors, the need for it to capture attention is paramount. If a story will drive attention, then it will be treated as news. Social value or moral weight end up as secondary concerns, despite how journalism likes to see itself.

After the case of sub-postmasters wrongly convicted of stealing from their branches because of a fundamentally flawed computer system was turned into an ITV drama, *Mr Bates vs the Post Office*, it led to an explosion of front-page denunciations (the *Mirror*: 'Why still no justice?'; *The Times*: 'Post Office fury intensifies'; the *Daily Mail:* 'Shameless: National revulsion over Post Office scandal mounts') which might have given the impression that the national newspapers had been all over the scandal throughout the 15 years that had passed since it was first revealed.

In fact, as the veteran media commentator Liz Gerard wrote in the *New European*,[30] the story had been the subject of just one national newspaper splash since *Computer Weekly* started reporting it in 2008. That *Daily Mail* front page – '33 die without justice' – appeared in February 2022, bylined to Tom Witherow, who was reporting on the first day of the public inquiry into the case which began that month. Significant national newspaper coverage came only after the sub-postmasters had won two huge legal battles (a £58-million class action in December 2019 and the quashing of 39 convictions in April 2021). Witherow later moved to *The Times*, where there'd been no more than a whisper about the story until that point, with just a scattering of small stories deep in the paper, some of them tiny news in briefs (NiBs). Gerard pointedly quoted one of those NiBs in her piece. It was headlined 'Post Office legal bill' and read in its entirety:

WHAT'S THE STORY?

The Post Office has spent an estimated £5m in a legal battle with sub-postmasters. More than 500 people say computer glitches mean they were wrongly accused of false accounting and theft. The case will be heard in the High Court on Wednesday. The Post Office denies that the system was at fault. It may have to pay up to £1bn if it loses.

That's the Post Office – and ultimately the taxpayers – facing a £1-billion bill following a campaign of false accusations against more than 500 innocent people and it was shoved in a dark corner of paper, considered unworthy of more than 63 words. Once the story was a TV drama, that dismissive attitude from her own newspaper played no part in *Times* columnist Melanie Phillips' outraged op-ed. Beneath the headline 'Where's the outcry over postmaster scandal?', she hailed the outlets that did report on the scandal – *Private Eye, Computer Weekly* and the BBC – and wondered if there wasn't more outrage because 'the victims were just ordinary people from modest backgrounds'.

Nick Wallis, a freelance journalist, doggedly pursued the scandal for years in *Private Eye*, as well as fronting, producing and consulting on three BBC *Panorama* episodes, presenting a BBC Radio 4 series and writing a book on the case. But while he and journalists at *Computer Weekly* – notably Rebecca Thomson and Karl Flinders – stuck with the story for years, the words 'Post Office' and 'computer system' were enough to induce narcolepsy in national newspaper editors.

The *Daily Mail* only started to take the scandal more seriously when Wallis got a lucky break in late 2018. As he explained in

BREAKING

an interview with *InPublishing*,[31] he managed to get hold of the personal email address for the paper's then-editor, Geordie Greig. He got in touch and Greig replied that the local sub-postmaster in the village where he had a weekend cottage – what do you expect from a man whose family have been royal courtiers for generations? – had been pressuring him to look at the story. Greig assigned the *Mail's* chief reporter Sam Greenhill to look into it and the paper began one of its patented and enormously self-aggrandising campaigns on the issue.

While the *Mail* had reported on some aspects of the story from 2008 onwards, like *The Times*, it had confined its coverage to pieces buried deep in the paper. But once its 'campaign' kicked off, it was able to claim out-size credit for the sub-postmasters' successes in 2019 and 2021 ('Our £58m Post Office victory', 'Victory for the *Mail* as first postmaster cleared'). Had Wallis not got Greig's email address and the second-home adjacent sub-postmaster not been pushy, the *Mail* would have been as chronically disengaged as the rest of Fleet Street.

Similarly, once *Mr Bates . . .* had hit our screens, the newspapers howled for former Post Office boss Paula Vennells to be stripped of her CBE, leading her to agree to return it, but they said nothing when she was given the gong in 2019 New Year's Honours list, a year before the sub-postmasters won their £58-million class action. The honours coverage that year was dominated by a damehood for the model Twiggy, a knighthood for the cricketer Alastair Cook and another for the author Philip Pullman.

Almost all of the national newspapers – bar the *Sunday Express* – failed to notice until January 2024 that Fujitsu, the firm that built the faulty Horizon IT system that led to the injustices

WHAT'S THE STORY?

and the hounding of hundreds of people, had won more than 150 government contracts since the Post Office stopped prosecuting staff. *Computer Weekly* and *Private Eye* noticed, of course.

After *Mr Bates vs the Post Office* put the Post Office scandal at the top of the bulletins, two familiar strains of bullshit splattered all around the place. The first was the claim that journalists simply didn't report the story at all and that it took the ITV midweek drama to reveal it. But as the writers and producers of the series were scrupulous in pointing out, it simply wouldn't have existed without the work of Nick Wallis, *Private Eye* and *Computer Weekly*. The nationals didn't ignore the case entirely but they did a bad job of concealing their yawns, treating it as just one more example of corporate failure and huge figures rather than a human story of individuals crushed beneath corruption and bureaucratic indifference. The second line was the one promulgated by the national newspapers as they attempted to insert themselves into the story as late-in-the-day heroes or waved their hands around, pointing to everyone but themselves when apportioning blame for why a vast and calculated injustice hadn't been bigger news earlier.

So why was it that this story was ignored so long? It's a question of resources and focus. Specialists often struggle to get their news lines taken seriously or, in a lot of cases, simply aren't in their jobs anymore. It's why, following the almost total death of the industrial correspondents who focused on the trade unions, strikes are so badly covered. It's also why scandals in the NHS tend to emerge from trade titles such as *Health Service Journal* and *Nursing Times*; why crumbling concrete in schools was a surprise to Fleet Street reporters even after Jessica Hill at *Schools Week* had been raising the issue for months, and why only *Inside Housing* was sounding the alarm on dangerous cladding and high-rise buildings for years before Grenfell.

A fast-food diet of confected culture-war rows, Westminster horse trading, abject bollocks about the royal family and trend stories ripped from press releases and what's happening on TikTok is unfulfilling. But it's cheaper to run, easier to produce and simpler to explain than long investigations. There is an appetite out there for that kind of journalism – the resilience and growth of *Private Eye*'s circulation prove that – but national newspaper editors and their proprietors prefer to pretend that their readers are as bored and disconnected as them. Yes, there are still successful investigations in the papers, but they are thin on the ground.

The circle-the-wagons tendency among journalists at 'big' newspapers and broadcasters was obvious in their analysis of why the *Horizon* scandal didn't attract proper attention earlier. A conversation in early 2024 between the ex-BBC hosts of *The News Agents* podcast was a case in point:

> **Lewis Goodall:** At the moment, the brutal truth is there's not much else in terms of news. And if this story had happened, if the [ITV] drama had aired on, I don't know, 6 October 2023, just before the 7 October attacks, would we be in the place we're now in? The answer is: probably not. And that is, in a way, a bit disturbing, right? But it just shows this kind of contingency of news and politics sometimes.
>
> **Jon Sopel:** Look, I spent a third of my career as a foreign correspondent and what you learned was that there is a

WHAT'S THE STORY?

lighthouse beam and that beam is continually going around the world. And sometimes it is on you.

When I was in the US and Donald Trump was president, it was pretty much on you the whole time. There were other times when the beam goes somewhere else – Israel, the Middle East – and there's no point in ringing up the editor and saying, 'Put me on the news tonight' because the story would have to be so colossal.

And this [Post Office scandal story] landed just at a time after Christmas/New Year when people are still at home watching TV, maybe not at work, and have more downtime . . . Great moment in the schedules. There is no big competing new story that is taking it off the air – I'm sure people will say to me, 'Come on, Gaza has been huge' – it was a domestic story and it got attention. And that is the way we work . . .

Emily Maitlis: I also think many [previous disasters] were focused around events. Hillsborough was an event, it was appalling, it is actually sawn into my memory as a Sheffield girl . . . Grenfell the same, I can still see the building, see the flames at the top, we covered it on *Newsnight*, we were standing there. I think the ITV drama became that event in the absence of one thing that was memorable . . . that was the problem with the Post Office scandal, the stories and the testimonies were emerging to build a picture in a jigsaw way but it didn't focus around one day, one moment, one catastrophic emergency . . .

We talk in the industry about 'a peg' . . . 'What's the peg for that?' is the question that we're all asking, which

BREAKING

is: What does this hang on? What is the new piece of information that allows you to kick off your day's discussion or your news or your bulletin or your programme with that today? The truth is that the journalists did do their job, the paper editors did do their jobs, they did run the stories, they did put it prominently in their papers, but until you have new news, you're not going to lead with it.[32]

There's a complacency there that will be familiar to anyone who has worked in an office where things could be improved but won't be because people shrug and say, 'This is how we've *always* done it.' It's there in Sopel's 'and that is the way we work' and Maitlis's reassurance that journalists and editors did their jobs even when most of them didn't. Paying brief and half-hearted attention to a major scandal for years is not 'doing your job' but failure wrapped up in the tissue paper of an excuse.

Where some stories barely get the attention they deserve, others become media obsessions. The 2021 Census of England and Wales included two voluntary questions on sexual orientation and gender identity for the first time. The results showed 0.5 per cent of the population – 262,000 people in England and Wales – reported a gender identity different from the one originally listed on their birth certificate. When that number is broken down, trans women and trans men each account for 0.1 per cent of the population surveyed (48,000) with 0.6 per cent of people listing themselves as non-binary (30,000) and another 18,000 writing in a different gender identity. The point of giving you those figures – which are themselves subject to heated debate – is to illustrate

WHAT'S THE STORY?

that trans people are a tiny minority. However, over the past 15 years, coverage of that tiny minority has exploded to the point that not a day goes by without multiple stories about trans people in the British newspapers.

In November 2020, the press regulator IPSO published research[33] into news coverage of trans people which found that the volume of newspaper articles on the topic had grown significantly in the previous decade. In the five years up to April 2014, the researchers found that an average of 34 stories involving trans people were published per month in the UK. Between 1 May 2014 and 1 May 2019, that number swelled to an average of 176 per month – a rise of 414 per cent – and by the last year analysed (1 May 2018–1 May 2019), 224 stories were being published per month. The political debates triggered by the Gender Recognition Act in 2017 were an obvious catalyst for that change but that doesn't explain the sheer weight of coverage. The IPSO report included a quote from a managing editor at a national daily tabloid which is instructive:

> The types of stories we carry have changed. When the trans thing first started 10 years ago, we used to do simple stories about trans pioneers – the first trans pilot, for example . . . But the public has lost its appetite for those stories and they have dried up. Now it's all about the political debate, schools, Karen White (a trans woman who was admitted to the female prison estate and sexually assaulted inmates).

The phrasing used there – 'when the trans thing first started 10 years ago' – betrays a lack of knowledge and seriousness

BREAKING

combined with the cynical desire to treat a small group of human beings as little more than a handy wedge issue, a means of creating lots of heat and very little light. When Roberta Cowell became the first British trans woman to have gender affirmation surgery in 1954, the *Lancashire Evening Post* ran the story under the headline 'He Changed from "Bob" to Roberta' and opened by saying: 'Father of two children, and a wartime fighter pilot, 35-year-old Bob Cowell, of Croydon, has now become attractive blond-haired Roberta Elizabeth Cowell, "Betty" to her friends.'

The notion that 'the trans thing' began in 2010 is belied by that kind of historic coverage and even far more recent stories involving trans people – the 1998 introduction of the trans character Hayley Cropper in *Coronation Street* (although the actress Julie Hesmondhalgh herself was not trans) or Nadia Almada winning *Big Brother* in 2004, for example – were treated as novel and largely positive stories. Even newspapers that are now extremely well known for their hardline anti-trans stances were writing mostly sympathetic stories as late as 2016. That may just explain why the number of stories about 'trans pioneers' has 'dried up' – faced with a largely antagonistic media climate, a lot of trans people don't want to put themselves up for interview.

According to analysis by data journalist Ell Folan,[34] the *Daily Telegraph* published just ten articles related to trans people in January 2016, six of which were actively positive. Seven years later, in January 2023, the paper produced 75 articles about trans people across the month, 73 of which were negative. At the *Daily Mail*, January 2016 saw the publication of 22 pieces related to trans issues – five of which were positive or neutral. In January 2023, the *Mail* published 115 articles about trans

WHAT'S THE STORY?

people, 100 of which were straightforwardly negative. One trans contributor to the IPSO research summed up the shift in the representation of trans people in British media like this: 'It was going OK in terms of coverage – respectful, good language – and then the tone shifted to questioning. There was then a focus on the worst-case scenarios for everything.'

You could write a whole book unpicking the debates created by the British press about the very existence of trans people – indeed, many people have. Instead, I want to focus on how the media justifies a rise of more than 400 per cent in the number of stories about a group of people who represent at most 0.5 per cent of the population over the course of a decade and why that number continues to grow. I'm not arguing that trans people shouldn't be written about in the media but the sheer weight of negative coverage suggests a moral panic rather than a discussion of competing rights. The state of the 'debate' reached such a low that nominally 'left-wing' magazine the *New Statesman* promoted an article by writing about 'the trans question'[35] – a distinctly unsettling turn of phrase with deeply unpleasant historical connotations.

Editors defend the disproportionate focus on trans people by saying that public interest in such stories has grown, but that's because the press's focus on telling those kinds of stories has grown. Day after day, papers are presenting this particular story in terms of a huge threat and so it's unsurprising that a significant proportion of their readership comes to believe that is true. While newspaper op-eds and news stories talk often of the 'trans lobby', there's very little talk of the newspaper columnist lobby – a group with a lot more power and ample opportunities to present their arguments. The British press's stories about trans people cannot be

BREAKING

separated from the structure of the press itself and its demand for topics that cause fear and unease.

As well as creating and sustaining threads of news by repetition, the media has always made news through investigations. One of the most fascinating historical examples took place in Chicago. While The Mirage looked like any other 1970s Chicago dive bar, it was an illusion hiding an audacious act of undercover investigative journalism. The name of the bar was a clue left in plain sight. Pam Zekman, a reporter at the *Chicago Sun-Times*, heard that city inspectors were shaking down business owners for money and favours, but the victims were too afraid to go on the record. She persuaded her editor that the only way to get the story was to live it. He agreed and in 1977, collaborating with a non-profit watchdog group, the Better Government Association, the newspaper bought the derelict tavern and began running it themselves.

Every part of The Mirage was set up for the sting: the owners were reporters, as were the bartenders, the repairmen were photographers, a space was built into the ceiling for cameras and the bar stools were placed to ensure they'd get clear images of city inspectors accepting bribes. The effort paid off with a 25-part series that began in January 1978; it turned a spotlight on rampant bribery, skimming and tax evasion. In the end, it being Chicago, no one went to jail – though several city and state employees were fined and some were convicted of bribery – but the articles provoked a serious overhaul of the system and the city's codes.

The Mirage series was nominated for a Pulitzer Prize for Local Special Reporting with the jury lauding the *Sun-Times* for using 'resourcefulness, initiative and [an] imaginative approach' to

WHAT'S THE STORY?

'[expose] corruption in a powerful and effective way'. However, the editors of the *Washington Post* (Ben Bradlee) and the *St. Petersburg Times* (Eugene Patterson), who were both on the Pulitzer board, argued strongly and successfully that the *Sun-Times* should be disqualified from contention because its story was based on deception. Bradlee told *Chicago Reader* writer Michael Miner that reporters should not be allowed to 'misrepresent themselves in any way . . . [or] be the hidden owners of anything'.[36] Patterson compared the *Sun-Times* series to police officers posing as sex workers to entrap johns. The root of Bradlee and Patterson's objection was that the story could have been reported in another way where deception wasn't needed.

In an oral history of the project, Zekman explained it had been triggered because the paper had been 'getting phone calls from businesses that were complaining about having to pay a steady stream of inspectors . . . looking for payoffs to ignore city violations'.[37] The *Sun-Times* didn't orchestrate the situation, it merely came up with a way of witnessing and capturing that behaviour. It was the journalistic equivalent of setting a mouse trap, but Bradlee worried that the tactics used in The Mirage would send journalism on a wrong course. Bradlee's concerns, despite being back in the 1970s, still typify one of the major differences between journalism in the US and the trade in the UK: in the UK, undercover reporting is used far more often, even after one of its most notorious practitioners, the *News of the World* and *Sun on Sunday*'s 'Fake Sheikh' Mazher Mahmood was convicted of conspiracy to pervert the course of justice in 2016.

The difference between valuable and justified undercover reporting – exposing exploitative working practices at major corporations or revealing failings in government agencies – and the exploits Mahmood engaged in is that in those examples it's about infiltrating an organisation and observing what's happening inside. The Fake Sheikh set up his victims by dressing up as a member of Arab royalty and promising riches. He was engaged in exactly the kind of entrapment that Patterson wrongly suggested the *Sun-Times* had been indulging in. The story that finally brought the self-described 'King of the Sting' down involved encouraging the singer and former *X-Factor* judge Tulisa Contostavlos to arrange for him to be supplied with £800 worth of cocaine, a trick he'd used on many other fading stars in the past. Contostavlos was arrested and charged with involvement in the supply of a class-A drug. But when the case came to trial, it became clear that Mahmood's driver, Alan Smith, had initially told the police that the 'hyper-drunk' singer had made anti-drugs comments while he was taking her and two of her equally inebriated friends home from a meeting in London. The next day, he asked for his statement to be amended to remove the detail which, it later emerged, he had done after emailing it to Mahmood. Both men were found guilty of conspiring to pervert the course of justice; Smith was sentenced to 12 months, suspended for two years, and Mahmood was jailed for 15 months.

Five years earlier, Mahmood told the Leveson Inquiry that he'd committed illegal acts to get a story – 'I've purchased child pornography, for example, which clearly is an illegal act, and that led to a conviction' – and argued that 'clearly the end [justified] the means'. It revealed him as one of the more extreme results of a newspaper mentality that says getting the story is all that matters. Mahmood was at the far end of the spectrum of media behaviour,

WHAT'S THE STORY?

but he repeatedly won awards for his work and was handsomely paid for it. At times, he revealed real wrongdoing, notably when he exposed match-fixing by members of Pakistan's national cricket team, but on many other occasions, he created a fictional world to exploit his target's desperation.

Fiction, in the modern media, is not always confined to the methods of individual journalists. Despite proof being one of the fundamental bases on which journalism is, or should be, founded, occasionally the hunger for a story takes over. When the media is obsessed with a particular narrative, it's easy for fictoids – fictions that gain the credence of fact through repetition – to take hold.

On 26 November 2001, a report in *The New York Times* was headlined 'Heavily Fortified "Ant Farms" Deter bin Laden's Pursuers', and quoted an interview with a retired Russian sapper, Colonel Viktor Kutsenko, who had been in charge of destroying a cave complex in Zhawar during the Soviet occupation of Afghanistan. He claimed that behind the base's 'iron doors' there was a bakery, a hotel, a hospital with an ultra-sound machine, a library containing books in English and Farsi, and a garage that was home to a well-serviced Second World War-era Soviet T-34 tank. Essentially, in only a matter of months since the terror attacks of 11 September 2001, it became an accepted truth that Osama bin Laden was hunkered down in an elaborate bunker burrowed into the Tora Bora mountains of Afghanistan. *The New York Times* report quoted from a paper that had appeared that September in the *Journal of Slavic Military Studies*, which was, in turn, quoting from an interview translated from the Russian version of *Soldier of Fortune* magazine (*Soldat udachi*). *The New York*

BREAKING

Times bolted an unsourced claim that bin Laden '[was] reported to have upgraded [the base] and a nearby camp in the 1990s' onto that historical recollection. It wasn't fact but a translated anecdote mixed with an unsourced rumour.

The following day, Richard Lloyd Parry filed a report for the *Independent*[38] that told the story of a similar bunker in the Tora Bora mountains:

> It has its own ventilation system and its own power, created by a hydroelectric generator. Its walls and floor in the rooms are smooth and finished and it extends 350 yards beneath a solid mountain. It is so well defended and concealed that – short of poison gas or tactical nuclear weapon – it is immune to outside attack. And it is filled with heavily armed followers of Osama bin Laden, with a suicidal commitment to their cause and with nothing left to lose.

That story, balanced on one unnamed source, went on to claim that the so-called fortress was built using resources from the bin Laden family's Saudi construction empire and was home to 'as many as 2,000 Arab and foreign fighters' living in conditions 'like a hotel'. Curiously, while Lloyd Parry's reports from preceding and successive days remain in the *Independent*'s online archive, that particular Tora Bora story is long gone.

From here, things really began to snowball. It was *The Times* that made the story fly when it literally painted a picture of the 'lair'. An illustration published by the paper on 29 November 2001 depicted a cut-out view of a mountain with a complex network of tunnels, offices, bedrooms, ventilation shafts, ammo dumps

WHAT'S THE STORY?

and secret entrances. A label claimed that 'the complex of caves at Tora Bora is carved 1,150ft into a 13,000ft mountain and can accommodate up to 1,000 people'. Like Lloyd Parry's report, *The Times*' Bond-villain style vision of the 'mountain fortress' featured no named sources.

By 2 December, *The Times*' flight of imagination was being used on NBC's *Meet the Press* as an explanatory tool for viewers during host Tim Russert's interview with US Secretary of Defence Donald Rumsfeld. Russert talked through the graphic as though it was a photograph, pointing out Taliban guards, noting secret exits and presenting a vision of a highly technically advanced bunker. 'It's a very sophisticated operation,' he concluded, teeing up Rumsfeld to continue with the fantasy, nodding that it was 'serious business'. Russert described a *picture* drawn in London, based on *rumours* shared in Afghanistan as though it was an unquestionable representation of reality. And Rumsfeld encouraged the fantasy because US intelligence had been talking up the stories of complex tunnel systems to justify the vast bombing campaign.

Nine days later, when *Time* magazine's Matthew Forney followed Afghan forces into the now abandoned caves, the fantasy of the impenetrable fortress was broken:

> These weren't five-star accommodations with internal hydroelectric power plants and brick-lined walls, areas to drive armoured tanks and children's tricycles, and tunnels like capillaries that have captured the world's imagination. Such commodious quarters might exist higher in the White Mountains, but these were simply rough bunkers embedded deep into the mountain.[39]

BREAKING

There were no other more 'commodious' quarters higher up and the 'rough bunkers' were natural tunnels. There were also no *mea culpas* from the *Independent*, *The Times*, *NBC News* or any of the other media outlets that had spread the propaganda story of Bin Laden's hi-tech lair. Over two decades later, the idea of the Tora Bora bunker abides, still referenced and alluded to in news reports whenever the authorities warn of new terrorist threats. Starting with unrelated facts from the past mixed with rumour and speculation from motivated sources in the intelligence agencies, each new story had accreted new details, building an ever more baroque picture of a new, and entirely false, reality.

The fairy story of 'Bin Laden as Bond villain' was, in large part, a product of anonymous briefings. And it's not the only one that's been shaped by the hidden hand of storytellers whose names never appear in a byline or referenced in copy. The involvement of shadow influencers hugely reduces the amount of genuine journalistic inquiry in the newspapers and the wider media that feeds on them. So despite the existence of academic criteria – be they aspirational or reflective – sometimes the values of those eager journalists and how they shape the news take a back seat entirely. When stories are dropped pre-digested into reporters' beaks, the result is a regurgitation of someone else's line.

The ranks of those shadow influencers include public relations (PR) people, government communications teams, politicians' special advisors, representatives of foreign governments, think-tankers and spooks. The telltale signs are there, but only if you know where to look. News stories based on some survey or other are a good sign that they've been punted towards a desperate news

WHAT'S THE STORY?

desk by a PR company. Briefings on what a politician will say, or a party's future policies, come from 'a senior source', 'people in a position to know' or 'sources close to the leadership'. And when the security services are the source, reports tend to talk more obliquely about 'fears' or 'indications'. But readers and viewers who are not adequately aware of how a story has come onto the agenda are not able to properly judge how much credence they should give it. What a politician *might* do shouldn't be news but it is often treated as if it is, allowing parties and individual politicos to use the front pages of newspapers and the news bulletins that closely follow them as a means of testing the response from pundits and the public alike.

On any given day, a huge amount of news coverage is about the results of surveys or polls commissioned by companies or political players, events that haven't happened yet and might not happen at all, and inconsequential comments spun into controversies. On the less controversial end, there are the topics that come around every year like clockwork: just after New Year, it's time for the stories bemoaning that Easter eggs are already on the shelves; spring is for pieces about storms and flooding – a surprise every single time; summer is for 'phwoar, what a scorcher!' coverage of heat waves that ignores climate change and dubious photos of attractive girls getting their exam results; autumn brings the annual debate about people wearing/not wearing the remembrance poppy; and winter is the most wonderless time of the year with the perennial comment pieces about whether you can still say 'Christmas', depressing news stories about rip-off Winter Wonderlands and perpetual debates about which popular songs are now 'cancelled' over questionable lyrical choices.

BREAKING

Sometimes, what turns something into a story is a catchy piece of branding. In the early 2000s, there was a rash of reports in the British media claiming child hoodlums were committing unprovoked assaults purely to record them on their mobile phones before distributing the footage via Bluetooth. It may never have reached the national newspapers or become a folk panic in the wider media had the act not been given the snappy (or rather slappy) name 'happy slapping'. The two-word description was used by Michael Shaw, a reporter at the *Times Educational Supplement*, in a January 2005 story, pulling together anecdotes about the nascent trend from teachers in London schools.[40] Twenty years later, one of Shaw's social media profiles reads: 'Still blamed, among other things, for helping to coin the phrase "happy slapping".'

Shaw told *Vice*, for its oral history of the phenomenon: '[The night before publication] my editor said, "You do realise the kids who aren't already doing this out there are going to be doing this when it comes out?" The next day, the story actually did get picked up by all the national daily papers. It did start getting talked about that weekend, and from then on.'[41] Despite flaky home internet and the complete absence of even 3G mobile data, reports howled about thousands of 'happy slapping' videos being uploaded. The press had a new crime to fear *and* it was tied to a device that was increasingly going to be the newspapers' greatest frenemy – the mobile phone.

In December 2005, the *Daily Mirror* reported on an assault against the pop singer/TV presenter/newspaper fixture, Mylene Klass, under the headline 'Mylene's Happy Slap Hell':[42]

WHAT'S THE STORY?

Shaken TV presenter Mylene Klass was recovering last night after being attacked by a vicious gang of 'happy slappers'... First referring to Hear'Say's No. 1 hit, they sang at her 'Pure and Simple', adding menacingly, 'I'm going to kill you'. Then one of the girls dumped a bag of chips on her head before terrified Mylene, 27, was hurled roughly to the ground. As she lay stunned another of the thugs, laughing at her misery, said, 'Shall I bitch slap her?', a reference to 'happy slapping'. The gang then tried to snap her on their mobile phones before running to a nearby Tube station.

Klass had recently launched an anti-bullying campaign and her then-PR man, Jonathan Shalit, and spokesman, Simon Jones, were quoted extensively. An assault, especially against someone with a degree of professional notoriety, is definitely news but the story was given an extra frisson because the *Mirror* could tie it to the 'happy slapping crime wave'. Many more serious attacks, including several which resulted in the deaths of the victims, were attributed to 'happy slapping' by the press because of the involvement of a mobile phone; the definition became so loose as to be meaningless.

'Happy slapping' is just one of the press's successes in rebranding old crimes as new scourges: street robbery morphed into 'muggings'; vigilantes became 'have-a-go heroes'; assaults by motorists became 'road rage' and using cars as tools to rob shops turned alliterative as 'ram raiding'. A rebrand can give an old idea new life just as much in journalism as it does in advertising: 'New! Improved! Road Rage: Now with Smartphones!' After an idea has been repeated enough, the weight of coverage often trumps evidence.

BREAKING

With print sales in terminal decline, the (largely unspoken) truth about media brands is that they are not in the information business but competitors in the entertainment industry. Where once they were challenged by radio and TV, publishers face competition from an ever-expanding army of online distractions. The sheer number of screens in the world means there are more readers than ever but the demands on the audience's attention have grown too. Newspapers' greatest friends in the pre-internet age were boredom and disconnection. Now, with boredom almost extinct, grabbing attention requires a carnival barker's instincts and a stand-up comedian's ... timing. In turn, the hyperbolic tone that used to be largely confined to the tabloids has infected every publication – an endless, foot-stomping toddler tantrum that grows louder as their advertising revenue declines.

Owing to this pressing need to entertain, the news industry is also subject to fads and obsessions. In the introduction to his memoir published in 1978, the British foreign correspondent and war reporter Edward Behr wrote: ' ... the content of newspapers and magazines, like the shape of women's clothes, follows the vagaries of fashion.'[43] That's as true now as it was in the 1970s but the speed of the news industry's hype cycle is far faster. The news gets *bored*. When a war begins, the conflict will sit high on the news agenda, but as it goes on and its horrors become routine, it will slip down the bulletins and be given less space, deeper into the newspapers. It's hard to get editors to address long-term trends and ongoing stories because they are usually driven by novelty. A big storm – with the attendant opportunity to stick a reporter out in the driving rain – is more immediately interesting than spending months

WHAT'S THE STORY?

and years on a dogged commitment to reflecting the realities of climate change.

At the other end of the entertainment spectrum, we find the slightly more salacious content. Noam Chomsky says that 'when the press focuses on the sex lives of politicians [you should] reach for your pocket and see who's pulling out your wallet because those are not the issues that matter to people'.[44] I admire Professor Chomsky's high-mindedness but, in this case, I think he's dead wrong. People want to kid others – and often themselves – that they aren't interested in gossip, celebrity news or trivialities of any kind, but data, experience and the existence of MailOnline's 'Sidebar of Shame' tell us otherwise. Human beings are a nosy species and journalists are the nosiest subset of that species. While the French tend to respond to their politicians' affairs with a Gallic shrug (and, in fact, eye them suspiciously if they don't stray), the Protestant heritages of Britain and America provoke a continual interest in what happens behind prominent people's bedroom doors and elsewhere besides. The public interest defence for delving into politicians' private lives is usually hypocrisy but the long history of British political scandals shows the press haven't always needed that excuse.

In *Enquirer*, a 2012 play produced by the National Theatre of Scotland and the *London Review of Books* consisting of interviews with 43 working journalists, most of them anonymous, a character says: 'The group of people who haven't been on trial in the Leveson Inquiry are the British public, three million of whom bought the *News of the World* every week because they wanted to read that stuff. How did they think they got their pictures?'

BREAKING

It's an uncomfortable point but not an untrue one. A lot of people will pantomime distaste for the output of the tabloids but still have MailOnline in their browsing history with its greasy fast-food diet of paparazzi pictures of vaguely famous people daring to go outside and women accused of 'flaunting their curves' simply for existing in corporeal form.

The calculus behind whose suffering becomes a news story has always been brutal, as evidenced by the title of Behr's book – *Anyone Here Been Raped and Speaks English?*. The line was attributed by Behr to a BBC reporter who shouted it at a group of Belgian nuns after they had been airlifted out of Stanleyville – now Kisangani – in 1964 during one of a series of civil wars in Congo. The Indian writer, Farah Naqvi, called it 'the gold standard for journalistic crudity',[45] while Christopher Hitchens wrote in his memoir, *Hitch 22*, that it was the unofficial motto of the *Daily Express* foreign desk for which he briefly worked as a correspondent around the time that Behr's book was published. The spirit of the question is soaked deep into the newsrooms of Britain; when a plane crashes, news editors are quick to check if there were any British people on board before deciding whether and how prominently the story is covered.

Lists, like the ones we started this chapter looking at, can provide a framework for defining what's news, but there's always a gap between theory and practice. As we've seen, the news is subject to human obsessions and the fickleness of trends. What makes the headlines doesn't always reflect what serves the widest possible audience but rather the concerns of smaller groups of interested parties. Think back to how the newspapers largely failed to reflect the public's rejection of war in Iraq or how

WHAT'S THE STORY?

happy slapping and road rage became major worries rather than a selection of largely unconnected incidents. Into this melee, I would like to take the opportunity to suggest my own method for categorising the news: think of it like food – organic, processed and totally artificial. Organic news is when events are reported as they happen with a strong emphasis on facts. Processed news is where a story is heavily shaped by the agenda of the news organisation presenting it to you. Artificial news is where the story only exists because the outlet wished it into existence, presenting the few facts it might contain in the most bad faith way possible. If you have a population that has a news diet heavy with processed and artificial reporting, you end up with a malnourished society.

4.

An Anatomy of The News

Stripping Stories Down to Their Constituent Parts

'Reading the morning newspaper is the realist's morning prayer. One orients one's attitude toward the world either by God or by what the world is. The former gives as much security as the latter, in that one knows how one stands.'
– Hegel, *Miscellaneous writings of G. W. F. Hegel* (2002)

We're so familiar with the phrase 'news story' that we tend not to think about its meaning that closely, but the combination of words deserves more scrutiny. Whether they're on a screen in front of you, a voice emerging from a speaker, or concealed behind the written word, there are storytellers behind every piece of news. Just as fiction writers make choices to build a world for you, journalists and editors make hundreds of little choices in every report. No news story is entirely neutral because every story requires an angle and is subject to the perspectives of those creating it.

BREAKING

As we saw in the previous chapter, the first choice is deciding when an event becomes a story. Most things that happen, including wars and disasters, remain unreported in most places. I often think of the scene in the sitcom *Peep Show*, where the performatively hippyish Nancy complains about a TV news report on a bus crash ('What about all the buses that made it safely to their destinations, huh?') and is shut down by Mark, the finger-wagging fun sponge: 'Yes, I suppose the news should just be a dispassionate list of all the events that have occurred the world over during the day. That would be good. Except, of course, it would take forever!'

Every story has an angle, a point of view informed by the people working on it and the outfit for which they work. Watch coverage of the same event on the BBC, ITV, Channel 4 News, CNN, Al Jazeera and Fox News and you'll find common ground buried beneath each station's angle on a particular story, the corporate perspective mixed with the choices and interests of the reporters, producers and editors involved. While the BBC will agonise more about questions of impartiality – something we'll explore more later – and show less obvious bias than some of the other outlets mentioned, absolute neutrality is impossible. The angle is always present and the choices and, crucially, compromises that have been made to get a report on the air are always discernible if you stop to examine them closely.

At the most basic level a news story needs to contain the answer to five Ws and an H: Who? What? Where? When? Why? And How? Then comes the structure needed to contain them. In school, you're taught to tell stories chronologically, beginning at the beginning. That goes out of the window when

AN ANATOMY OF THE NEWS

you're learning to be a journalist. The first and simplest form of story structure you're taught is the 'inverted pyramid', presenting the material in descending order with the most interesting and important elements at the top. That's fine to begin with – it'll give you the tools to write perfectly serviceable news reports – but to be *good* at journalism, you need to go beyond that basic media Meccano and master more complex constructions.

The challenge comes when you're dealing with a story that doesn't have an obvious chronology or a clear protagonist to focus on. It's like opening a jigsaw box, tipping out the pieces and discovering that some of them could slot in anywhere and others don't seem to fit at all. Oh, and then you realise there's no picture on the lid to refer to, one voice is shouting at you to get it finished and there are multiple others telling you that the image you're putting together is not at all what you think it is.

One of the benefits of picking up a newspaper in print is that the physical organisation of it is revealing. By comparison, online news stories are constantly changing, with many news organisations being shady about showing where and when they have been updated. Print is a snapshot of choices and traps excellence and errors in equal measure, like ancient mosquitos in amber, making them easier to examine and dissect. A newspaper is not just a series of the previous day's most pressing stories arranged in order of importance but an overarching story in itself. It tells you what its editors thought would entice and incite. The front page is a statement of intent and an advert for what's inside. Each story's placement and relationship to other stories tells you something about that publication's priorities but also its restrictions. And the glaring absence of some event that you expect to be covered is equally telling.

BREAKING

Despite the huge advancements in the physical processes of printing presses, the structure of a print newspaper is still dictated in large part by the demands of this technology. Sending pages to the printworks in a staggered order means that there are 'early' pages which go first and include the material that's least time sensitive and not likely to change at the last minute, such as features and columns. Sports news is usually placed on the back pages to account for last-minute scores and other late-breaking details. The front page and the big domestic stories that tend to follow are printed on the same sheets of paper as the sports reports – these are the 'late' pages.

And so, as they race to make the presses, newspapers are not so much finished as consciously abandoned; they could always be tweaked to include more detail or fine-tune the language, but that effort has to stop when the print deadline arrives. It's the perpetual quest to fill the pages in time that produces the anxious energy of the newsroom. Even with the constant demands of online news, a publication that retains a print version tends to work to that rhythm to some extent. The rather quaint term for sending an edition to print – 'going off stone' – is a hangover from the early days of printing when type was set into a layout on a piece of metal called an imposing stone to align the text. While print newspapers are now frequently out of date by the time they hit the shelves, second or third editions which are sent later can allow them to catch up with developments.

While the media goes well beyond the newspapers, they still play a major role in defining the grammar of news and feeding into broadcasters' agendas. These agendas are about as varied as it is possible to get, each publisher with their own unique brand

AN ANATOMY OF THE NEWS

and bias. One particular scene from *Yes, Prime Minister* remains a useful guide:

> **Jim Hacker:** Don't tell me about the press. I know exactly who reads the papers: the *Daily Mirror* is read by people who think they run the country; the *Guardian* is read by people who think they ought to run the country; *The Times* is read by the people who actually do run the country; the *Daily Mail* is read by the wives of the people who run the country; the *Financial Times* is ready by people who own the country; the *Morning Star* is read by the people who think the country ought to be run by another country and the *Daily Telegraph* is read by people who think it is.
> **Sir Humphrey**: Prime Minister, what about people who read the *Sun*?
> **Bernard Woolley**: *Sun* readers don't care who runs the country, as long as she's got big tits.
> – *Yes, Prime Minister*, 'Conflict of Interest', series 2, episode 2 (1987)

In many respects, Jim Hacker's newspaper monologue – written by Antony Jay and Jonathan Lynn – holds up 38 years later, even though it was technically out of date then (the *Independent* launched in October 1986). But there have inevitably been changes in the intervening decades. Here's a quick, partial and biased guide to the political alignment of British newspapers and what they represent in 2025:

BREAKING

Daily Mail

In 2019, Channel 4 announced that the Mail's long-term editor Paul Dacre – then in a brief period away from the paper – was going to front a documentary that promised to reveal how he 'shaped the *Daily Mail* as the voice of middle England'. When Dacre returned to the *Mail*'s parent company, Associated Newspapers, as editor-in-chief, the documentary was put on ice, but that promotional text was instructive. 'The voice of middle England' is exactly how the *Mail* sees itself. The documentary was called *The World According to Paul Dacre* and, despite Ted Verity now being in the editor's chair, that's what you get when you pick up the *Mail*.

It's the paper that will always tell you how much a murder victim's family home is worth, a permanently outraged and paranoid personality that will switch from warning of Britain's decline to cooing at a cute puppy. *MailOnline*, it's online incarnation, has the same instincts but wielded by a sweaty-palmed voyeur training a telescope on the world in an endless hunt for vaguely well-known women out 'flaunting their curves'. Though the *Sun* was the paper that politicians most chased for approval in the 1990s and 2000s, the *Mail* has long been the title they fear.

Sun

The newspaper equivalent of the TV series *Life on Mars* but with the modern cop forced to exist in a 1970s police station replaced with contemporary journalists cosplaying as hard-bitten hacks permanently in the 1980s. Though the paper's most notorious editor, Kelvin MacKenzie, left the building for the first time in 1994, his spirit remains like cigarette smoke soaked into an old pub's walls.

The *Sun* speaks for an imagined and homogenous working

AN ANATOMY OF THE NEWS

class, for a stereotypical version of the white van man who is never less than livid. It's a hugely diminished beast, trading off the inflated myth of its former influence but rarely breaking big exclusives or defining the news agenda as it once did. The *Sun* is a paper in its dotage, alive in print only because of Rupert Murdoch's nostalgic fondness for it as a product of his own creation and formerly a major source of the profits that allowed him to expand his empire in the 1980s.

Daily Mirror

The *Mirror* has never really recovered from being in the grubby hands of Robert Maxwell, who raided its credibility almost as much as he plundered its pensions funds. Historically a paper of the left, it can now only really claim a place in the flabby centre with Labour, the political party it supports almost entirely out of habit, like a football fan buying the new strip each season whether they're keen on the design or not.

While the *Mirror* is often treated as though it's the 'nice' one compared to its natural enemy the *Sun*, its instincts are almost as reactionary as the rival red top. As its parent company, Reach, tries to produce more identikit celebrity news with fewer and fewer journalists – it made 700 redundant in 2023 alone – the paper struggles to set the news agenda.

The Times

I've often described *The Times* as the *Sun* with a more expensive thesaurus, but that's not quite right. Currently edited by Tony Gallagher, a former *Mail* man who also spent time in the chair at the *Sun* and the *Daily Telegraph*, its instincts have been increasingly

BREAKING

Mail-like in recent years. Its politics are solidly right wing and its stable of columnists (and presenters on its spinoff radio station, Times Radio) is heavy with former Tory ministers and advisors. Its daily feature supplement, Times2, is as committed to making women feel paranoid about their lives, bodies, families and careers as the *Mail's* censorious and scaremongering Femail section.

The *Times* has been growing its online subscriptions as its print circulation declines, but partly on the back of permanent promotions that sometimes make it seem like the newspaper equivalent of one of those furniture warehouses where the big sale never ends. That said, its paywall has turned it into a profitable title for its parent company, News UK, while its tabloid cousin, the *Sun*, which was once the company's pay pig, has haemorrhaged money (partly as a result of huge financial settlements in phone hacking cases).

Financial Times

If *The Times* was once the paper read by 'the people who actually run the country', that title is arguably now held by the *Financial Times* because the people who *actually* run the country are the stock markets. While undoubtedly a centre-right publication with an almost fanatical devotion to free markets, the *FT* is the most reliable player in the British press if you want to read news that presents the world largely as it is rather than through the prism of the proprietor's preferred ideology. That's because people whose focus is making money want facts to help them make their bets.

The *FT* is not without its grotesque elements. Its How to Spend It magazine – a glossy bit of fluff full of hyper-expensive geegaws for bankers to spunk their bonuses on – could easily be

AN ANATOMY OF THE NEWS

a very blunt piece of Marxist propaganda designed to foment bloody revolution.

Daily Telegraph

Having just written about a newspaper which presents the world largely as it actually is, we come to one which lives in a paranoid world of its own. Where the *Daily Telegraph* was once the rather staid house journal of the Tory Party, it has shifted over the past ten years to become a paranoid fanzine for the most unhinged members of the right and far right.

In the view of the *Telegraph*, Britain and the wider world are going to hell in a handcart and that handcart is being pushed by the woke left, despite governments that the paper vigorously supported having held power for the majority of the last hundred years. A Labour government is not so secretly delightful to the *Telegraph* as it can go even further in its paranoid rantings while also getting plenty of mileage from the Conservative Party's ongoing psycho-dramas.

Guardian

There's a gap between the *Guardian's* stereotypical reputation and the reality. In October 2022, then Home Secretary and frequent resident of liberal nightmares Suella Braverman made a speech in Parliament that put the blame for Just Stop Oil protests on '*Guardian*-reading, tofu-eating wokerati'. Casting aside the fact that even *The Times*' readership undoubtedly contains a large number of tofu-eaters, the notion of *Guardian* readers as hippies who knit their own muesli is a throwback to the mid-1990s. A 20-year-old comment from Sir Max Hastings, the former

Telegraph editor, about why he wrote for the paper is more on the money: 'It is read by the new establishment.'⁴⁶

While the *Guardian* still likes to see itself as a paper on the centre left, that new Establishment position means it tends to be rather less left and a lot more centrist. While the paper undoubtedly cares about and covers social issues, breaking stories about injustices like the Windrush scandal, and has writers who are passionately on the left, it has a tendency towards what Adam Curtis defined as 'oh dearism' in a 2009 short film of the same name, making reading the paper like 'living in the mind of a depressed hippie'. Although, in the *Guardian*'s case, that depressed hippie will often go from telling you about the homelessness crisis to extolling the virtues of some extremely expensive cushions.

Daily Express

Once the *Daily Mail*'s great rival, the *Daily Express* has long been an also-ran. Formerly the butt of jokes for its frequent tenuous front pages on Princess Diana, Madeleine McCann and snow – though never managing to produce a story that combined all three – it's now part of the Reach stable of papers. While it's always been a resolutely Tory paper, apart from blip in 2015 when it endorsed UKIP, the *Express* increasingly serves as a print companion to GB News. And where it was once obsessed with his mother, the paper now chases traffic by constant coverage of Prince Harry and his wife, Meghan.

Independent

Founded in 1986 by three former *Daily Telegraph* journalists, the *Independent* once tried to embody the promise of its title and

AN ANATOMY OF THE NEWS

managed to challenge both the *Guardian* to its left and *The Times* to its right. But those days are long gone. Now a limp and liberal-ish paper, the *Independent* became a more depressing kind of pioneer in 2016 when it published its final print edition and went online only. Decent traffic figures disguise the fact that the title relies heavily on deceptive clickbait headlines and has a website that's choked with ads and sponsored content.

Evening Standard

Like the *Independent*, the *Evening Standard* is owned by Lord Lebedev. While he seems to have largely lost interest in the former, he frequently pops up in the latter, interviewing celebrities and 'thinkers' he wants to meet, dictating op-eds, and featuring in many pictures taken at events sponsored by the *Standard*, which give him further opportunities to pal around with the prominent and powerful. Despite London being largely a Labour-supporting city, the *Standard* tends to support Tories, going so far as letting the former Conservative Chancellor George Osborne edit the whole thing for a few years. It has now shifted to a weekly print schedule, having struggled with a reduced commuter audience and the arrival of WiFi on Tube trains.

i

A spin-off from the *Independent*, the *i* is now owned by DMGT, the *Daily Mail*'s parent company, but shares little with the *Mail* politically. It's the most resolutely centrist newspaper and therefore generally the most boring. Its love of fence sitting is best exemplified by the paper's decision to back neither 'leave' nor 'remain' during the Brexit referendum, as well as an ongoing

BREAKING

refusal to endorse a party in general elections. With its very concise articles, reading the *i* tends to feel like visiting a restaurant that refuses to serve proper portions and leaves you almost as hungry as you were when you arrived. To needlessly extend that metaphor, if the *i* was a person, it would think mayonnaise is spicy.

Now we've looked at the character of the various papers, what about the nuts and bolts that you find inside them? I have compiled a classic A to Z to break down some key components:

Adjectives
A news story stuffed with adjectives is a news story that's trying too hard to persuade you of its importance. Henry J. Smith discouraged the tendency to overwrite in his 1921 pamphlet, *It's the Way It's Written: Notes on the literary equipment of a newspaper man*:

> To belong to the distinguished company of real newspaper writers you must *rein in*. A great tragedy . . . needs no artificial colouring. A story of a lost child of a tramp dying in the country hospital must be simply told. The bigger the story, the more it reaches into the complexities and mysteries of the human soul, the less it needs embroidery.

'After . . .'
The word 'after' is a handy tool for glomming together two unconnected events in a story. For instance, 'Prince William is

AN ANATOMY OF THE NEWS

getting back to work *after* footage of him and his wife Catherine was published this weekend.' The first part of that sentence has no relation to the second but it allows the writer to cut-and-shut two facts together as if they flow naturally.

Below the line
See 'Comments'.

'Breaking'
Meant to denote a fresh and unfolding story, but often added to news alerts just to make the outlet sending them seem like they're on the ball. Increasingly, extremely ordinary stories are pimped up with the promise that their content is 'breaking' when they were never that interesting in the first place.

Bylines
The byline on a story – literally the line that tells you who a story is by – can reveal a lot about how it was put together. If it says 'PA Wire', '*Daily Mail* Reporter' or some variation on that theme you're looking at copy that has been written by a news agency and bought in. It may have had some primping and plumping up by the publication you're reading but there's a high chance it won't have. If you see multiple names in the byline, it may mean that a team of journalists has written the story but it could also be down to the fact that senior journalists want credit for the inclusion of a single fact they contributed or simply because they were around and have *been around* longer. Bylines will also tell you if the report you're reading is from a general reporter or one of the paper's specialist correspondents.

BREAKING

Captions
Pay attention to picture captions. You can get a sense of what the sub-editors think of the subject of a news story by the way they describe them in these often-overlooked bits of page furniture.

Columnists
See chapter five.

Comments
In the pre-online age, readers had to write a letter, stick it in an envelope, shell out for a stamp and hope that their views would be printed in the paper via a process that was entirely opaque to them. Online, the comments section has long been the bane of hacks, who tend to tell each other never to venture **below the line** because there be monsters as well as an even more frightening category of people – the ones who actually know more about a topic than the writer and have the facts to prove it. Moderators who are employed to keep conversations on track and on the right side of the law can also be used to delete contributions that are uncomfortable for the writer or the publication as a whole.

Conference
Most newsrooms have at least two conferences a day – morning and afternoon – where stories to be included in the paper are discussed. These are where the editorial agenda is set but are also an arena for the internal politics between different sections of the organisation to play out.

AN ANATOMY OF THE NEWS

Copy
Normal people write sentences. Journalists hammer out copy.

Curiosity gap
Headlines that deliberately leave out information to induce you to click on them. They were extremely popular in BuzzFeed's boomtimes in the 2010s but you'll still encounter them today. Example: 'This type of headline is dying. You'll never guess what killed it ...'

Dog's dick
Increasingly archaic journalistic slang for an exclamation mark. Yes, it truly is a grown-up industry.

Elegant variation
Writers and sub-editors are desperate to avoid repetition so you'll often find them using shonky synonyms in news stories. The practice was defined as 'elegant variation' by H. W. Fowler and F. G. Fowler in their grammar guide, *The King's English* (1906), but it's often anything of the sort. It's why a story in the *Guardian* about bananas ended up referring to 'the ubiquitous yellow fruit', and the *Daily Telegraph* turned *The Great British Bake Off* into 'the sweet-toothed ratings hit' and dubbed Venice 'the famed lagoon city'. Inevitably, there's an elegant variation for elegant variations – second mentions – and an account by that name on Twitter/X has been collecting the best examples of the seriously laboured synonyms (shit, there's another one) for years now.

BREAKING

Errors

Seek out the 'corrections and clarifications' box. While newspapers shout their original accusations and insinuations, placing them on their front pages or in other prominent locations, they whisper their apologies. Though the regulator's guidelines say corrections should be given due prominence, you'll generally find them hidden deep in the paper, shoved in the corner of the letters page or nestled at the bottom of a boring spread near the back. 'Clarifications' is just another way of saying 'we cocked up' but with even less contrition.

Headlines

If a headline ends in a question mark, you can usually respond with the answer 'no'. This old and relatively reliable maxim was discussed by both Andrew Marr, in his book *My Trade* (2004), and veteran technology journalist Ian Betteridge in a 2009 article,[47] which led to him lending his name to Betteridge's Law of Headlines. A question headline is a good indication that a story is pushing its luck, hoping to create controversy where there is none, or make some uncertain prospect seem more likely.

Treat quote marks in a headline as a warning sign. Load-bearing quote marks – 'Wright "betrays" journalism' – are a way of smuggling an opinion into a headline without the newspaper having to take responsibility for it. Investigate the copy beneath a headline sprinkled with speech marks and you'll usually discover that the claim at the top is not supported by the facts beneath it. The sneaky hope of a headline with quote marks is that your eyes will skip over them and you'll be left thinking that the suggestion they are supporting is actually a fact.

AN ANATOMY OF THE NEWS

Headlines, hammer
Especially large headlines designed to produce maximum impact. The *Sun*'s response to the sinking of the Argentine battleship *Belgrano* during the Falklands War is probably the most notorious hammer headline in British media history: 'Gotcha'.

Hidden details
Watch out for page two stories. Stories bumped from the front page by the night editor, or which the paper wants to say it reported but would rather didn't get too much attention for political or business reasons, are often shifted to page two. A lot of people turn the page and move straight to page three, even in papers other than the *Sun* which don't use the space for a gratuitous picture of a woman in a bikini.

Similarly, read the NiBs. The 'News in Briefs' are the one- or two-line stories in columns at the side of a page. You can often find interesting and significant pieces of news shoved there by news editors and subs who, through blind spots, bias or just limited space, decided to boil them down to nearly nothing.

Human interest
'Human interest' is one of those strange journalistic descriptors which should really apply to everything a media outlet publishes – if there's no human interest, why care? In reality, human interest stories are where an emotional hook – an individual or individuals affected by the events of a story – is put ahead of the cold facts. The upside of human interest stories is that they're a good way of making people actually care about an issue. The downside is that they can reduce wider structural issues to a question of individual suffering.

BREAKING

Injunctions

You can spot injunctions by their influence on a story. If you read a story that's especially coy on naming names or which leans heavily on vague innuendo, there's a good chance that an organisation's desire to report something has smashed into the immovable object of a well-off individual's ability to pay for lawyers capable of persuading a judge to put a stop to it. It's worth noting that these are much less common than you might expect.

Kiss-and-tells

In the 1980s and 90s, if you had a 'romp' or, in fact, many 'romps' with someone well known, there would be a tabloid newspaper ready and willing to pay you to 'reveal all'. Tales of 'love rats' have become decidedly lesser-spotted since 2012 when Mr Justice Eady awarded £60,000 damages to Max Mosley after the *News of the World* published extensive coverage and secretly filmed footage of his five-hour S&M party with five women. The judge concluded that sexual conduct that didn't break the law was not a matter of 'genuine public interest'.

Where you come across – ooh err, etc. – what looks like a kiss-and-tell story now, it's likely to be highly flattering to the celebrity it names (people rarely sue when they're made to look like a sexual superhero) and may even have been sold into the paper by their publicist.

Leader columns

Whether you're reading a newspaper in print or online, the leader columns – or the 'editorial page' if you're in the US – are a good place to start. Published without individual bylines,

AN ANATOMY OF THE NEWS

these are the institutional voice of the newspaper and will give you a good idea of the paper's current political positions and what it cares about – or, at least, what it is claiming to care about – on any given day.

Lede, The
The lede is just a news story's initial sentence or paragraph. Its purpose is to summarise the main point and keep you reading. It's the home of the five Ws and that solitary H. 'Burying the lede' is failing to put the key information at the top of the story but it's not always done through ignorance or inexperience. Sometimes the lede gets buried because an outlet doesn't want to draw too much attention to it but also wants to avoid being accused of ignoring it.

Letters
Taking a look at the letters page is a good way to see how a publication polices the bounds of debate and what it considers legitimate criticisms or responses to its output. It's also fairly common for letters editors to go out and solicit letters to push a debate forward or get a specific kind of response. Letters pages are never an organic reflection on any article. For that you have to go diving into the **comments** section before the moderators get in there and clean up.

Obits
The best bit of any national newspaper is the obituaries. They can be dead funny, dead moving or dead wrong, but they're also pretty much guaranteed to be dead interesting. While being a beloved

figure is a good way to get yourself a prominent memorialisation, monsters who make their mark on the national and international consciousness get in there too – Henry Kissinger got lavish spreads and the death of the Yorkshire Ripper, Peter Sutcliffe, made several papers' obit sections.

Photographs

A picture may be worth a thousand words but how many of those words are lies? Without even taking into account the increasing influence of imagery created by generative AI, photos featured in the news can be deceptive in a number of more prosaic ways. Watch out for 'handouts' – pictures taken by an official photographer and distributed to the press following a judicious edit. Increasingly, images of politicians out and about are taken by someone on their payroll in an attempt to avoid embarrassments like the infamous (and ludicrous) case of then-Labour leader Ed Miliband being humiliated for committing the unthinkable act of . . . eating a bacon sandwich as millions of other people would.[48]

PR puff

Is the fact that Marks & Spencer launched knickers with built-in padding to 'give backsides a bit of oomph' (not my words, the words of the *Daily Mail*)[49] or the actress Sofia Vergara releasing a swimsuit collection with Walmart[50] news? No. But in both cases, those stories gave newspapers an excuse to run pictures of shapely women, while also doing advertisers a favour. Not all reports provoked by press releases will be as obvious but if there's an incongruous reference to a company in the copy that's a sure sign that they had a hand in it.

AN ANATOMY OF THE NEWS

Pull quotes
Taken from the main body of a news item or feature, pull quotes are designed to draw you in to reading the rest of the copy. Like reviews quoted on movie posters, they can be quite unrepresentative of the actual story.

Reverse ferret
If you spot an organisation's editorial line on an issue has changed from one week to the next, or even one day to the next, you've caught it in the act of a reverse ferret. Another of former *Sun* editor Kelvin MacKenzie's dubious contributions to the English language, it comes from his description of making life uncomfortable for public figures – especially politicians – as 'sticking a ferret up their trousers'. Consequently, if the paper then found itself on the wrong side of public opinion, MacKenzie would then race around declaring that it was time to 'reverse ferret!'. The term was picked up by *Private Eye* and has now jumped the Atlantic, with *The New York Times* describing anti-Trump Republicans who suddenly converted to his cause when he first secured their party's nomination as indulging in a reverse ferret.[51]

Riddle
Another way of describing newspapers' practice of bunging a question mark on the end of a headline when they're insufficiently sure of the story – i.e. 'If we don't know, make it a riddle.' Is this the REAL story?

BREAKING

Right of reply

When a news story ends with a line like 'Lord Bastard's representatives declined to comment' or 'We put these allegations to Baroness God-Awful of Great Corruption but she hadn't responded at the time of publication', this is a sign that the outlet in question has given the subject(s) of a story a right of reply – putting the details to them and asking them to comment. This isn't a shield against legal action but it's looked upon far more favourably by the judiciary than hitting 'publish' and laughing to yourself demonically.

Scare stories

If there's a worst-case scenario, that's what the newspapers will focus on. Take, for example, the *Sun*'s front-page story on 11 January 2023: 'Nuke Plot Smashed at Heathrow'. The headline was illustrated with a stock image of a dirty yellow nuclear warning symbol emerging from inky darkness. A strapline warned of 'deadly cargo fears' and bullet points hammered home how scared the reader should be with increasing panic: 'Uranium Shipment Intercepted' > 'Probe By Spooks and Terror Cops' (cue the scary music) > 'Package Was Sent to Iranian'.

The copy warned 'counter-terror cops and security services [were] investigating after a deadly shipment of uranium was seized at Heathrow'. But Scotland Yard told several other news outlets that the material that had been seized was an 'extremely small' amount of contaminated scrap metal. It could only have been 'a deadly shipment' if someone had tried to eat it.

The *Sun* report went on to suggest that 'the undeclared nuclear material [could] be used in a dirty bomb'. The notion of a 'dirty bomb' – a conventional explosive with radioactive material added to it – is one of journalism's most resilient scare stories. There is no record of a successful 'dirty bomb' attack ever happening. In 2001, the Wisconsin Project on Nuclear Arms Control passed a document to *The New York Times* that appeared to show the Iraqi Army had tested a 'dirty bomb' in 1987. The device was 12 feet long and weighed more than a ton. The Iraqis abandoned the project after concluding that levels of radiation produced were too low.

The following year, José Padilla was arrested in Chicago on suspicion of planning a 'dirty bomb' attack. He was held in military custody without charge for four years and later convicted of conspiring to commit murder and funding terrorism – though neither charge related to the alleged plot. A 2014 US Senate investigation of CIA interrogations uncovered emails from the agency that revealed Padilla had referred to a satirical online article headlined 'How to Make an H-bomb', which advised readers to fill a bucket with liquid uranium and swing it around their head as fast as possible for 45 minutes. Another CIA email admitted that trying to follow the article's advice would 'likely result in death' but 'definitely would not result in a nuclear explosion'.

The *Sun* was also trying to make something explosive without the correct ingredients. The game was to pretend that an 'Iranian dirty bomb plot' had been foiled – despite lacking evidence of any plot, Iranian or otherwise. Inside the paper, a further story – 'Uranium flown into London on a passenger jet' – which added crime reporter Mike 'Sully' Sullivan and defence editor Jerome Starkey to the byline, gave the impression that the package was *only* uranium and leaned heavily on the phrase 'UK-based Iranians'.

BREAKING

Anyone engaged in honest journalistic inquiry would have asked three questions: why would anyone trying to smuggle uranium into the UK send it through Heathrow, which has specialist scanners for detecting radioactive material? Why such a small amount? And why in the form of contaminated scrap metal?

In situations where journalists promise a plot, it's always worth asking if it's actually just a cock-up. Professor Michael Clarke, a defence and security analyst, told *Sky News* that it was 'almost certainly an accident'[52] but his quote was placed just beneath speculation from a former head of the British Army's Joint Chemical, Biological, Radiological and Nuclear Regiment, who said while there was no indication of Al Qaeda involvement, it '[had] their trademarks and fingerprints on it'. Their trademark move of *not* making 'dirty bombs'?

The *Sun* got its scare story for that day but never followed up on the plot because ... there was none. No arrests were made and no hidden cells of crazed fanatics were revealed.

Sources, anonymous

There are lots of ways of referring to unnamed sources which are being used to support a story. Here are some formulations and how to translate them into plain language:

'Sources close to [the star / the CEO / the minister / the Prime Minister ...]' = someone who works with that individual and is pushing a line that they want out there but with the added benefit of deniability.

'Friends of ...' = Either the person in question or someone paid by them. In only a vanishingly small number of cases does this mean a 'friend' in the sense that you or I might understand it.

AN ANATOMY OF THE NEWS

'A government source . . .' = Someone relatively junior.

'A senior government source . . .' = This might mean that they're actually senior or the journalist simply wants the story to sound more impressive.

'A government source in a position to know . . .' = Someone who probably works in the same office.

'The minister is said to believe . . .' = The minister definitely thinks this but doesn't want to say it on the record.

'I understand . . .' = This is definitely happening but I can't let on how I found out.

'The BBC understands . . .' = Another organisation has already reported this fact but we really don't want to credit them.

'I hear . . .' = This is gossip but I believe it.

'It's believed . . .' = I know this is true but I'm hedging my bets.

Sources, on the record

When a story quotes named sources, it's always worth considering their angle. Opinions expressed by spokespeople from think tanks – which usually have names like the Institute of This or The Centre for That – should be taken with such a large pinch of salt that your doctor will worry about your blood pressure. Similarly, PR people from companies that offer quotes with their name attached should provoke an arched eyebrow. And if you keep a careful eye on the news section of papers, you'll see the names of the same coterie of tame backbench MPs over and over again – every newspaper has its list of politicians who can be relied upon to get angry about a given issue and provide an outraged quote on command.

BREAKING

Strapline
A secondary headline used to further sell a story.

Surveys and studies
Companies and their PR people know that an eye-catching survey result is an easy way to get a free mention in the papers. Equally, hacks know that recently published academic papers are a good source of striking tales. You should be deeply sceptical of stories that purport to bring you the results of an important survey, rigorous study or exciting new research. For example, on the day I was writing this section, two out of three stories on page three of the *Daily Mail* were about shaky study results. The headline on the first thundered 'Warning over risk to pets from human painkillers'[53] and claimed that 'animal lovers [were] putting pets at risk by giving them human painkillers'. The fact that 'research' was from a pharmaceutical packaging company who based this on a mere 1,930 online searches of Ibuprofen-related pet questions per month was buried at the end of the report. The second story ('A canine companion can result in fewer dog days'[54]) on the stress-relieving benefits of being with 'a well-trained poodle' was lifted from a paper from researchers at a South Korean university which reported on an experiment involving just 30 volunteers, all of whom ... liked dogs.

Topline
Another way of describing the angle of story, e.g. 'What's the topline for this one about the bears shitting in the woods?'

AN ANATOMY OF THE NEWS

Zinger
A word that tends to appear in print to describe a quip the writer thought was good and which I've included here as a cheap means of making this a proper A to Z.

This chapter is an attempt to give you a kind of toolkit for reading the news. Disassembling the language used to present a story to you can make it easier to see the motivations behind it. No outlet, no matter how loud its claims, is without an agenda. While the vocabulary of journalism continues to evolve in the same way as language more widely, it stubbornly retains terms and turns of phrase tied to much older versions of itself. And the characters who comment on the news are also products of that knotty history, as we'll discover next.

5.

A Matter of Opinions

On Columns and Columnists

*'People seem not to see that their opinion of the world
is also a confession of character.'*
– Ralph Waldo Emerson, *The Conduct of Life* (1860)

Opinions are like arseholes – everyone's got one and some people make good money from sharing theirs with the public. Despite the perennial complaint from a persistent section of their readership that papers should simply report the news and 'stick to the facts', opinion journalism, as delivered by that curious creature known as the columnist, drives attention, creates loyalty and differentiates one publication from another. Columnists can be the moral centre of a newspaper or the literal personification of its cruellest, basest and most amoral inclinations.

Since there have been newspapers, there have been columnists, but the word 'columnist' itself is a relatively recent descriptor. Daniel Defoe's essays in his eighteenth-century periodical *Review* were arguably the first informal and chatty newspaper columns. They were strongly partisan – he was imprisoned for libel and thrown in the stocks on several occasions – and designed to entertain and provoke. Similarly, Jonathan Swift's scathing satires, Alexander Hamilton's broadsides for the *New York Evening Post* (which he founded) and Mark Twain's comic (and only semi-factual) newspaper dispatches resemble contemporary column writing.

The modern concept of the columnist began to solidify in the early years of the twentieth century. By 1920, it was familiar enough for C. L. Edson, himself the writer of a humour column for the *New York Evening Mail*, to publish a light-hearted guide to doing the job: 'The successful columnist puts his own personality into his column. It is not a case of impersonal jesting and heaping up of cold, blue-lit diamonds of wit. The reader likes the column because it reveals a daily insight into another man's soul – and he finds this other soul likeable.'[55]

It's a beautifully naive and utopian definition. If you combed through the output of today's columnists in search of soul, you'd come back with very slim pickings. In general, modern columnists are carnival barkers, trolls with a bigger megaphone than those stuck on social media or locked down in the comments section. The demands of producing a fresh take weekly (or, occasionally, multiple times a week) in a ruthless attention economy lead most columnists to rely on the cheapest tricks, like emotional e-numbers meant to make the reader angry with either them or the targets of their ire. To succeed as a columnist, you have to get a reaction. And to analytics, editors and advertisers, a click made in anger counts as much as a delighted one.

A good columnist should be willing to say things that will surprise the reader but not simply as a shock tactic. They should

A MATTER OF OPINIONS

use their head but write from their heart. Columns can and should be funny when the topic can stand it, but a great columnist will avoid the temptation to be glib and will be serious when the story demands it. The best columns leave the reader seeing a subject differently and stick in their head long after they've put down the paper or closed the tab.

The great temptation for columnists is to become a character writing in a heightened register, ignoring facts that don't fit with your angle. It's one that most long-term opinion writers cannot resist. Nesrine Malik, a *Guardian* columnist who I think bucks that trend, explained her approach to me:

> One thing I've learned over time is that a column has to provide a service. It has to be useful in some way. It's tempting to see a column as just a place to say what you think, but that's not useful. In my head, I have a schematic with four windows, each one a type of column – analytical, reported, channelling (making the reader feel seen and understood) and logical (taking something complicated that's been mired in confusion and simplifying it).

If we apply the Malik Matrix (patent pending), most columns in the British press exist on the outer edge of the 'channelling' category, reflecting their readers' existing views right back at them, before diving into the empty void of 'just a place to say what you think'. The traditional refrain of British papers promoting their star columnists is that they 'say what everyone else is thinking' and, in some respects, that's true: columnists tend to play to the prejudices and beliefs of their readership while making out that they are engaged in well-remunerated acts of bravery to a fixed word count and specific deadline. And while they tend to be enormous fans of the mantra 'no one tells me what to write', columnists who attempt to stray too far from the company line will soon find themselves out of a job. In my time contributing instant comment pieces to the *Telegraph*'s Blogs section, I quickly realised how often you're required to have an opinion on topics about which you actually have no strong feelings.

Another *Guardian* columnist, Marina Hyde, gave a blunt reply when asked about her process by Press Gazette: 'It's a trade. And you just have to fill the space. And it's good if you can do it better. But if you can't, it must nonetheless be filled.'[56] It's not for nothing that one of *Private Eye*'s generic columnist characters is punningly named Phil Space, whose 'will this do?' style is reflected in the real world by lifers such as the *Guardian*'s Tim Dowling, whose column has been recounting the mundane aspects of his daily life for nearly two decades.

Private Eye's female version of the terrible columnist, Glenda Slagg – a name more than a little tinged with a particular eighties brand of misogyny – began as a pastiche of that era's dominant Fleet Street women (Jean Rook of the *Daily Express* and Lynda Lee-Potter of the *Daily Mail*) but has come to represent the Doctor Who of demonic, vitriolic and wildly inconsistent column queens, reincarnated for each new generation. The *Mail*, home to Liz Jones, Sarah Vine and Jan Moir among many others, is like an academy for new Glendas – though the *Telegraph*, where Allison Pearson looms over the opinion pages, is no slouch.

To illustrate the fundamental issue with columnists, I want to tell you four stories – two about male columnists, two about

A MATTER OF OPINIONS

female columnists (one of whom plies her trade in the US at that apparent bastion of propriety, *The New York Times*).

In 2009, Stephen Gately, a member of nineties boyband Boyzone, died suddenly, aged 33, as the result of an undiagnosed heart condition. On 16 October 2009, three days after a post-mortem confirmed the singer died of natural causes, Jan Moir – a woman still not in possession of a medical degree – wrote in the *Daily Mail*: 'Healthy and fit 33-year-old men do not just climb into their pyjamas and go to sleep on the sofa, never to wake up again. Whatever the cause of death is, it is not, by any yardstick, a natural one.'[57] Moir tried to connect Gately's death to drugs ('he at least smoked cannabis on the night he died') and implied that being gay was another factor in his demise ('Gately's death . . . strikes another blow to the happy-ever-after myth of civil partnerships'). The reaction was immediate: Moir's article led to 25,000 complaints to the Press Complaints Commission – the toothless voluntary press regulator – that day, sending its website into temporary meltdown. Celebrities, notably Stephen Fry and Derren Brown, used the then-nascent Twitter to encourage readers to complain and other columnists condemned the column. In the *Guardian*, Charlie Brooker wrote that Moir had tried to 'gay-bash a dead man'.[58] And then . . . nothing.

After a brief scuffle in which advertisers demanded the *Mail* ensure that their ads weren't served on Moir's column and the headline was changed from 'Why There Was Nothing Natural about Stephen Gately's Death' to 'A Strange, Lonely and Troubling Death . . . ', the columnist sailed on. She issued an outraged statement wondering 'how many of the people complaining have fully read [my column]' and complained, 'in what is clearly a heavily orchestrated internet campaign I think it is mischievous in the extreme to suggest that my article has homophobic and bigoted undertones'. It was a classic columnist's reversal – she had painted herself as the victim rather than the victimiser.

Of course, Moir's next column capitalised on the upset she had created. She apologised for the timing of her previous contribution then ploughed on, arguing again that she was just asking questions, complaining about 'a roaring ball of hate fire, blazing unchecked and unmediated across the internet', before trying to turn it into a wider social problem: 'Can it really be that we are becoming a society where no one can dare to question the circumstances or behaviour of a person who happens to be gay without being labelled a homophobe? If so, that is deeply troubling.'[59]

What was missed by both Moir's pompous self-justification and the justified outrage that preceded it was that her kneejerk and cruel opinion about Gately's very recent death was just one of a series of ill-thought-out opinions formulated for that week's column. It was followed by items in which Moir decried the 'socialite' Tara Palmer-Tomkinson's choice of outfit at *Tatler* magazine's 300th birthday celebrations, made snide comments about the Nolan sisters, offered her banal thoughts on autumn, talked about her taste in baked goods, complained about women having too much maternity leave and burbled on about school sports. For Gately's family, his death was a tragedy; for Jan Moir, it was fodder for filling her allotted space.

These pieces from Moir are a perfect example of columnist derangement syndrome (CDS), a common condition where the demand for new and controversial opinions every week on deadline leads someone further and further into unhinged

A MATTER OF OPINIONS

territory. And at the *Daily Mail* in particular, that mindset appears to be encouraged and rewarded. At the Leveson Inquiry in 2012, Moir's editor, Paul Dacre, blithely explained that the column 'could have benefited from a little judicious sub-editing' but that he had been at the opera for his wife's birthday the evening it was filed. He went on to declare that he would 'die in a ditch to defend a columnist's right to have her views' – don't threaten me with a good time, Paul – and that 'there isn't a homophobic bone in Jan Moir's body', as though it was her skeleton and not her writing that was in question. Sixteen years after the Gately column, Jan Moir is still one of the *Mail*'s star attractions. While there's outrage in the moment, there are rarely long-term consequences for this behaviour.

Another symptom of CDS is an addiction to making outrageous (and deeply unpleasant) statements that would lead to any normal person being sacked and ostracised from what passes for polite society. Outrage provokes attention and, for many columnists, attention is their key metric for success. Over time, the line between what a columnist genuinely believes and things they've written purely to be provocative becomes a smudged and indistinguishable mess. With columns in the *Sun*, *Sunday Times* and *Spectator*, Rod Liddle is a repeat and unrepentant offender. While his career as a columnist is a graveyard of shambling zombie opinions, one immediately springs to mind: the 2012 column in which Liddle explained he couldn't have been a teacher because he would have slept with the children.

There's every chance the previous paragraph has brought my publisher's lawyers to the brink of a breakdown. Only, it's true and completely legally defensible. Writing for the *Spectator* under the

BREAKING

headline 'A Teenage Girl, a Maths Teacher and Righteous Tabloid Fury', Liddle opened his column by confessing:

> I seriously contemplated being a teacher once upon a time, when I was a lot younger. It seemed to me an agreeable doss, and one didn't have to be too bright or too ambitious, or possess any great quality of knowledge ... I never found out because the one thing stopping me from being a teacher was that I could not remotely conceive of not trying to shag the kids. It seemed to me virtually impossible not to, and I was convinced that I'd be right in there, on day one. We're talking secondary school level here, by the way – and even then I don't think I'd have dabbled much below year ten, as it now called.[60]

In England, pupils in year 10 are between 14 and 15.

The hook for Liddle's column was the then ongoing story of teacher Jeremy Forrest – now a convicted sex offender – who had absconded to France with a 15-year-old pupil. Liddle went out of his way to draw a distinction between Forrest, a middle-class white guy ('the witless maths teacher'), and sexual abuse cases in Rotherham involving Asian men which were also in the news at the time, arguing that what the former did was 'surely not grooming as we have come to understand the term'. Who is 'we' here? While Liddle could bring himself to admit that 'what Mr Forrest did was wrong', he followed that verdict up with a horrifyingly glib rejoinder: 'I suspect – and it is only a guess – that thousands of teachers up and down the land conduct sexual relationships with their older charges and that in most cases no harm comes of it.'

A MATTER OF OPINIONS

In a 2014 interview with the *Guardian*, Liddle talked about his initial response when another of his more controversial columns drew criticism: "'I'm just joking, don't you understand?' I try to get away with things too often by saying that. It's a flaw."[61] It's also a strategy that he and his editors rely on all the time and which is present all over the wider media. If you take the columns of a provocateur like Liddle seriously, you're told he's only joking. If you dismiss him *as* a joke, you'll be told you don't listen to different opinions and he is just saying what many others wish they could.

The 'I don't think I'd have dabbled much below year ten' column has stuck in my mind ever since – and resurfaced on social media often – because it is such a clear illustration of that professional advantage of having it both ways. Liddle expects to be treated seriously when he wants and given the latitude of a clown when he doesn't. He can be cruel and crass because he knows that's exactly what his editors want. For all the talk of 'not being able to say that anymore', Liddle can and does say whatever he likes, free of professional or personal consequences.

My third example comes from another man who has been drinking in the last chance saloon so long that he has a usual seat in the corner and is on more than nodding terms with the landlord. A hereditary columnist whose father, Alan Coren, was a multi-talented satirist whose many columns included a long-running slot in *The Times*, Giles Coren has been a columnist and restaurant critic for the same paper for 23 years. Running your eye down his Wikipedia page where the 'Controversies' section is by far the largest, it's not surprising that his position at the paper often seems more like a sinecure than a job.

I could have looked at any one of those controversies – the

BREAKING

sock puppet Twitter account he used to attack critics, sharing his graphic fantasy about murdering a neighbour's noisy child on social media, the time he risked contempt of court to break an injunction, his violent threats to an older journalist on another paper over another row on Twitter or his god-awful novel, the nearly unreadable *Winkler*. However, it is his behaviour after the death of the fine journalist Dawn Foster at the age of just 34 that sticks most in my mind.

I knew and liked Dawn. The last time I saw her was after the funeral of our mutual friend, Lyra McKee. After Dawn's sudden death in July 2021, as a result of complications related to her long-term health problems, Coren tweeted and deleted two messages about her in quick succession. The first, posted at 13.15 on 20 July 2021 read: 'When someone dies who has trolled you on Twitter, saying vile and hurtful things about you and your family, is it okay to be like, "I'm sorry for the people who loved you, and any human death diminishes me, but can you fuck off on to hell now where you belong"?'

The second, 'milder' version – posted at 14:16 on the same day – cut the section about 'fucking off to hell' and replaced it with 'HA HA HA HA HA HA'.

Dawn hadn't 'trolled' Coren. She'd corrected him when he was wrong on the facts and three years earlier, she'd tweeted: 'Giles Coren: a prime example of how the "if I've heard of yer da, I don't need to hear from you" rule holds for almost every man bar Jesus.'

The Times and its parent company, News UK, ignored requests from journalists for comment. Internally, the paper rushed to put up the virtual barricades, with an email from *The Times*' night editor to all staff working on the paper's website, leaked to and

A MATTER OF OPINIONS

published by *Private Eye*, which read: 'Sorry for the mass email. I've been asked to ensure comments are [pre-moderated] for all Giles Coren pieces from now on please, including reviews, until told otherwise.'

The paper wanted to make very sure that none of its paying subscribers could object publicly to the behaviour of one of its star columnists. For his part, Coren followed a familiar pattern – he disappeared from social media before skulking back at a later date, pretending nothing had happened, like the Keyser Söze of dickheads. In the column published before the tweets about Dawn, Coren wrote sardonically about the life of a columnist: 'I hate banging out column after column ... The fact that I am paid quite well for this job is what keeps it this side of bearable. Makes me feel less of a mug for trawling through the newspapers every single morning of my life for stories I can bark my opinion about to total strangers ...'[62]

It's dressed up like a joke but reads like an unwise revelation. The column he wrote after the backlash against his tweets about Dawn – and after 'Dawn Foster Forever' was painted on the wall outside his house – had the headline 'Did you really expect to turn over a new page?',[63] which felt like the sub-editor's revenge, but it contained no reference to what he'd said, let alone anything resembling an apology. Coren only made a half-hearted attempt at that much later, during an appearance on *Times* Radio to provide his edgy insights on the news of the day. He told the hosts that he 'did a terrible thing 18 months ago on Twitter', wouldn't say exactly what that was and made a point of saying he was 'sorry but never apologised'.

Why does this matter beyond the upset of Dawn's friends?

BREAKING

Because Coren works for a company whose papers are never shy of criticising individuals. If he were someone in anything resembling a normal job – including people who work in normal jobs *at* News Corp – he would have been sacked years ago for bringing the company into disrepute. But because he is a columnist, he's courted and praised for his unpleasant behaviour, egged on by editors and colleagues, and allowed to be a permanent teenager making 'edgy jokes' for his mates, even as he's handed the megaphone of a national newspaper three times a week. He's what happens when the character escapes the page.

If Coren has been rewarded with the columnist's equivalent of a long-service medal for his most unseemly thoughts and actions, the final columnist I want to talk about was awarded one of journalism's highest prizes for committing gross acts of cruelty in print. In 1999, *The New York Times* columnist Maureen Dowd received the Pulitzer Prize for Commentary with a citation that read: 'For her fresh and insightful columns on the impact of President Clinton's affair with Monica Lewinsky'. Exactly how fresh do those insights seem 26 years later? And were they perhaps rotten from the start?

In 1998, the year began with Clinton's infamous televised speech in late January ('I did not have sexual relations with that woman, Ms Lewinsky') and ended with him being acquitted on impeachment charges of perjury and obstruction of justice in a 21-day Senate trial in December. Through the long months that the scandal dragged on, Dowd almost completely gave her column over to the topic and it was Lewinsky, the young intern gave staffer, who gave her most sport rather than the 52-year-old president.

A MATTER OF OPINIONS

To start with, Dowd was sympathetic towards Lewinsky and strongly critical of the Clinton administration's attempt to smear her: 'Inside the White House, the debate goes on about the best way to destroy That Woman, as the President called Monica Lewinsky. Should they paint her as a friendly fantasist or a malicious stalker? ... It's probably just a matter of moments before we hear that Ms. Lewinsky is a little nutty and a little slutty.'[64]

But by February 1998, Dowd had joined Team Nutty & Slutty, calling Lewinsky, who was just 22 years old when the affair started, 'a ditsy, predatory White House intern who might have lied under oath for a job at Revlon'[65] and 'the girl who was too tubby to be in the high school "in" crowd'.[66] When the FBI asked Lewinsky to submit a handwriting sample, Dowd penned a stinging satirical column that imagined her 'girlish scrawl, with loopy letters, little hearts and breathless punctuation'.[67]

In June, Dowd compared Lewinsky's appearance in a *Vanity Fair* photoshoot to the murdered American toddler beauty queen JonBenét Ramsey.[68] The same month, she encountered her target at the Bombay Club restaurant in Washington and noted down the contents of Lewinsky's plate for the benefit of her readers ('veggie appetizers and chicken tandoori'), castigated her for choosing Chelsea Clinton's 'favourite restaurant' and claimed her presence there 'suggested the former intern was trying to grab the President's attention, like some love-struck teenager, loitering outside Billy Clinton's biology class'.[69]

The same column found Dowd listing the things she *should* have said when Lewinsky said to her: 'Do you mind if I ask you something? Why do you write such scathing articles about me?' With the columnist's advantage and no small amount of what the French call *'l'esprit d'escalier'* – thinking of the ideal reply far too late – Dowd filled out her word count with snide rejoinders before revealing what she had actually said during the confrontation: 'I wimped out. "I don't know," I shrugged, lamely. She sashayed away, looking triumphant. Hell hath no fury . . . oh, never mind.'

As the summer of 1998 shifted into autumn, Dowd switched from painting Lewinsky as naive to framing her as the real harasser. In a column that August, she compared Lewinsky to the character who brought the phrase 'bunny boiler' to life: 'Like the Glenn Close character in *Fatal Attraction* Monica Lewinsky issued a chilling ultimatum to the man who jilted her: I will not be ignored.'[70] What had Lewinsky done to 'provoke' this comparison? Well, she'd agreed to appear in front of a grand jury as requested. In September, Dowd doubled down, writing: 'It is Ms. Lewinsky who comes across as the red-blooded predator, wailing to her girl friends that the President wouldn't go all the way . . . It is Mr. Clinton who behaves more like a teen-age girl trying to protect her virginity . . . Ms. Lewinsky is the one who bristles with testosterone.'[71]

Bristles. With. Testosterone. This is the commentary that earned Dowd one of her industry's most prestigious prizes. Eight years later, casting around for a topic for her column, she wrote about the use of the word 'slut' and opined: 'Republicans denigrated the prim law professor Anita Hill [who testified about sexual harassment] by painting her . . . as "a little bit nutty and a little bit slutty." Clinton defenders demonized Monica Lewinsky the same way.'[72]

There's the tactical amnesia that is so handy to the professional

A MATTER OF OPINIONS

columnist. Dowd could have looked back at her award-winning columns in the *New York Times* archive but that would have required her to reflect on her past decisions. Instead, when Lewinsky reemerged in 2014 as an anti-bullying campaigner, Dowd sneered at the development in her column and wrote that: 'It was like a Golden Oldie tour of a band you didn't want to hear in the first place.'[73] Responding to criticism of her writing in a 2016 interview with *Business Insider*, Dowd claimed the only column she regretted writing was one that criticised the sitcom *Seinfeld* and said: 'I was the one who found out and pointed out that it was the White House that was bullying Monica Lewinsky, as Hillary Clinton later called her, a narcissistic looney-tune.'[74]

It was as though Dowd blacked out at some point in February 1998 and didn't return to full consciousness until she had the Pulitzer in her hand. As of 2025, she will have been a *New York Times* columnist for 30 years. Tenures of that length, which are common in the UK too, are damaging for the business of column writing. Being a columnist should be treated more like a tour of duty, with a defined end. Even the most popular columnists should take an enforced break now and then, reassigned to features, interviews or any other kind of writing that removes the weekly demand for a novel opinion.

Nesrine Malik believes 'there is a way to delay that sense of "columnist senility" by trying to be as diverse as possible in your interests. What keeps a column fresh is that your thinking keeps on evolving.' She went on:

> One of the things that makes me despair about the media in general but column writing in particular is that it should

BREAKING

be a fresh, exploratory genre. I have this very gothic, earnest view of what the ideal column should be. How will that happen if the way to end up being a columnist is by being someone's kid or spending years spinning your wheels in low-paid jobs subsidised by your parents? Column writing is like academic tenure, it bestows a level of trust upon you. That's betrayed by those routes in.

Malik argues for a distinction between columnists who want to connect with and inform their readers and another sort of opinion writer who isn't truly a columnist. She explained: 'With the culture wars and motivated right-wing stewards, lots of columns have become propagandistic. Those people aren't columnists; their purpose is to create controversy and to become the protagonist.' That's undoubtedly the case with Coren and Liddle – they keep their spots by always being willing to say things that will titillate and appal in equal measure.

There are many other kinds of columns beyond the most straightforwardly propagandistic screeds, but one that I want to particularly focus on is a category that I think of as the 'origami castle'. They're less obviously problematic but are worth highlighting due to their prevalence and underlying perniciousness. Origami castles rely on arguments which, at first glance, appear to be elaborate and impressive but which, on closer inspection, can't stand up to scrutiny. To explain, I want to look at a *Times* column[75] written by Juliet Samuel following King Charles III's coronation in May 2023. She wrote:

A MATTER OF OPINIONS

What [globalist liberals] don't grasp is why the institution at the centre of this weird ritual, the monarchy, has lasted on and off for more than a thousand years. It is because it embodies ideas that are necessary to keep together a community beyond the immediate sphere of family and friends. Ultra-liberals tend to take for granted the idea that humans can and should be loyal to an abstraction like 'humanity' or 'freedom', but this is not at all obvious. In fact, our everyday lives are ruled by personal relationships, chores and emotions. Collective loyalty beyond this is built by communal experiences – like the coronation – shared culture and a sense of who would stand with us in the face of adversity or attack. The only political unit that commands this abstract sense of loyalty is the nation.

Consider the unshakable confidence of that prose. Observed from a distance, the origami castle looks to have impressive ramparts and towering walls capable of withstanding the harsh winds of trendiness and fashion. But get closer and you'll see it's starting to sag. Take the assertion that '[the monarchy] has lasted on and off for more than a thousand years'. Subject it to scrutiny and it starts to crumble. What's lasted? Perhaps the idea, but it has changed substantially in that time, sloughing off the 'divine right of kings' stuff when that became untenable and having much of its actual power drained away in a series of parliamentary bloodlettings. And has the *family* lasted? Of course not.

For hundreds of years, Britain's most murderous bastards (surely a TV show that Danny Dyer could front) bumped each other off for legitimacy and eventually the country had to import a ragtag collection of German, Dutch and Greek royals to give the whole enterprise a refresh. They were rebranded as 'the British Royal Family'. During the First World War, the branch of the family reigning over the UK fought another one which was leading Germany before a third branch was killed by the Bolsheviks in Russia because their British cousins decided that saving the Tsar and his children would be troublesome.

Even Samuel's insistence that coronations are 'a communal experience' is the result of a marketing triumph. Queen Victoria's coronation was a damp squib and many monarchs who came before her were barely bothered with the rigmarole. The pageantry served up now is a product of public relations and the realisation that a certain degree of razzmatazz is required to keep eyeballs on the Firm. Just because voices like Samuel's tell us the royals bring us together does not make it true. But in the most common register of the columnist's voice a tone of unshakeable belief is key.

Subject an origami castle to a cold rainstorm of analysis or a lukewarm jet of pissy derision and you're left with the same result: a soggy, indefensible mess. But despite the presence of comment sections where readers can respond and object to the arguments columnists put forward, most of them do not engage with feedback. Instead, critics tend to be framed as at best kooks – the digital version of what previous generations of writers derided as 'the green ink brigade' – and at worst trolls and bullies.

There are, of course, some attempts to be exceptions to that rule, one such being Malik. She says, 'One of my driving fears as a columnist is talking down to people from above the line. The less imperious and quarantined the columnist, the better. It's a good

A MATTER OF OPINIONS

way to mitigate against ego. I genuinely learn from the comments, including ways in which I could have communicated better.'

So why is it that this fairly major part of our media landscape is failing in its basic purpose? A look at the polling company YouGov's rankings of the most well-known columnists in the UK suggests that in a world where anyone can promote their opinion, professional bigmouths are in decline: two of the top ten are dead: the third best-known columnist Jimmy Young died in 2016 and seventh-placed Michael Winner passed away in 2013. A further six of the individuals listed no longer have a regular column in a mainstream newspaper, maintaining their fame either through TV/radio shows (Mariella Frostrup) or desperate controversy-baiting on social media (Katie Hopkins).

Exempting the famous dead, the average age of columnists in the top 20 of the YouGov chart at the end of 2024 was 60. The idea of columnists as influential voices in public discourse is approaching retirement, if it hasn't already headed off to tend its allotment and shout its unhinged opinions at the pigeons. Columnists have shifted from influential to influencers, fighting for the same space in the attention economy as Instagram personalities, YouTubers and TikTok stars.

Where influencers – in the most general sense of the term – tend to hawk meal kits, weight-loss tea, hair products and the dubious charms of Dubai, columnists are in the business of advertising ideas – sometimes their own but more often those that reflect the interests of their proprietors and their political tribe. As mentioned previously, the classic columnist's catchphrase is 'no one tells me what to write'. That's untrue in two different but related ways. Firstly, in a practical sense, the comment desk on a paper will veto ideas or make suggestions of things it would like a particular writer to consider. Secondly, there's no need for an explicit ban on any particular topic because any columnist aiming to keep their job will know implicitly what the paper's line is and when taking a particular stand would provoke a P45.

Malik suggests a technique for getting something even from columnists with whom you don't agree. She goes out of her way to read columnists that she disagrees with and attempts to understand their logic as well as unpick what makes others read them:

> I try to read people who I think others take in good faith but actually write in bad faith. It's easy when you feel strongly about something to just follow your argument and take shortcuts. The more you take shortcuts, the more it becomes bad faith. The current economics of column writing and the nepotistic quality reproduces conventional wisdom.

She also believes that there is scope for hope:

> Sometimes, if you've constantly got the 'state of British media' in your head, it can feel quite defeatist. But there is space – a tiny space – in this system to do more than you think. When you do crack it through luck or persistence, the public is open to it. There is a willingness to explore different ideas that is higher than you expect. There is an appetite for conceptualising other ways of doing things.

A MATTER OF OPINIONS

On the whole, I agree, but the problem is in that interaction between luck and persistence. In a time of media contraction, opportunities retreat and diversity of both background and perspectives goes with them. Remember, in 2019, The Sutton Trust found that 44 per cent of newspaper columnists had been to Oxbridge and that 'newspaper columnist' was among the top ten professions with the most Oxbridge graduates.[76] As Malik says, column writing is like tenure and if the small number of columnist slots in the British press are dominated by ageing Oxbridge graduates their contribution to national debate will be narrow.

Beyond the moral and social questions, the commentariat's homogenous nature is a *business* error. Executives in media companies often throw their hands in the air and lament that young people are simply not engaging with their products, even as their columnists spend an inordinate amount of time framing those very young people as a bunch of lazy, feckless and fundamentally unpatriotic parasites. The British press's approach to reaching a younger audience is akin to a cafe only offering shit sandwiches to the under-40s then raging that they don't know what's good for them when they choose to eat elsewhere.

It's not that we need a *Logan's Run*-style system where columnists are marched off to their deaths when they hit 30, but rather that the chance to write an opinion piece twice a week shouldn't be a job for life which you can retain however you behave. Spending years and years being treated as an oracle for opinions can only lead to complacency and an underlying contempt for your audience. A permanent place on a pedestal doesn't leave you open to new perspectives or able to see how things are shifting. It's the equivalent of a band having years to write their first album based on a wide range of experiences then getting stuck producing a run of records about tour buses and eating indifferent buffet platters in identical concrete backstage areas.

Salman Rushdie, a man with no shortage of strong opinions and perhaps more experience than anyone of how they can translate to violent actions, explained in a 2012 *Globe and Mail* interview: 'I used to write a monthly column for the *New York Times* syndicate. But I stopped because I found it really hard to have one extreme opinion a month. I don't know how these columnists have two or three ideas a week; I was having difficulty having 12 things to say a year.'[77]

The interviewer, Rick Groen, suggested that 'columnists may have a more forgiving notion of what constitutes an idea'. It was an astute observation. For a columnist, an idea has to work that week, across 800 to 1,000 words, and for long enough to keep the reader engaged. Columnists aren't rewarded for consistency or the accuracy of their predictions; they're rewarded for drawing attention.

Stephen Bush, currently of the *Financial Times* and formerly of the *New Statesman*, is an outlier in writing a yearly assessment of what he got right and, crucially, what he got wrong over the previous 12 months. When I asked Bush why he started writing the review, he told me he had to write something to run between Christmas and New Year that could be edited before the festive period and not require any further changes: 'I thought, "Well, I'm not going to get any less wrong between then and now."' But he's kept up with the exercise because he finds it useful and also because 'it's quite freeing to know that I can always throw my hands up in the air and say, "Look, I got that wrong."'

A MATTER OF OPINIONS

Were columnists treated not as serious figures but as a form of entertainment, this would all matter much less. But just as America is a nation that has turned a movie star (Reagan) and a TV caricature of a mogul (Trump) into presidents, the UK made a columnist (Boris Johnson) into a prime minister. Things are so unserious that I'm certain it could happen again.

6.

Political Theatre

Understanding Political Journalism

'Objectivity is a fallacy. In campaign reporting more than any other kind of press coverage, reporters aren't just covering a story, they're part of it – influencing outcomes, setting expectations, framing candidates – and despite what they tell themselves, it's impossible to both be a part of the action and report on it objectively.'
– Michael Hastings, 'Hack: Confessions of a Presidential Campaign Reporter', *GQ*, 1 October 2008

Let's start with professional wrestling. If you understand professional wrestling, a self-contained world where muscular men and women in spandex throw themselves around in a ring that commentators call 'the squared circle', you will have a far better understanding of politicians, the people who report on them and the stories they tell. Whether your focus is Washington or Westminster, the situation is the same: there is the narrative that makes its way onto broadcast news and into the papers, and then there's what is actually happening. The two intersect but often only by accident.

Professional wrestling has two layers – the cold reality of the business and the fantasy of 'kayfabe'. With a hazy etymology that most plausibly points to carny slang or Jewish argot from interwar east London, kayfabe is the collective agreement to maintain the illusion that matches aren't predetermined and interactions between wrestlers aren't scripted storylines. Before the internet and ubiquitous streaming video, kayfabe was ruthlessly observed by the wrestling industry. Now, it's almost a shared agreement between the companies and the fans; it is maintained during events and broken in the coverage around them.

Wrestling could not exist if there was no kayfabe. The feuds, friendships and frantic antics of a wrestling show require a particular kind of suspension of disbelief – that is kayfabe. A wrestler can switch from a heel (villain) to a face (a hero) according to the franchise's need, thanks to the media's cooperation and in line with the demands of the fans, but observers, be they professional commentators or simply fans, know that there is a deep connection between the scripted storylines and the real politics of the company behind them.

The relationship between politicians and the press is almost the same. Just as every wrestling match has an angle – as simple as a tag team clash between two pairs of wrestlers, or as complex as a 'rumble' between dozens of wrestlers where only one can prevail, or as extreme as a no-holds-barred ladder match conducted in a cage – political reporting is about narratives, politicians as characters, and parties as long-running and interconnected soap operas.

In the British media and politics, kayfabe extends to letting the

POLITICAL THEATRE

public in on the relationship between many of the central players. Every year on Valentine's Day, the London branch of Politico, the political news website, publishes a list of Westminster 'power couples'. It makes for queasy reading, especially when you realise how many of the relationships are comprised of a prominent journalist and a politician, special advisor or think-tank wonk. The easy retort from the denizens of the eight square miles they call 'the Westminster village' is that people often end up sleeping with, dating and marrying people they meet at work. But in many more normal work environments, where the stakes are far lower than the state of public debate and the future of the nation, conflicts of interest are dealt with more simply and transparently. The same goes for more platonic connections.

One instructive recent example is that of James Forsyth, political editor of the *Spectator* and a columnist for *The Times*, whose best friend, Rishi Sunak, whom he met when they were both pupils at Winchester public school, became Chancellor and subsequently Prime Minister. Forsyth's wife, Allegra Stratton – formerly a journalist for the BBC and ITV – was director of strategic communications in Sunak's Treasury before becoming Boris Johnson's Downing Street press secretary. Forsyth continued to analyse the government's fortunes when his best mate (who'd also been his best man) and wife worked at the heart of it. The situation became even more ludicrous when a leaked video of press conference prep that featured Stratton asking how she might handle questions about law-breaking gatherings in Downing Street during the UK's Covid restrictions kicked off the Partygate scandal. How could Forsyth effectively judge the serious failings of the government when his wife was at its heart?

BREAKING

In November 2022, just a month before Forsyth was hired as one of Sunak's most senior advisors, he was still writing columns for *The Times* discussing his friend's policies and sticking with the style of referring to him as 'Sunak'. That he had known Rishi for decades by this point – something he noted on podcasts with a mumbled '. . . who I've known for years' – was not flagged in the paper. It was such a well-known fact in the political and media worlds that it was unremarkable, but it should never have been assumed that readers, listeners and viewers would be similarly clued up. Every time Forsyth discussed his buddy, he should have made it explicitly clear that he did not just *know* Sunak but that the politician is his best mate, was his best man and would give his wife her best possible reference.

With Forsyth now the one in Downing Street, Stratton – who resigned over Partygate – hopped back into the revolving door and returned to journalism with a job writing Bloomberg UK's political newsletter. She used it to attack her former boss, Johnson, and write positively about her husband's current boss and their shared family friend. In a sane political climate, the whole barn dance would be unthinkable. In Britain, it provokes, at best, some tutting about 'chumocracy', which is a cutesy way of talking about corruption while pretending that sort of thing only happens in foreign countries.

The green rooms of radio and TV stations – backstage holding pens where you'll get indifferent coffee and slowly curling sandwiches if you're very lucky – provide another opportunity to see how political kayfabe works. There, commentators and politicians who are nominally on different sides will often chat quite amiably, joshing with each other and reminiscing about

POLITICAL THEATRE

previous encounters, before going on air to perform their assigned roles – the bolshy lefty, the plummy Tory backbencher, the insipid Lib Dem or tub-thumping, tax-cut obsessed think-tank goon. The outcomes of 'debates' on political shows are not preordained in the way that wrestling matches are but it's close. Subjected to pre-interviews by producers before they're booked, guests' opinions are not a surprise; having cast a Punch and Judy show, it's always a disappointment to editors when an unexpected bout of consensus breaks out.

But despite these colourful displays, away from the kayfabe, an air of ideological stagnation has indeed broken out in the mainstream of British political journalism, caused in part by the growing ability of politicians to totally avoid particular papers, shows or even entire outlets if they feel that engaging isn't to their advantage. Broadcast television and publications that are ideologically aligned with your party are still useful if you're a politician, but you can get directly at voters online with almost total control of the format and message. This ability for the politician to avoid the spotlight has in turn impacted the way in which these interviews take place. Political journalists' need for access has blunted their teeth, bringing an end to an era where it was common to see major political figures metaphorically battered and bruised by interviewers.

To understand the current relationship between politicians and the press it's useful to look back. This relationship has never been stable; in fact, it has been quite the opposite, with different players influencing changes in sentiment over the years. In television's early years, politicians could decide when to subject themselves to its scrutiny. An infamous Conservative Party

BREAKING

election broadcast in 1951 featured the BBC's Leslie Mitchell opening his interview with the Prime Minister, Anthony Eden, by obsequiously enquiring: 'Well now, Mr Eden, with your very considerable experience of foreign affairs, it's quite obvious that I should start by asking you something about the international situation today, or perhaps you would prefer to talk home. Which is it to be?' Can you imagine a politician today being offered the option for what they wanted to discuss?

But by the late-1950s things started to change, with TV journalist Robin Day spearheading a new, more blunt and direct style of political interview. Though Day was rather dismissive of his previous experience as a barrister, it fed into his prosecutorial style. His 1958 interview with the Prime Minister, Harold Macmillan, was a star-making turn. Day later wrote that 'it was the moment when my life as a political journalist on TV really began',[78] while the next day's edition of the *Daily Express* hailed it as 'the most vigorous cross-examination a Prime Minister has been subjected to in public'. This was not to say that this change in style was welcomed in every quarter – Day's polite but pointed questioning provoked a storm of criticism from many columnists. The very fact that he had *dared* to ask Macmillan about whether he intended to dispense with Foreign Secretary Selwyn Lloyd was unbearable to some. Bill Connor, writing under the pseudonym Cassandra in the *Daily Mirror*, thundered that 'the Idiot's lantern is getting too big for its ugly gleam',[79] while a *Telegraph* leader column asked, 'Who is to draw the line at which the effort to entertain stops?'

Those columns were pearl-clutching and bore little resemblance to the overall relationship between press and politicians; another prime ministerial encounter with Day produced a more

POLITICAL THEATRE

worthwhile prediction. When Day interviewed then-Prime Minister Sir Alec Douglas-Home in 1964, he asked him whether – as the papers were reporting – he would take part in a TV debate with the Leader of the Opposition, Harold Wilson. Douglas-Home replied: 'I'm not particularly attracted by, so to speak, confrontations of personality. If we aren't careful, you know, you will get a sort of (what's it called?) *Top of the Pops* contest – I daresay I should win it, I'm not sure. But at any rate, I'm not really attracted by this. You'd then get the best actor as leader of the country and the actor will be prompted by a scriptwriter.'[80] Douglas-Home's comments were prescient given how personality-driven our political contests have become.

In print, Bernard Levin, who also played a striking role in the cast of the satirical TV show *That Was the Week That Was*, almost single-handedly created the modern form of parliamentary sketch-writing. Sketches, which began as a means of circumventing eighteenth-century restrictions on reporting proceedings in Parliament, were intended to give a sense of political goings-on. At the beginning of the fifties, they'd become quite soft and amenable to MPs, but Levin had no truck with that. The *Spectator's* then owner and editor Ian Gilmour brushed aside Levin's initial objection that he wasn't any kind of political expert by telling him to 'review it as you would review television'. Taking the pseudonym 'Taper' – lifted from the name of the corrupt political insider in ex-Prime Minister and sometime-novelist Benjamin Disraeli's 1844 novel *Coningsby* – Levin took Gilmour's advice on board: 'I was watching a farce, from the front row of the stalls, with a glass of champagne in my hand.'[81] Under the mortar bombardment of Levin's typewriter, the Tory grandee Sir Reginald Manningham-

BREAKING

Buller was renamed Sir Reginald Bullying Manner. When he was knighted as Lord Dilhorne, Levin honoured him as Lord Stillborn. Meanwhile, Labour's Sir Hartley Shawcross, who had been the UK's chief prosecutor at the Nuremberg Trials, was granted no more respect: Levin dismissed him as Sir Shortly Floorcross.

The age of deference was done and politicians' need to harness television's publicity power coupled with booming newspaper and magazine sales meant political reporters could revel in the new rudeness. In 1973, three days after Lord Lambton, Douglas-Home's cousin, was forced to resign as a minister in Edward Heath's government after the *News of the World* printed photos of him in bed with two sex workers, he made himself available for an interview with Day. 'Why,' the interviewer asked, 'should a man of your social position and charm and personality have to go to whores for sex?' Lambton, unruffled and rather louche, replied: 'I think that people sometimes like variety. I think it's as simple as that and I think that impulse is probably understood by almost everybody. Don't you?' It's impossible to imagine a political presenter putting such a blunt question today, nor a politician – disgraced or otherwise – answering it so directly.

That period of frankness didn't last. The shift in tolerance for harsh questioning can be seen in a later Robin Day interview from October 1982. Margaret Thatcher's Defence Secretary, John Nott, removed his microphone and stalked off set after Day, who was questioning the minister about cuts to the Royal Navy and the First Sea Lord's criticism of them, asked: 'But why should the public, on this issue, as regards the future of the Royal Navy, believe you, a transient here-today – and if I may say so – gone-tomorrow politician rather than a senior officer of many years

POLITICAL THEATRE

experience?'. In 2002, 20 years after the walkout, Nott wrote for the *Daily Telegraph* about what he was thinking:

> As [Day] questioned me, the major part of my brain was dwelling on my farm – the autumn colours, the conclusion of the harvest, the green fields of England – and here was this famous controversialist, desperately trying to generate a row out of something that, as far as I was concerned, was already part of history. My brain reacted: 'What the hell? I don't need to sit here refighting the Defence Review with a journalist, however famous.'[82]

The political class was running out of patience.

Irrespective of the waning tolerance of polticians, political interviewers' tactics continued to evolve. Day was the John the Baptist of the blunt political broadcasters leading the way for what was to come. The generation that followed him included more ferocious evolutions of the style he pioneered. On the radio there was John Humphrys, taking lumps out of politicians on Radio 4's *Today* programme, and on the TV, Jeremy Paxman of *Newsnight*, whose impatient, frustrated style was summed up by the political sitcom *The Thick of It* as a 'big, rubbery horse-face of mock incredulity'. Paxman's style of interviewing reached its apotheosis during his combative 1997 encounter with Michael Howard, the former Home Secretary who was running to become leader of the Conservative Party, then newly in opposition. Paxman asked the ex-minister if he had 'threatened to overrule' the head of the Prison Service and received an evasive and legalistic response in return ('I was entitled to express my views.

BREAKING

I was entitled to be consulted . . . '). So he asked him the same question a further 11 times.

In the face of this hardline approach from the media, politicians began to realise that they needed allies if they were to escape the grilling. Nowhere is this fevered need for approval between politicians and the media more clearly concentrated than it was with the New Labour governments in the late 1990s. New Labour was swept into power in 1997 by a huge public desire for change, but the years of being battered by the right-wing press, and particularly the Murdoch papers, had persuaded the party's leadership that they needed the ageing Antipodean and his editors on side. The myth created by the *Sun*'s headline after the 'shock' Tory win in 1992 ('It's the *Sun* Wot Won It') was abiding. So, in July 1995, Tony Blair travelled to a News Corp corporate retreat on Hayman Island, off the coast of Australia, to make a deal and break the curse. On stage, Murdoch introduced the Labour leader with a queasy metaphor: 'If the British press is to be believed, today is all part of a Blair-Murdoch flirtation. If that flirtation is ever consummated, Tony, I suspect we will end up making love like two porcupines – very carefully.' In time, those pricks would get so close that Blair, out of office by then but still cultivating power, became godfather to Rupert Murdoch's daughter Grace. Curiously, he was cut out of the pictures of that blessed event – which was rather crassly performed at the spot on the River Jordan where Christ was reportedly baptised – when they were published by *Hello!*. Nonetheless, it was a bizarre but somehow logical conclusion to a long decade in which the Murdoch machine backed Blair in three elections and several wars.

During the grotesque pre-fight promo stage for one of

POLITICAL THEATRE

those conflicts, the 2003 invasion of Iraq, 174 of 175 Murdoch newspapers offered their support for the coming attack. The one hold-out was the Hobart *Mercury*, one of ol' Rupert's smaller Australian titles, which, on 12 September 2002, published a passionate anti-war editorial. It argued: 'It would be wrong for the US pre-emptively to attack Iraq. It would be wrong for Australia to ride shotgun to any unilateral assault on the hated regime of Saddam Hussein ...' Emphatic to say the least. It continued with the damning statement that any such invasion would be 'Osama bin Laden's dream come true.' But only four months later, on 17 January 2003, with war inching closer, the Hobart *Mercury* started singing with the choir, in a rather familiar voice: 'No one wants a war. But the alternative – to let a madman thumb his nose at the rule of international law is an obscenity. Nations who live by the rule of law ... have an obligation to confront these dark forces.' The pressure from the top was just too much.

With the Murdoch papers on side, New Labour's desire for control over the media was at its most deranged during the Iraq era. What had started in 1995 with such innovations as the bluntly named Rapid Response and Rebuttal Unit to 'anticipate and neutralise bad news and, wherever possible, turn a negative attack into a positive storyline' turned into a running war with BBC News. This culminated in Blair's chief spin doctor Alastair Campbell turning up live on Channel 4 News, his eyes black with fury, to condemn the BBC and make himself the story in the process. We'll come to the BBC's complicated role in the British media later.

By the end of the New Labour era, politicians tended to believe that they had the measure of combative interviewers, a view that was summed up again by *The Thick of It*, when chocolate-guzzling junior minister Ben Swain blithely dismissed the threat of a Paxman grilling: 'Yeah, look, we all know the cheat codes for Paxman now. That aggressive style is just old-school. All you do is play the honest Joe, just trying to humbly get your point across.' For plot purposes, Swain ended up skewered by the great inquisitor, but in reality, he'd never have been put up to defend the government in the first place. Political operators were increasingly realising that not engaging was an option. Paxman stepped down from *Newsnight* in 2014.

In August 2015, just over a year after Paxman relinquished the chair, his replacement, Evan Davis – possibly emboldened by the reduced likelihood of bumping into his former colleague in the lift – used an interview with the *Independent* to suggest the combative style of interviewing was 'overdone, worn out . . . [and] not a particular public service'. He went on: 'Politicians get better defences as interviewers get better attack techniques. Politicians now sound defensive and boring instead of making gaffes.'

Earlier that same summer, another BBC man, Andrew Marr, had also taken a pop at the champ. Speaking at a London School of Economics journalism conference, he discussed Paxman's interviews with the Prime Minister, David Cameron, and Leader of the Opposition, Ed Miliband, ahead of the May general election:

> Replacing a [head-to-head debate] with a good 'Pax-maning' for both of them, while entertaining was not a good replacement . . . the thing about Jeremy is that he is a genuinely tortured, angry individual – and you get the real Jeremy. He looks disdainful and contemptuous and furious

with his guests because he, by and large, is. You can't fake these things on television.[83]

I wonder if Marr was faking his enthusiasm for Tony Blair when back on 9 April 2003, Huw Edwards threw to him standing outside 10 Downing Street, 20 days after the invasion of Iraq began. He slobbered:

> ... all the usual caveats apply, there could be some ghastly scenes in the future; there could be terrorist attacks, all sorts of things could go wrong. But frankly, Huw, the main mood is unbridled relief. I've been watching ministers wander around with smiles like split watermelons ... I think this does one thing: it draws a line under what had been, before this war, a period when a faint air of pointlessness was hanging over Downing Street. There were all these slightly tawdry arguments and scandals; that is now history.
> Mr Blair is well aware that all his critics out there in the party and beyond aren't going to thank him – because they're only human – for being right when they've been wrong, and he knows there might be trouble ahead as I've said. But I think this is a very, very important moment for him: it gives him a new freedom and a new self-confidence. He confronted many critics. I don't think anybody after this is going to be able to say of Tony Blair that he is someone that is driven by the drift of public opinion of focus groups or opinion polls. He took all of those on. He said that they would be able to take Baghdad without a bloodbath and that, in the end, the Iraqis would be celebrating. And on

both of those points, he has been proved conclusively right. And it would be entirely ungracious for his critics not to acknowledge that tonight he stands as a larger man and a stronger prime minister as a result.

I've quoted that at such length because it is such a perfectly grotesque example of horrific real-world events simplified through the prism of Westminster soap opera. As Marr was pontificating outside Number 10, his then colleague, BBC foreign correspondent Huw Sykes, was witnessing very different scenes. This was his 9 April 2003, as recalled in his book, *War Crime*:

> We come across a tour bus, empty and abandoned. The windscreen has been cracked and punctured by shrapnel from an explosion ... There's a company name on the side of the bus, and its slogan: *Happy Travel*. The front and rear doors are open. There's no obvious evidence of death or injury. I learned later that it had been a civilian bus, with three passengers killed and several wounded when a bomb was seemingly dropped in error by an American plane. The Pentagon apologised.

In Marr's commentary, the war was a Westminster event, abstracted from the reality on the ground. Sykes was experiencing that reality.

Travelling back in time to Marr's earliest appearances on the BBC brings us to a useful analysis of the wider problem with the British political media. In February 1996, four years before Marr joined the corporation as its political editor, he presented a BBC

POLITICAL THEATRE

series called *The Big Idea*. In recent years, a clip from one of its episodes – Marr's interview with the linguist and political thinker, Noam Chomsky – has gained a second life on YouTube.

It begins with Marr asking Chomsky to explain his view of the media as a silencing force: 'If the press is a censoring organisation, tell me how that works. You're not suggesting that proprietors phone one another up or many journalists get their copy spiked, as we say.' In reply, Chomsky paraphrased 'The Freedom of the Press', an essay by George Orwell originally intended to appear as the preface to *Animal Farm* but which was first published by the *Times Literary Supplement* in 1972, pointing out that the press is owned by wealthy men who have an interest in not having certain things made public and that the whole educational system tells children there are certain things you don't say.

Marr says he was 'brought up, post-Watergate film and so on, to believe that journalism was a crusading craft and that there were a lot of 'stroppy, disputatious people in journalism' and asks how Chomsky can know that he is 'self-censoring'. That's when the moment that has become almost cliché through repetitive quotation occurs. With a cold politeness, Chomsky replies: 'I'm not saying you're self-censoring; I'm sure you believe everything you're saying. But what I'm saying is that if you believed something different, you wouldn't be sitting where you're sitting.'

Putting the idea of self-censorship to someone working on a national newspaper is a bit like trying to ask a fish about what they think of water. One columnist I spoke to for this book quipped, 'I guess you don't know you're not in the water until you're choking.' Much like columnists, when political journalists say, 'No one tells me what to write,' they are, on the whole, being honest. But this is

BREAKING

only because the culture of a newsroom makes the lines that you cannot cross quite clear without the need to state them explicitly.

The idea that the UK has a pluralistic and heterodox media was central to Marr's argument in 1996 and is still trotted out by reflexive defenders of the industry even after it has substantially contracted. It's a comforting myth that's not remotely borne out by the media landscape that exists. In Britain's political media, the Overton window – the range of policies that are politically acceptable to the mainstream population at any given time – has shrunk so much that we're dealing with the Overton cat flap. The underlying framing of major issues like the housing crisis, food poverty or immigration doesn't differ greatly across the available outlets. BBC News is almost as keen to dispatch a reporter to commentate on small boats in the Channel as GB News was to send Nigel Farage out there like a malign member of the *Dad's Army* cast.

This being said, the opportunities presented on the latter for right-wing politicians has reached a new level of chumminess. A senior broadcaster from a more established news channel told me the GB News set-up of Tory politicians interviewing other Tory politicians on TV and presenting their own shows was 'disgusting'. They went on to recall when Labour MP turned independent firebrand George Galloway, who was then representing Bethnal Green and Bow, made his infamous appearance on *Celebrity Big Brother* in 2006: 'There's a better argument for Galloway donning a Lycra catsuit and drinking milk from the outstretched hands of [the actress] Rula Lenska as a means of engaging with the electorate than [frontline politicians like] Lee Anderson, Jacob Rees-Mogg, Nigel Farage et al. having their own programmes on

POLITICAL THEATRE

a TV channel.' Where Galloway's antics were treated as an oddity, the blurring of the line between politicians and onscreen political commentators has created a new norm.

In March 2024, Ofcom – the broadcast regulator so toothless that it resembles an old man searching for his dentures – issued the latest in a string of rulings against GB News. This time, it found that the channel had breached Rule 5.3 of the Broadcasting Code ('No politician should be used as a newsreader, interviewer or reporter in any news programmes unless, exceptionally, it is editorially justified') five times, in shows hosted by the married Conservative MPs Philip Davies (who lost his seat in the subsequent general election) and Esther McVey, and Tory backbencher and Victorian undertaker cosplay fanatic Jacob Rees-Mogg. The consequences for GB News amounted to a mild ticking off rather than fines or a requirement to read the regulator's judgements out on air. It was in line with Ofcom's approach to previous misdemeanours from GB News: five previous breaches were dealt with by reminding the channel to 'take careful account' of the regulator's words and, in the case of ex-presenter Mark Steyn broadcasting unadulterated anti-vax conspiracy theories, requiring executives from the channel to attend a compliance meeting. That's the corporate governance equivalent of being called into the head teacher's office and asked if you're having 'problems' at home.

Even as GB News continued to rack up regulatory rulings, others in the media convinced themselves that it was slowly but surely moving into the mainstream. Former BBC Editor of Live Political Programmes Rob Burley told the political news site *Politics Joe* that the channel now had 'people like [former Labour MP] Gloria De Piero – who's a friend of mine – who I think is very good. They've got [*Telegraph* columnist] Camilla Tominey. They've got [former *Telegraph* political editor] Chris Hope. So they are becoming more conventional . . . more establishment, in that these people are proper journalists.' Another way of looking at the growing crossover between *Telegraph* journalists and GB News is that the newspaper has moved further and further into the unhinged territory occupied by the TV channel, rather than the broadcaster mellowing.

GB News takes the political journalism/professional wrestling parallel to its most extreme form in Britain so far. It is never happier than when it is reporting on itself, creating its own multiverse of meta-news. When the GB News host and then-Tory MP Lee Anderson was preparing to defect to Reform in the spring of 2024, Hope, the channel's political editor, found himself excitedly reporting that one GB News host (Anderson) was having 'secret' talks with another (Richard Tice) about joining a party whose honorary president and spiritual leader was also a GB News host (Nigel Farage). Inevitably, Farage then talked about the two other GB News hosts on *his* GB News show and as a guest on a selection of the station's other output.

While GB News has taken it to a new and farcical level, the revolving door installed between the world of political reporters and the adjacent dungeon dimension full of political advisors, MPs and think tanks has long spun so fast that its whirr is a permanent background noise in Whitehall. In December 2022, when Sebastian Payne, then the *Financial Times*' Westminster editor, announced he was making the short leap across to a think tank it provoked an avalanche of congratulations from colleagues and rivals alike.

POLITICAL THEATRE

Payne, who had been scouting around for a safe seat that might make him its Conservative MP – ultimately stymied by the fact that the party was about to have fewer safe seats than a condemned rollercoaster – became director of Onward, a Tory think tank inspired by Emmanuel Macron's En Marche movement and funded by corporate backers including BAE Systems, Shell, Uber Eats and Diageo.

A healthy political and media culture would have asked some more questions about that kind of career move. They might have included: why was everyone pretending that Payne – formerly of the *Daily Telegraph* and *Spectator* – had not been deeply committed to the Tory agenda while he was employed as a supposedly neutral observer? And wasn't this just a sign that he was jumping ship now his best sources were likely to be either out of Parliament soon or languishing in opposition? Instead, reading the replies beneath Payne's social media announcement revealed a long queue of political journalists and politicians taking their turns to applaud as if no one else could see the backslapping, sweaty chumminess in progress. The presenter of BBC Radio 4's influential evening political news programme *PM*, Evan Davis, congratulated Payne on a 'fascinating move' and hoped he'd 'still come on [the programme] as regularly'. Emily Maitlis, co-presenter of Global's *News Agents* podcast, wrote she was 'sad and happy'. That's the same Maitlis who, in her MacTaggart lecture at the Edinburgh International Television Festival, had warned against being 'cosy with those in authority and disconnected from those we are trying to serve'.

The list of 'congrats' was long and covered all corners of the print and broadcast spectrum. One dissenting voice stood out: the veteran political correspondent Peter Oborne wrote 'strongly disapprove' and asked about Onward's funding. It's striking that a profession so addicted to saying it 'speaks truth to power' said so little about another defection to the think-tank world. But people like to keep their options open. These eruptions of delight when a journalist skulks off to a think tank or to lobby for the gambling industry or a corporate giant make that flea-bitten promise of 'speaking truth to power' look even more ratty. It doesn't do to even acknowledge the revolving door in case it stops spinning before you decide to step into it. Payne has subsequently slipped back through it, becoming a leader writer and columnist at *The Times*.

Back when Robin Day was in his pomp, there remained a discomfort with blurring the line between the personal and the professional. The Labour Prime Minister James Callaghan said that he didn't 'care for too much mateyness on the television between interviewer and interviewee, otherwise the viewer will get the impression it is a set-up job'. The 'impression' is the key word there and why Callaghan was careful to refer to Robin Day as 'Mr Day' on screen rather than 'Robin' as he did when the camera was off. There was a distinction between private politeness and public scrutiny.

Today, there is a pervasive sense of class solidarity between the media and the politicians it covers. It's common for Labour and Tory MPs to publicly declare themselves friends and for journalists to be photographed at politicians' weddings or chuckling along with them at the *Spectator*'s summer party or one of Rupert Murdoch's seasonal shindigs. There is often a complete lack of embarrassment about this collapse of the already paper-thin walls between journalists and the people they write about.

POLITICAL THEATRE

That chummy media environment is further bolstered by the growth of podcasts presented by people who are nominally political rivals. The pattern was established by *The Rest is Politics*, where former Labour spin doctor Alastair Campbell and ex-Tory minister Rory Stewart promise to disagree amicably but tend to agree furiously, interspersed with the odd bout of playful rhetorical mouthing. Following Campbell and Stewart's example, former Chancellor George Osborne (who spent a period as the *Evening Standard*'s least qualified editor) and former shadow Chancellor and *Strictly* star Ed Balls launched *Political Currency*, a show in which every chuckle-smothered episode appears to confirm the conclusion that parliamentary debate is so much pantomime posturing.

When I put my 'political reporting as professional wrestling' analogy to a political journalist at one of the nationals, they ran with it but said: 'Yes, we'll cover Triple H clothes-lining the Undertaker but if we see Vince McMahon doing something dodgy, we'll cover that as well.' Decoded for the non-wrestling minded, that means that while they'll write about the surface level clashes, they don't believe that they avoid covering the screw-ups of people who are good sources for them or members of a party their paper broadly supports. But given the many cases above showing how closely these worlds are linked, does this hold water?

One of the problems with trying to explain how political reporting works is that in simplifying the interactions between hacks and politicos, you can end up giving the impression that what ends up in the newspapers is the result of careful consideration. One criticism of my analysis of British political journalism from several people I spoke to was that I tend to attribute too much competence to hacks. A political correspondent put it to me this way: 'Often, things come out a particular way as a result of disorganisation and a total shitshow, rather than because of some concerted or planned political manoeuvre. Sometimes, we've just cack-handedly followed another paper's story.' The need to present a coherent narrative and one that goes beyond details that could be pumped out as social media posts across the day tends to lead political journalists to give the impression that they know far more than they actually do about the current state of the government or the internal workings of the opposition. It was summed up for me by another political hack who concluded: 'Even the most senior political journalist knows fuck-all compared to the most junior minister about what's going on in the government. Even the good ones can't help but write simplified narratives because there's always that imbalance of knowledge.' That's strikingly honest and a tone that's usually missing from the assured predictions that usually make up British political commentary. If reporters leaned into that friction rather than overly empathising with their subjects, political journalism would be in a much healthier state.

In 2023, the *New Statesman* gathered six of its former political editors and writers for a round table which was posted on YouTube and printed in the magazine. It threw up a very interesting piece of dissonance between how political journalism tends to think of itself and how it actually functions on a day-to-day basis. Time for another guest appearance by Andrew Marr:

Marr: I think what unites us is that nobody told or tells us what to write.

POLITICAL THEATRE

Steve Richards: My period was that early New Labour period. Ian Hargreaves, the editor, wanted two things that were slightly contradictory. He wanted us to find out what was happening behind the scenes of this project. And he also wanted scoops and exclusives which pissed off the very people that you needed to get behind the scenes. That was a never-ending dilemma.[84]

There's a dissonance between Marr, the recipient of Chomsky's disdain all those years ago, posturing as thoroughly independent and Richards explaining that his editor made it abundantly clear what he wanted. It's what editors do, some with a light touch and others with a heavy hand. Just as every outlet has a house style – a set of guidelines for how copy should be presented – it has a house view, a sense of the political positions that the publication will take and the ones that it will dismiss.

Marr's belated response to Chomsky's critique came in a 2017 *Guardian* webchat when he replied to a reader's question about the incident:

> I was – quite rightly – nervous of Chomsky, who is a formidable intellect. When he suggested that 'if you believed something different, you wouldn't be sitting where you're sitting', I immediately realised that this was not so much brilliant as unanswerable . . . the conversation was taking place in the context of me expressing disbelief that, in his view, all mainstream journalists were essentially the same – I had said that it seemed to me the *Guardian* and the *Telegraph* posed very different world views. And that

journalists varied hugely in their politics and temperament. He is brilliant, but he is a brilliant conspiracist...[85]

This excerpt is a clear example of the immune system response of political journalism – and journalism in general – to criticism. The narratives that political journalism constructs and indulges in extend to the people who create them. Just as professional wrestling has its heels and faces, political journalists have to believe there is a vast difference between the world views of the various publications, even as the same people move seamlessly between them in a dizzying spectacle of ideological flexibility. Journalists have always changed titles – a job's a job – but there was a time in the mid- to late-twentieth century when to go from the *Daily Mirror* to the *Daily Mail*, or vice versa, you would have had to pass through some interim points along the way.

Based on their surface-level output alone, there's no doubt that the *Guardian* and the *Daily Telegraph* are very different publications, but on closer inspection, their political reporting accepts a lot of the same underlying assumptions – the Labour Party should not be *too* left-wing, being a buy-to-let landlord is socially acceptable, immigration is 'an issue' and people can have their 'reasonable concerns about it' etc. Newspapers in the twenty-first century are becoming more concentrated versions of what they always were, producing political journalism that's geared to their readerships' existing prejudices rather than seeking to challenge them. It's political discourse as fandom and newspapers as fanzines – each with their preferred set of politicians to cheer. When wrestling with the narratives presented, it's hard not to feel that the public are the ones getting pinned.

7.

The Impractical Question of Impartiality

On The Past, Present, and Future of The BBC

'He who prides himself on giving what he thinks the public wants is often creating a fictitious demand for lower standards which he will then satisfy.'
– **Lord Reith, memo to Crawford Committee on establishing the BBC (1926)**

In August 2022, shortly after she left the BBC after 21 years, but before launching Global's *News Agents* podcast alongside her former BBC colleagues Lewis Goodall and Jon Sopel, Emily Maitlis gave the MacTaggart Memorial Lecture, the keynote address at the influential Edinburgh International TV Festival. She took the audience back to 2016 and explained:

BREAKING

'... it might take our producers five minutes to find 60 economists who feared Brexit and five hours to find a sole voice who espoused it. But by the time we went on air, we simply had one of each. We presented this unequal effort to our audience as balance. It wasn't. I would later learn the ungainly name for this myopic style of journalism – both-sidesism – which talks to the way it reaches a superficial balance while obscuring a deeper truth. At this stage, I had never heard the term or indeed the criticism – I just thought we were doing our job.'[86]

The speech stretched my credulity so thoroughly that it felt like it had done a full hour of hot yoga by the time it was finished. It was bizarre to hear someone who had until very recently been one of the BBC's most prominent political interviewers claim that she hadn't encountered the idea of false balance, or it being wielded as a criticism of the corporation until Brexit and Trump.

Two years before the Brexit referendum, a year-long inquiry by a UK Parliamentary select committee concluded that BBC News teams consistently engaged in false balance when reporting on climate change stories. So for a senior news journalist to suggest they weren't familiar with the concept felt like a very stark confession. Head back even further, to the misty, almost unimaginable past of 2006, and you'll find Rob Corddry on *The Daily Show* parodying journalists who bend over backwards to establish balance where there is none: 'How does one report the facts when the facts themselves are biased? ... From the names of our fallen soldiers to the gradual withdrawal of our allies to the

THE IMPRACTICAL QUESTION OF IMPARTIALITY

growing insurgency, it's become all too clear that the facts in Iraq have an anti-Bush agenda.'

Maitlis's speech was rightly praised for highlighting the influence of Conservative Party appointees on the BBC, but it also contained a series of confessions about missing the elephant in the room even as the stench of dung must have been stifling. Recalling the morning after Donal Trump was elected President, Maitlis said: 'We did not yet understand that it was not replacing one man with another but one set of rules with another. We didn't realise we would need to change too.'

By election night, 509 days had passed since Trump had announced his candidacy, a period during which he had fought the bitter Republican primaries and spent months campaigning against Hillary Clinton. How could someone who spent so much time observing and analysing those events claim they 'didn't realise' things would be so different? One reason for that blind spot could be how the world looks refracted through the prism of the BBC as an organisation with its particular and longstanding principles and hang-ups.

Fundamentally, the BBC and the newspapers are different beasts with different aims, but they share the same habitat and draw on many of the same sources and resources. However, while newspapers can be predators, the BBC has had to behave more like a large and slightly lumbering omnivore; papers can deal in red meat, in bloody absolutes, while the BBC has to seek balance and is largely unable to defend itself. It's to BBC journalists' credit that they tend to investigate scandals at the corporation with even more vigour than their rivals (and enemies), but it can end up seeming more farcical than *W1A*, the satire set at and broadcast by the BBC.

In 1922, the BBC was born as a commercial enterprise created by a consortium of British and American electrical companies that made radios. It wasn't until January 1927, when the company's assets were transferred to a non-commercial organisation with a royal charter, that the BBC as we know it began. The BBC's founder and first Director-General, Lord Reith, boiled its purpose down to four words: it should 'inform, educate and entertain'. Those Reithian principles are embedded in the BBC's royal charter and form a kind of constitution for the corporation. But, as with the US Constitution, there are always arguments about the framer's intentions and how the meaning of those words – inform, educate and entertain – has shifted over the years. Even the order in which Reith laid out the principles is up for debate. When the somewhat stereotypical dour Scot opted to put 'inform' and 'educate' first, did he mean to make 'entertainment' subordinate to learning? Reith wrote in his book, *Broadcast Over Britain* (1924), that 'to have exploited so great a scientific invention for the purpose and pursuit of entertainment alone would have been a prostitution of its powers', so it seems fairly likely.

However, the early BBC audience didn't always agree with him. In February 1923, the debut edition of the *Radio Times* – the world's first listing magazine, itself also founded by Reith – contained a complaint from a listener who signed off as P. J. from Birmingham:

> Frankly, it seems to me that the BBC are mainly catering for the 'listeners' who . . . pretend to appreciate only and

THE IMPRACTICAL QUESTION OF IMPARTIALITY

understand only highbrow music and educational and 'sob' stuff. Surely, like a theatre manager, they must put up programmes which will appeal to the majority and must remember that is the latter who provide the main bulk of their income.[87]

Even in those earliest days, the debate over the BBC and value for money was live.

This conflict over the importance of the directive to 'entertain' could be seen on multiple occasions in those early years. In 1927, Reith appointed the journalist, former spy and ex-political secretary to the UK's first sitting female MP, Nancy Astor, Hilda Matheson, as the BBC's first director of talks. Matheson is a fascinating character – her achievements and adventures could fill the rest of this book – but it's for her impact on the BBC that she warrants mention here. Determined and principled, Matheson soon came into conflict with the more traditional Reith, their power struggle crystallising the clash between popular concerns and more niche content. Matheson persuaded literary heavyweights including H. G. Wells, George Bernard Shaw, Rebecca West and Harold Nicholson to give talks but she also introduced features such as 'The Pudding Lady', a recipe segment that led to the BBC being inundated with requests for copies, and 'The Day's Work', in which people described their jobs.

Matheson was also central to the BBC's early coverage of politics and parliament. After a ban in the BBC charter on covering controversial and political topics was lifted in 1928 – a sense of caution that has nonetheless lingered in the organisation's culture – Matheson launched a new programme to coincide with all women over 21 getting the vote. *The Week in Parliament*, which quickly became *The Week in Westminster*, began with Mary Hamilton MP explaining the events of the last seven days in politics. Reith, however, was not impressed. On 6 March 1930, he complained in his diary: 'Developing a great dislike for Miss Matheson and all her works.'[88] The final breakdown in their relationship came when Matheson commissioned a series of talks by Harold Nicholson on modern literature trends. He proposed talks about James Joyce and D. H. Lawrence but Reith forbade it because he did not want 'banned books' discussed on air. Matheson resigned in exasperation. Nicholson wrote in his diary that Reith had 'a head of bone'.

If you could stick Reith in a time machine and bring him forward to 2025, plonking him in front of the reboot of *Gladiators* or an episode of the betrayal-based, Claudia Winkleman's fringe-focused gameshow *Traitors*, it would probably provoke a massive heart attack. But much as in the time of 'Miss Matheson' and 'her works', entertainment is key; if you see news and information as the BBC's primary purpose, it makes its continuing existence harder to defend. Most people are a lot less keen on eating their vegetables than enjoying a pile of cream cakes (in this analogy, at least one of the cakes is shaped like Doctor Who).

When the BBC was still a toddler – not even four years old – it rolled over and showed its belly as a result of government pressure during the General Strike of 1926. In an essay written 36 years after the fact (and 25 years after he left the corporation), Lord Reith wrote: '... if there had been broadcasting at the time of the French Revolution, there would have been no French Revolution; the Revolution came from Marseilles to Paris as rumour. The function of the BBC was fully as much to kill falsehood as to

THE IMPRACTICAL QUESTION OF IMPARTIALITY

announce truth; and the former can derive automatically from the latter.'[89] But the 'truth' Reith announced – literally, as he took over reading many of its news bulletins – was defined by the government; he had been flattered into accepting that it was 'in the national interest'. In his reflections, written in 1963, Reith admitted that the BBC had been 'neither commandeered nor free'.

The BBC has always been engaged in juggling a complicated and often contradictory mix of demands. When George Orwell – or Eric Blair, as his personnel file had it – worked there between 1941 and 1942, composing propaganda to be broadcast to occupied Europe, he wrote in his diary that the atmosphere was 'something halfway between a girls' school and a lunatic asylum'. In a public critique of the corporation, published by the *Tribune* in January 1944, he expanded on that thought in a way that should feel very familiar in 2025: 'People are broadly aware that they don't like the BBC programmes, that along with some good stuff, a lot of muck is broadcast, that the talks are mostly ballyhoo and no subject of importance ever gets the honesty of discussion that it would get in even the most reactionary newspaper.'[90]

So it is that the newspaper columnists of today who, like the *Daily Telegraph*'s Allison Pearson, complain of left-wingers '[shoehorning] their tedious, progressive ideas into programmes about pot plants or food or puppies'[91] are engaged in a long-standing British tradition – BBC bashing.

Despite those early signs of conflict in the ranks, both at the top with the likes of Reith and Matheson and between those working below, the BBC continued to flourish, creating formats and shows which hit home with the public it aimed to serve. In March 1940, the BBC began *Postscripts*, a series of talks that went out after the

BREAKING

news on Sunday evenings designed to counter broadcasts from Hamburg by the traitorous William 'Lord Haw-Haw' Joyce. The novelist J. B. Priestley took over as host in June after the original presenter, the eminent lawyer and raconteur Maurice Healy, was deemed to be only a moderate success. Priestley made his first appearance on 5 June 1940 – the day after Churchill delivered his 'we shall fight them on the beaches' speech in Parliament – and made the evacuation of Dunkirk his theme: 'What strikes me about this is how typically English it is. Nothing, I feel, could be more English both in its beginning and its end, its folly and grandeur ... What began as a miserable blunder, a catalogue of misfortunes ended as an epic of gallantry.' Imagine how the modern British press would explode if a writer used the BBC's airwaves to make what they would doubtless present as an unpatriotic attack on 'our boys'. This was a talk delivered while the wounds were fresh and the country faced the imminent threat of invasion. It was sensational and deeply necessary.

But despite the success of Priestley and his show, the political right considered him to be unacceptably radical. Both the former Chairman of the Conservative Party Lord Davison and senior Ministry of Information official Lieutenant-Colonel Norman Scorgie complained about his political messages. Priestley lasted until October before the critics succeeded in getting him removed. His response, recorded in a letter to the political theorist Harold Laski, sounds as modern as Orwell's analysis of the BBC: '[The Tories] are pretending that everything on their side is non-political and not tendentious, but anything on the outside must be barred because it is political and tendentious.' As then, so now.

*

THE IMPRACTICAL QUESTION OF IMPARTIALITY

Impartiality is such an important concept for the BBC because it's tied directly to the idea of universal provision. If the BBC isn't an impartial voice that speaks for the whole nation, then it can no longer justify the existence of the licence fee as a compulsory charge. The notion of impartiality is what gives the BBC authority. It's important that – Wizard of Oz style – we don't look at the man behind the curtain. It's also why BBC journalists are often comforted by the idea that if they are criticised by both left and right for bias then they must be doing OK. But that falls apart when you notice that the right, which dominates the press, whines about bias while being pandered to endlessly.

Reading the definition of 'due impartiality' in the BBC's editorial guidelines is headache-inducing. It explains that 'due impartiality usually involves more than a simple matter of "balance" between opposing viewpoints'. The BBC is meant to be inclusive, taking a broad perspective on any issue, and ensure that the existence of 'a range of views is appropriately reflected'. That doesn't mean it has to be neutral on any issue – it certainly isn't on the monarchy and tends not to be when UK forces are involved in military action – or detached from 'fundamental democratic values'.

These requirements and the huge scope for interpreting them in different ways mean the BBC is continually pulled in different directions by forces both within and outside the corporation. For newspapers, and the people behind them, who are ideologically opposed to the BBC's existence, no version of impartiality will ever be impartial enough unless the broadcaster simply capitulates to every aspect of their worldview. The majority of complaints that the BBC receives are related to the corporation's objectivity and

BREAKING

what the complainant perceives as a lack of it. 'Perceives' being the operative word here.

The gulf between the perception of bias and having evidence of it was highlighted when, in January 2022, the then Culture Secretary Lucy Frazer was skewered by Kay Burley on *Sky News*. After Frazer told Burley that 39 per cent of complaints to Ofcom about the BBC in the previous year were related to impartiality, up from 19 per cent the year before, Burley pointed out that 'perception isn't necessarily reality'. Frazer replied that 'perceptions of the BBC by the public are important'. When Burley asked for evidence, Frazer offered again: 'The evidence of bias is what audiences believe about the content of the BBC.' She didn't have evidence; she had vibes. Interested parties – be they rival media organisations or politicians – spend a lot of time pushing that perception of bias and with the press's perspective coming predominantly from the right, it's complaints *from* the right that are given most column inches and credence.

In its effort to commitment to impartiality, the BBC can take a step too far. In 2023, the launch of BBC Verify, the corporation's highly publicised fact-checking initiative, was arguably a counter-productive move. Viewers and listeners already expected the BBC to be transparent and clear about how it did its journalism. The idea that BBC News needed what its chief executive, Deborah Turness, described as 'a new brand within our brand' to build audience trust made already distrustful audiences more suspicious. It felt like a 'the lady doth protest too much' moment. Journalists should check their facts without the need for a dedicated team with its own special area in the newsroom. When the BBC's Disinformation and Social Media Correspondent Marianna

THE IMPRACTICAL QUESTION OF IMPARTIALITY

Spring introduced Verify on *BBC Breakfast*, she used a graphic which included 'alternative media' alongside labels marked 'far-right figures', 'foreign links' and 'UK conspiracy movement'. It was a conflation that suggested that the BBC was using its power in the media market to stamp on much smaller competitors.

Impartiality is most often scrutinised when it comes to the BBC's political reporting. After the *Telegraph* columnist – the paper's former editor and official biographer of Margaret Thatcher – Charles Moore wrote that 'the national broadcaster [needed] to show super-impartiality' (which is presumably impartiality that eats its greens), BBC presenter Nick Robinson wrote a letter in reply:

> When as BBC Political Editor, I reported night after night on the loans for honours scandal which damaged Tony Blair – or as presenter of *Today* on Theresa May's fight over Brexit with her own backbenchers, or Jeremy Corbyn's battles over antisemitism – I heard no call for 'super-impartiality' from Lord Moore. I wonder why not.[92]

Robinson was right – Moore's demand for 'super-impartiality' was ludicrous – but his defence of the BBC boiled down to another variant of that old favourite 'if both sides are criticising us, we must be doing something right'. This doesn't hold. Right-wing columnists and the papers they serve consider their views to be the normal and natural state of things and object when they feel coverage doesn't hew to that line. Right-wing newspaper attacks on the BBC are generally in bad faith, inspired by ideological opposition to the existence of a public service broadcaster and their proprietors' commercial considerations. Hardliners on the right don't want impartiality – whatever that means to them – but rather the BBC's total capitulation followed by it being dismantled at high speed.

Time and time again, the right pushes the idea that the BBC is a nest of Marxist revolutionaries, the broadcast vanguard of the woke, ramping up the coverage whenever an 'enemy within' is required. As a result, anything remotely left-wing tends to be treated with an underlying suspicion by the BBC. How might Tory politicians and their supporters have responded if one of their leaders was depicted as the *Harry Potter* villain Voldemort, as *Newsnight* did with Jeremy Corbyn in 2016? Of course, the Corbyn-era was far from the first time that a Labour leader got an extra-special kicking from the BBC.

Over the years, Labour had frequently been the butt of the joke – this casual mockery was typified by an incident in 1971 when Harold Wilson, who had returned to opposition the previous year, was treated to a specially composed satirical song by the comedy band Scaffold that was woven through the BBC documentary, *Yesterday's Men*. Wilson and his shadow cabinet took part in the film believing that it would go out under a different title and be a rather straighter piece of work. Oddly, the companion BBC film on Edward Heath's government, *Mr Heath's Quiet Revolution*, was free of comic songs. The years of constant ribbing had engendered a party-wide suspicion of the BBC which runs deep. Labour's deep psychological scars around the BBC from years of slights, both real and perceived, were thoroughly reopened around the Iraq War after a series of events which led to terrible consequences for the BBC in particular, the media in general and

THE IMPRACTICAL QUESTION OF IMPARTIALITY

the nation. And the public battle between the government and the BBC ended in a horrible personal tragedy.

On 18 July 2003, Dr David Kelly, a biological weapons expert and UN weapons inspector, was found dead on Harrowdown Hill in Oxfordshire. His body was discovered by a volunteer search team after his family reported him missing. He was 59 years old.

Earlier that year, in February 2003, just over a month before the Iraq War began, US Secretary of State Colin Powell had addressed the UN Security Council with striking assertions about the status of Iraq's chemical and biological weapons programmes. He claimed that the country had mobile weapons laboratories which 'could produce a quantity of biological poison equal to the entire amount that Iraq claimed to have produced in the years prior to the Gulf War'.

Kelly, who had examined the very vehicles that the US government claimed were 'mobile labs', spoke off the record to the *Observer*. His quote, attributed to a 'British scientist and biological weapons expert', contradicted Powell's speech: 'They are not mobile germ war laboratories. You could not use them for making biological weapons. They do not even look like them.'[93] Kelly suggested that the US claims were literally overblown: 'They are exactly what the Iraqis said they were – facilities for the production of hydrogen gas to fill balloons.'

Peter Beaumont, one of the journalists bylined on that *Observer* story, confirmed to the Hutton Inquiry, the judge-led investigation into the circumstances surrounding Kelly's death, that the scientist was the source. Also in February 2003, Kelly himself wrote an anonymous article for the *Observer*, which the paper republished with his name on the byline after his death.

BREAKING

In it, he wrote: 'War may now be inevitable. The proportionality and intensity of the conflict will depend on whether regime change or disarmament is the true objective. The US, and whoever willingly assists it, should ensure that the force, strength and strategy used is appropriate to the modest threat that Iraq now poses.'

US and UK forces entered Iraq on 20 March 2003. On 1 May 2003, standing on the flight deck of the USS *Abraham Lincoln*, which had been in the Persian Gulf but was now anchored in marginally less scary waters off San Diego, President Bush declared 'mission accomplished'. The following Wednesday – 7 May 2003 – BBC *Newsnight*'s Science Editor Susan Watts phoned Kelly, who she'd spoken to for earlier stories, and asked about various topics surrounding the war, including a UK government claim, attributed to the security services, that Saddam Hussein could deploy weapons of mass destruction (WMDs) against Britain 'within 45 minutes'. The latter claim became known as the '45-minute dossier'. Watts' shorthand notes from this conversation recorded that Kelly had called the claim 'a mistake' and said that Tony Blair's Press Secretary, Alastair Campell, had '[seen] something in there' that 'sounded good' but which was from 'a single source ... not corroborated'.

On 22 May 2003, Kelly met journalist Andrew Gilligan at the Charing Cross Hotel in London. Gilligan, who went on to become a major supporter of and advisor to Boris Johnson as well as working at the *Sunday Times*, was then the defence and diplomatic correspondent for the BBC's *Today* programme. He had met Kelly twice before, but this was a much more serious conversation. Gilligan asked Kelly why WMDs hadn't been

THE IMPRACTICAL QUESTION OF IMPARTIALITY

discovered in Iraq. Gilligan later claimed that after 30 minutes, the discussion had tuned to the 45-minute dossier and how it had been edited to make a greater impact. Gilligan took notes not in shorthand on a pad – standard practice for a BBC reporter – but on an unsuitable and, crucially, unreliable electronic organiser. Armed with the lines from Kelly, he appeared on the 29 May 2003 edition of *Today* at 6.07am, interviewed by its most senior presenter, John Humphrys, to trail a report later in the show. He said:

> ... we've been told by one of the senior officials in charge of drawing up that dossier that actually the government probably ... erm ... knew that the 45 minutes figure was wrong, even before it decided to put it in. What this person says is that a week before the publication date of the dossier, it was actually rather ... erm ... a bland production. It didn't, the draft prepared for Mr Blair by the intelligence agencies actually didn't say very much more than was public knowledge already and ... erm ... Downing Street, our source says, ordered a week before publication, ordered it to be 'sexed up', to be made more exciting and ordered more facts to be ... er ... to be discovered.

Gilligan had a single source: Kelly. *Today*'s producer Kevin Marsh later wrote that Gilligan deviated from his pre-planned script, breaking a rule that anonymous single-sourced stories '[had] to be reported word perfectly'.[94] In the blandest possible managerial assessment, Marsh said that 'Gilligan had lost control of that precision.' Downing Street had not been contacted for comment

BREAKING

before Gilligan made his claims and, at 7.32am, its press office – home to a red-faced and raging Alastair Campbell – issued a statement: 'Not one word of the dossier was not entirely the work of the intelligence agencies.'

Gilligan doubled down in a report for BBC Radio 5 Live's *Breakfast* programme. Kelly didn't initially recognise himself as Gilligan's source because the description simply didn't resemble him. He hadn't been 'in charge of drawing up the document' and had only been asked to comment once its contents had already been established. The day after Gilligan's reports, Susan Watts called Kelly at home. Her recording of the call was later featured as evidence in the Hutton Inquiry. Kelly told her that he didn't think he would be suspected of the leak and they discussed the 45-minute claim again:

> **Watts:** OK, just [going] back momentarily on the 45-minute issue; I'm feeling like I ought to just explore that a little bit more with you ... So, would it be accurate then, as you did in that earlier conversation, to say that it was Alastair Campbell himself who ...
> **Kelly:** No, I can't. All I can say is that the Number 10 press office ... I've never met Alastair Campbell so I can't ... But I think Alastair Campbell is synonymous with that press office because he's responsible for it.

In the coming days, Gilligan doubled down again. In an article for the *Mail on Sunday*, he named Campbell as the catalyst for the 45-minute claim, saying he'd asked his source why Blair had 'misled us all over Saddam's weapons' and received a one-word

THE IMPRACTICAL QUESTION OF IMPARTIALITY

reply: 'Campbell'.[95] It was the story spreading from the BBC to the Middle England-focused *Mail* titles and the continued attention on Campbell that provoked a meltdown in government with furious meetings about Gilligan's claims and a frantic search for someone to blame. Kelly told his line manager at the Ministry of Defence (MoD) that he had met Gilligan and that the 45-minute claim was discussed. He also told his bosses that Gilligan had mentioned Campbell but only in passing. He wrote: 'I did not even consider that I was the "source" of Gilligan's information.' He said he only realised he *might* be the source after Gilligan appeared before Parliament's foreign affairs select committee. Kelly's statement continued: '[Gilligan's] description of that meeting in small part matches my interaction with him, especially my personal evaluation of Iraq's capability but the overall character is quite different.'

After two interviews, the MoD concluded that Kelly *might* be Gilligan's source but that the journalist appeared to have exaggerated things. No official action was taken against him but he was warned that he might be named in the press. Tom Baldwin of *The Times* – who'd previously broken stories on scandals around the Blair government and went on to become a comms advisor to one Labour leader (Ed Miliband) and pseudo-official biographer of another (Keir Starmer) – wrote stories on 5 and 8 July 2003 that hinted heavily about the source's identity. Tony Blair decided that Kelly shouldn't be named unless a journalist correctly guessed it was him; it was less a strategy but more of a grim parlour game for the press. In a diary entry, 4 July 2003, Campbell wrote that it would 'fuck Gilligan' if Kelly was revealed as his source.[96]

BREAKING

On 8 July, the day that Baldwin's second story was published, the government issued a statement that said a staff member at the MoD had come forward to admit meeting Gilligan. The next evening, a *Financial Times* journalist called Chris Adams won Blair's guessing game, while a *Times* reporter also hit the target after submitting 19 failed guesses. Earlier the same day, veteran BBC journalist Tom Mangold, an old friend of the scientist, emailed Kelly privately to offer 'a dry shoulder to cry on'. Another old friend, Nick Rufford of the *Sunday Times*, visited Kelly at home to warn that his name would be published the next day. He told Kelly to get out of his house to avoid the media and offered to get him a hotel before trying to get him to write exclusively for his paper. That ruse failed when the MoD told Kelly to find somewhere else to stay. He and his wife headed to Cornwall.

Three days later, Kelly's boss, Bryan Wells, called him to say that he would have to appear in front of Parliament's Intelligence & Security and Foreign Affairs select committees. The latter would be televised, something Kelly's wife said caused him a great deal of distress and anxiety. He called Wells a further nine times that day.

When he appeared in Parliament on 15 July, Kelly was subjected to hostile questioning from both select committees. It later emerged that Gilligan had sneakily supplied the Lib Dems with questions which were put to Kelly by David Chidgey, an MP later elevated to the House of Lords as a life peer. Gilligan's memo to the MPs revealed Kelly's conversations with Susan Watts, even though he didn't know for sure at the time that the scientist had been her source. Writing for *Open Democracy* in 2017,[97] Tom Mangold called it 'an extraordinary betrayal' that contributed

THE IMPRACTICAL QUESTION OF IMPARTIALITY

to a catastrophic result. Mangold surmised that the most likely explanation for Kelly's death was that he had learned from 'a well-meaning friend' at the MoD that 'the BBC had tape-recorded evidence which, when published, would show that he had said things ... that he had formally denied saying'.

In a letter to the *Observer* in 2010, Gilligan denied that either he or the BBC betrayed Kelly. Responding to a critical article about him written by Nick Cohen, he wrote: 'Neither I nor the BBC ever revealed him as my source, either in public or in emails to an MP, until after his death. It was his employer, the Ministry of Defence, that effectively leaked his name – after he came forward, having been promised anonymity – to his bosses.'[98]

On the day that Kelly took his final walk to Harrowdown Hill, he replied to an email from the *New York Times* journalist Judith Miller. He wrote that he would 'wait until the end of the week before judging' and that 'many dark actors [were] playing games'. In the aftermath of his death, the Hutton Inquiry, chaired by Lord Hutton, the former Lord Chief Justice of Northern Ireland, was set up to investigate the circumstances surrounding it. In January 2004, after 22 days hearing evidence from 74 witnesses, it concluded that Kelly took his own life. The former Conservative Party leader Michael Howard and former Liberal Democrat minister Norman Baker – who wrote a book about the case – were among a vocal minority who have raised doubts about the verdict. Baker's book provoked anger from members of Kelly's family, who accused him of 'raking over old bones'.

The Hutton Report's findings triggered the resignation of then-BBC chairman Gavyn Davies – whose appointment had been controversial as he was a major Labour donor and married to Sue Nye, Gordon Brown's most senior aide – and Director-General Greg Dyke, who lost the support of the corporation's board. Andrew Gilligan also resigned but used his resignation statement to rage that Hutton had 'cast a chill over all journalism'. Subsequent official inquiries – the Butler Review (2004) and the Chilcot Inquiry (2016) – concluded that the 45-minute claim was 'included because of its eye-catching character' and the product of 'a deliberate policy of exaggeration and omission in the intelligence'. Gilligan's story had been right but that didn't vindicate how he went about reporting it nor how he treated Kelly as a source.

In *Shock and War: Iraq 20 Years On*, a 2023 podcast series presented by BBC Security Correspondent Gordon Corera, Sir Richard Dearlove, the former head of the Secret Intelligence Service (MI6), was so relaxed about the spin added to the case for war that he was almost horizontal. After Corera commented that journalists, including him, did not ask tough enough questions, Dearlove replied: 'There are precedents; look at what happened recently over Ukraine. The intelligence services have always been used [to sell policies] in certain cases.'

Research by Cardiff University[99] – commissioned by the BBC – into news coverage during the first three weeks of the Iraq War found that the corporation was the least likely to quote Iraqi sources, less likely than Sky News, ITV, or Channel 4 to talk to independent and sceptical sources like the Red Cross, and placed the least emphasis on Iraqi casualties. The notion that the BBC was somehow anti-war or even anti-government was dispelled by the reality of its reporting. When the shooting starts, the corporation tends to shift subtly from a public service

THE IMPRACTICAL QUESTION OF IMPARTIALITY

towards a state broadcaster. In the years since Hutton, BBC journalists on the ground have not become less brave or keen to find the truth, but the managers above them are often more cautious and craven.

In an LBC podcast introduction to her MacTaggart lecture with which we opened the chapter, Maitlis suggested that 'politics has massively changed [and] political actors have massively changed'. It was a compelling thesis but it starts to fall apart a little when subjected to scrutiny. It's comforting to pretend that Donald Trump's rise was a unique and terrible historical occurrence, but the Obama era, with a president who was 'presidential' in TV-friendly terms, slapped a veneer of civility over US foreign policy that remained as brutal as it had ever been. The earlier era of media distrust and 'alternative facts' under Bill Clinton and the Bushes (senior and junior) faded in the minds of goldfish-brained commentators. Similarly, in the UK, there's a good living to be made in pretending that Boris Johnson was a monster who came shambling out of the fog rather than a product and inevitable consequence of a long-standing system. And, as with the case of Kelly, the corporation's actions have played a role in shaping national events.

A key premise of Maitlis's speech was that government interference in the BBC had reached new and terrifying levels, focusing on former Tory comms boss Sir Robbie Gibb acting as 'an active agent of the Conservative Party' on the BBC board. It was a comforting claim for liberals who need a golden past to cling to. Yes, the Tories made a party donor, Richard Sharp, chairman of the BBC and were happy to have a former Tory council candidate, Tim Davie, as director-general, but this wasn't new. As previously mentioned, Greg Dyke was a Labour Party donor before he

BREAKING

became director-general in 1999. In 2013, former Labour minister James Purnell became the BBC's head of strategy. When he died, former Director-General Marmaduke Hussey was described by obituary writers as 'Margaret Thatcher's man at the BBC' sent there by her to 'sort it out'.

The sociologist Tom Burns argued in his 1977 study of the corporation, *The BBC: Public Institution and Private World*, that it is best understood as a 'quango' – a quasi-independent body expected to act 'in conformity with government purposes' and subject to 'essential instrument[s] of control'. Chief among those 'instruments of control' is the licence fee. But, in 2022, Maitlis worried: 'Things that for many decades were givens . . . a media free from interference or vilification now appear vulnerable.' That golden age never existed – there's never been a time when the BBC wasn't subject to political pressure or used as a convenient enemy by politicians.

The corporation's myths aren't limited to its political influences but can mean that many of the BBC's blindspots go uninterrogated. Why does it have a North of England correspondent but no South of England correspondent, as though anywhere past Watford is a frozen wasteland that requires specialist skills to cover, but the audience simply 'gets' the south? Why does it accept the status of the royal family as a given and refuse to cover the Windsors with anything like real scrutiny? On senior royals' birthdays, it still plays the national anthem on Radio 4, making many listeners feel like they've stumbled through a time portal to the mid-1950s. Or perhaps the 1850s. Why does the daily religious slot 'Thought for the Day' still exist and give space to newspaper columnists like the *Daily Telegraph*'s Tim Stanley and writers such

THE IMPRACTICAL QUESTION OF IMPARTIALITY

as Rhidian Brook simply because they're Christians? Why was Gary Lineker paid so much? Why did the BBC move so many of its operations to Media City in Salford but do so little to shift the corporate mindset away from London?

The supposed snobbery and London-centric nature of the corporation is criticism which is regularly hurled at the BBC. When the *Guardian* asked Paul Dacre, then editor of *the Daily Mail*, now its editor-in-chief, for his view on the corporation, he pointed it towards the Hugh Cudlipp Memorial Lecture he delivered in 2007. In that speech, he railed against the corporation, calling it 'snobbish [and] disdainful, in particular, of the values of the decent lower middle classes . . . [who] strive to raise their families, respect the traditions of this country, obey the law and get by on their comparatively meagre incomes'. Dacre – whose total pay package in 2007 was a 'meagre' £1.5 million – was describing *Mail* readers and advancing the idea that they had been left behind by the 'metropolitan elite' BBC. Despite *Mail* journalists appearing frequently as panellists on BBC shows like *Question Time* and *The Moral Maze*, as well as talking heads across its news programmes, Dacre claimed that 'the BBC's journalists, insulated from real competition . . . [consider] any dissenting views – particularly those held by popular papers . . . to be extreme and morally beyond the pale.'[100] The night before Dacre's speech, the *Mail's* front page will have been promoted on the BBC's newspaper reviews. On the morning of the speech, *Daily Mail* stories will have been discussed on BBC TV and radio broadcasts. And so strong is the BBC's disgust for the *Daily Mail* in return that it mentions it numerous times every day.

Dacre used his speech to accuse the BBC of being 'a closed

BREAKING

thought system operating a kind of Orwellian Newspeak . . . perverting political discourse and disenfranchising countless millions'. That line is reflective of the *Daily Mail* worldview, something which Dacre was so pivotal in developing and reinforcing, a narrative created for 'the decent lower middle classes', offering a cast of stock characters – devious immigrants, benefit cheats, cunning criminals, a dangerous underclass – designed to terrify them into picking up the next instalment. The BBC has to give space to its critics; the *Daily Mail* is under no such obligation. The *Mail* and other tabloids are the most consistent and successful 'closed thought systems' in the British media and the BBC's 'villainy' is an article of faith to them.

Sometimes it's insiders on their way out who offer the most strident analysis of the BBC. While Dacre lamented the closed-off nature of the BBC, others criticise its breadth. In the same article that featured Dacre's comments, just a couple of months before he presented his final edition of *Newsnight*, Jeremy Paxman gave a cutting critique of the corporation's scale to the *Guardian*:

> I don't really understand why it does Radio 1. Clearly, you can meet those needs commercially . . . the BBC has got an unfortunate history of never seeing an area of broadcasting or, increasingly, a web presence, without feeling the need to get into it itself. There's no argument that the BBC distorts the marketplace in online [news].[101]

The BBC *is* a many-headed hydra, but if you start to accept that it should lop a few of them off, the argument for putting the entire

THE IMPRACTICAL QUESTION OF IMPARTIALITY

creature down becomes easier to make. Paxman couldn't see the point of the BBC being in the business of playing pop music but many of its commercial rivals can't see why it has to produce news coverage either. After all, *Sky News* and *ITV News* are paid for with advertising.

This hydra-esque nature doesn't just result in a dilution of output but can have grimmer consequences; while the BBC leaves the more salacious headlines to other publications, it has not been exempt from scandal. The shadow of Jimmy Savile still hangs over the organisation. In 2011, one part of the corporation – *Newsnight* – was investigating subsequently proven allegations about the presenter's long history of rape and sexual abuse while another – the light entertainment division – was prepping a slobbering documentary on the recently deceased star and his long career at the broadcaster. The tribute programme won out over the news investigation, which was shelved. Instead, ITV broke the story with a documentary researched and presented by Mark Williams-Thomas, a former police investigator who had been involved in the original *Newsnight* investigation.

The calamitous divide at the heart of the response to the Savile scandal is a stark illustration of one of the biggest misconceptions about the BBC: that it's a monolith, controlled with a certain and unyielding grip from the top. If you've worked in any sort of large organisation, you'll know that's not possible. The BBC is a sprawling and often contradictory collection of departments and specialisms. It's a structurally difficult place to manage, full of people who are hard to wrangle working to the demands of strict and often frustrating editorial rules. A veteran BBC reporter put it to me like this: 'People strain every sinew to be impartial.

BREAKING

Due impartiality is an easy concept to understand but it's a very difficult one to put into practice.'

While the Savile case revealed horrific historical failings at the BBC, the revelation in 2024 that Huw Edwards, the BBC's most senior news presenter and its anchor for many historic events including the death of Queen Elizabeth II, had been charged with possessing images of child sexual abuse was a huge blow to trust in the modern organisation. Edwards was subsequently convicted of the offences. In the aftermath, BBC Director-General Tim Davie said on Radio 4's *Today* programme that no one at the corporation is 'indispensable' and that he had banned the use of the word 'talent' to describe big names in the organisation. He told Nick Robinson: 'We often refer to people like yourself as talent [but] you're a presenter, I'm a leader of the organisation and we're here to serve.'[102]

A BBC reporter told me they're personally committed to impartiality in reporting because they 'don't have a monopoly on truth'. It's a good principle to work from but not one universally held across thousands of BBC employees, particularly among its highly paid class of star 'talent'. The BBC has a presenter problem. There's a significant amount of frustration in the organisation from reporters and producers who are paid far less than the stars and often held to much higher standards. One BBC staffer told me: 'They get venerated to a point where it's exhaustion and counter-productive. Presenters hold too much power and are overpaid.'

Sarah Sands, who went from a long career in newspapers to editing Radio 4's *Today* programme (having been hired by another newspaper blow-in, former *Times* editor James Harding, then the corporation's head of news), brought an outsider's eye to the

THE IMPRACTICAL QUESTION OF IMPARTIALITY

proceedings. After spending three years at *Today*, from 2017 to 2020, she told *The Times* she was startled to find 'you've got a producer on £30,000 working 14-hour shifts and a presenter on £600,000. It's a shocker.'[103] Sands also criticised the BBC's use of the word 'talent' for star presenters ('You're a journalist so you need to behave like a journalist') and talked about being tasked with getting then long-serving *Today* presenter John Humphrys to take a pay cut. When she told him that he earned too much, he agreed: 'I don't know why they gave me all this money!'

While levels of pay at the top of the corporation are a problem, cuts on the frontline are another. The BBC has inherent biases and they're made much worse by financial cuts. The kinds of reporting which tend to get closer to the ideal of impartiality are expensive. They involve sending journalists further afield and giving them more time and resources to explore stories. The further from Westminster or Washington a reporter travels, the more likely they are to get an understanding of the political climate that breaks with consensus and draws on a wider set of sources rather than reflecting a soap opera of competing politico personalities. Cuts at the BBC always reduce the number of frontline staff who make programmes and actually do journalism, while strengthening the position of people in management, increasing the sense of authoritarianism within the corporation.

The size and level of complexity within the organisation continues to put the BBC in a difficult position on a daily basis, in ways that while less sinister are still troubling. It's meant to provide a universal service and represent all taxpayers, but shifting tastes and massive technological change mean fewer young people consume its output. It cannot wait for them to age into a penchant for public-sector broadcasting; it has to go where those audiences are. Turning the oil tanker is made harder by the continuing need to also produce shows that older listeners and viewers value, and a hostile environment in which many of the media reporters that cover the corporation might better be described as anti-BBC correspondents.

The BBC's continued existence is a good thing but like other sacred cows of the early twentieth century, including the NHS, it sometimes acts as though it should be exempt from proper criticism. To point out the corporation's faults is often treated by the comfy occupants of the political centre as akin to mentioning a hairy mole on a beloved maiden aunt's face or standing on an ageing mutt's injured paw. It has brilliant reporters – many of them in its increasingly beleaguered local news division – and retains a willingness to fund the obtuse and unusual. No one but the BBC would make *Desert Island Discs* or commission Adam Curtis's string of pugnaciously alternative documentaries on the history of ideas, culture and conspiracies.

A world without the BBC would be less informed, less culturally adventurous and less inclined to give chances to new talent in journalism and the arts alike. But all of this being said, the BBC often feels like a burgled house being circled by arsonists. There was a social media trend for a while of posting a licence fee advert from the 1980s called 'What has the BBC ever given us?' featuring John Cleese doing a version of *The Life of Brian*'s 'What have the Romans ever done for us?' riff – following each repetition of the question with more things the BBC has done for its audience – as a response to people criticising the broadcaster. That Cleese himself has frequently lashed out at the

THE IMPRACTICAL QUESTION OF IMPARTIALITY

BBC in his anti-woke late-life incarnation was beside the point, as was the fact that the BBC described in that advert, with more money to spend on drama and sports rights, is the BBC of then rather than of now.

What centrists and right-wingers have in common is a demand for a public service broadcaster that looks and sounds like them. The BBC is a creature of the Establishment, and the licence fee structure – which is now subject to renewed scrutiny under the new Labour government – means it is also beholden *to* the Establishment. Its natural state is defaulting to the defence of the status quo, a tendency that makes it bureaucratic, generally slow-moving and prone to being riddled by shots from both sides. If the BBC is destroyed, nothing like it would ever be rebuilt. It's the product of inter-war experimentation and post-war ideals. Those who want to burn it down are vandals but those who pretend that it does not need serious renovation are also contributing to the collapse. A BBC that cannot persuade younger people in particular that it speaks for them and is worthy of their attention cannot survive. One BBC reporter described the organisation to me as 'like a wounded beast' before swiftly adding the caveat that it is 'not a *mortally* wounded beast'. I hope they're right.

8.
Interviews and The Art of War

On the Fractious History and Preposterous Present of Head-to-heads

*'When you're interviewing someone, you're in control.
When you're being interviewed, you think you're in control,
but you're not.'*
– Barbara Walters in an interview with *Bloomberg* (2013)

In theory, interviews are about getting answers to questions. In reality, they're often a tussle between someone who wants to find things out and someone who's determined to make sure that doesn't happen. It might seem that a refusal to answer a straight question with a straight answer is a modern affliction but that's far from true. A study of televised interviews[104] by psychologists Peter Bull and Kate Mayer during the 1987 election found that the Tory Prime Minister Margaret Thatcher and Labour Opposition Leader Neil Kinnock both ducked more than half of the questions

BREAKING

put to them: 57 per cent for her and 59 per cent for him. They were interviewed for the same length of time by the same interviewers (Sir Robin Day, Jonathan Dimbleby, David Dimbleby and David Frost) and the researchers organised their non-replies into 11 categories. In the typology of non-replies that they created, you'll also discern the fundamentals of the media training which most politicians, business people and celebrities now undertake.

1. Ignoring the question
This is when the interviewee says what they intended to say anyway without being distracted by petty annoyances like the interviewer's concerns. Phrases like, 'Our message is very simple ...' or 'The real question is ...' are all good indications that the rhetorical bulldozer is revving up and the question is going to be shoved aside.

2. Acknowledging the question
This can arrive with an attempt at bamboozling flattery ('I'm glad you asked that ...'), a delaying tactic ('Before I come to that ...') or blatant deflection ('I don't think that's what people are really talking about/interested in/focused on ...').

3. Questioning the question
The researchers identified two variations of this approach – asking for clarification on a point of detail ('Which figures in particular are you referring to?') and kicking the question back to the interviewer ('Well, you tell me'; 'What do you think?').

4. Attacking the question
There are several ways this can manifest itself: suggesting the

interviewer is missing an important detail; dismissing the question as hypothetical or speculative; implying it's based on a false premise; trying to identify a factual inaccuracy; claiming it's deceptive, based on a misquote or sets up a false choice, and (faux) outrage, implying the question itself is objectionable.

5. Attacking the interviewer
This is a risky one but usually involves implying the questioner is biased, wouldn't put a similar point to an opponent or is unprepared.

6. Refusing to answer
Another multi-part option. In this case, the interviewee can argue they're in no position to reply *yet*; reject the question as a hypothetical or a demand to make a prophecy, or suggest they're the wrong person to ask. The last of those is difficult to pull off if you're the boss or even the prime minister. A common variant in recent years has been for politicians and other public figures to dismiss questions about ongoing controversies by spluttering that they're 'not going to give a running commentary'.

7. Making a political point
This will usually manifest as an attack on the opposition or another rival group ('We have a plan; they don't') or repeating an agreed line ('The Prime Minister is making long-term decisions for a better future') but it can equally be another form of reassuring but ultimately meaningless mantra. Tony Blair, facing a party funding scandal, once emoted, all Bambi-eyed: 'I think most people who have dealt with me think I am a pretty straight sort of guy.'

BREAKING

8. Only answering part of the question
Often, under time pressure, interviewers ask multi-part questions. It allows their guests to ignore parts they don't want to address and focus on the ones they're more comfortable with. Another variation is to say what you won't do, rather than what you will do.

9. Repeating a previous answer
When an interviewee has a line which they're particularly comfortable with or which they've been told to emphasise, they'll often avoid answering a question by simply repeating that. Former Prime Minister Theresa May and the rest of her cabinet were particularly guilty of this in the period after the Brexit referendum when, zombie-like, they used to repeat the mantra 'Brexit means Brexit'. They said it so much that it frequently metamorphosed into 'Breakfast means breakfast'.

10. Saying the question has already been answered
When an interviewee howls that they've 'been very clear', they almost certainly haven't.

11. Apologising
Truly the rarest of the non-answers, this option has been driven almost to extinction in British public life.

Bull and Mayer concluded Thatcher's most frequent tactic for parrying questions was to attack the interviewer. They wrote that she '[wrong-footed] interviewers and put them on the defensive by making frequent objections to interruptions, by personalising issues, and by taking questions and criticism as accusations'. They

INTERVIEWS AND THE ART OF WAR

also suggested that it was an effective strategy: in 83 per cent of the occasions that Thatcher attacked the interviewer, they asked a new question rather than attempting to reformulate the original one. By contrast, Kinnock, whose most common approaches were to claim he'd already answered the question or kick it back at the interviewer, failed to get the interviewers to drop it every time.

In 2000, in a paper published in the *Journal of Language and Social Psychology*, Dr Peter Bull applied the same approach to analysing Tony Blair's performance in televised interviews during Labour's winning 1997 general election campaign. But before he even got to Blair, he began by looking at reply rates in interviews with people who weren't politicians. In Martin Bashir's notorious 1995 interview with Diana, Princess of Wales, she replied to 78 per cent of the questions put to her. In another Bashir interview, Louise Woodward, the young British au pair convicted of the manslaughter of eight-month-old baby Matthew Eappen, answered 70 per cent of questions. Monica Lewinsky, interviewed by Channel 4 News's Jon Snow about her affair with President Clinton, addressed 89 per cent of the questions posed to her. The mean reply rate across the three interviews was 79 per cent, significantly higher than the rate observed in the Thatcher and Kinnock interviews.[105]

Blair, who presented himself as 'a pretty straight guy', learned from Kinnock's mistakes and Thatcher's tactics. Asked by David Dimbleby whether his 'new ally' Rupert Murdoch was right to take on the print unions in the Wapping dispute while Labour supported the industrial action, Blair simply said those days were over and 'there [was] no point in going back in the past'. He avoided answering either question by placing them as things that no longer mattered in the world of New Labour. In another interview, Peter Sissons pushed Blair to address a comment from the old enemy: '[Thatcher] was reported as saying there's nothing to fear from a Labour government under Tony Blair. Is that a compliment to you that you will cherish?' Again, Blair sailed through the middle, taking only what he needed from the question: 'Well, I certainly hope there is nothing to fear and I know there's nothing to fear from a Labour government.' He avoided offending members of his party and existing Labour supporters by praising Thatcher while skipping an outright denunciation of her as he courted former Tory voters. When confronted by Jeremy Paxman with a question that seemed to demand a yes or no answer – 'Do you still consider yourself a socialist?' – Blair danced around the danger of contradicting his claim to have reformed the party while avoiding seeming like he'd totally abandoned the positions he'd campaigned on under previous leaders and in previous elections: 'I do, in the sense of the values, but I don't share the idea that socialism's about some fixed economic prescription.' It's technically an answer but it rejects the premise of the original question because Blair changes the working definition of 'socialist'. In a 2022 conversation with Michael Sheen, who played him three times in *The Deal*, *The Queen* and *The Special Relationship*, Blair said he '[tried] to give Britain a different narrative'[106] and that's what you notice in his interviews, whether with combative figures like John Humphrys or Jeremy Paxman or more laconic questioners like David Frost: he may not be directly answering the questions but he is always focused on trying to tell a story.

Just as politicians learn to combat the techniques of political interviewers, the journalists come to understand the tricks

INTERVIEWS AND THE ART OF WAR

deployed by particular politicians. The halting, Bambi-eyed style that Blair used throughout his time as Prime Minister became less effective as hacks and audiences grew familiar with its faux-humbleness. This clash of avoidance tactics with awareness of those very tactics makes for one of the key failings of the political interview. When interviewing Robin Day in 1980, Bernard Levin raised this very idea, asking, 'Doesn't it then become a game, really? Almost like, in some respects, but only in *some* respects, advocacy in a courtroom: that everybody knows the rules?'[107] When this occurs, as a viewer, it feels more like you're witnessing a dance rather than a duel; the interviewer is less likely to draw out something unexpected and the subject can easily settle into drawing on prepared lines.

Writing for *The Times* in 2015, Jeremy Paxman also looked towards courtrooms as a comparison, but this time to draw a contrast between them and the court of public opinion in which he dominated the bench for so long. 'In an interview,' he argued, 'there should be no escape. But unlike a court of law, there are no rules of evidence and no judge to intervene to tell the interviewee to answer the question. You're on your own.'[108] Over the course of his long career, Paxman had clearly gleaned tips and tricks along the way, and while he was 'rather suspicious of experts dispensing advice' for a fee, he offered eight principles that he thought might make for better interviewers:

1. Remember you are there on behalf of the audience. 'The only difference,' he wrote, 'between the interviewer and any other citizen is not entitlement but opportunity.'

2. Decide what you want to know. Unsurprisingly, the man who hit Michael Howard with the same question 14 times in a

BREAKING

row advocates 'sticking at it until you get an answer or until it's abundantly clear . . . that no answer has been given.'

3. Do your research. The great interrogator admitted that he had been unprepared on many occasions and could have been 'holed well below the waterline' if an interviewee had asked him, 'Do you know?'

4. Know how to deal with the media trained. Paxman's advice to interviewers faced by someone prepared 'by some shabby member of our trade earning a few bob' – guilty! – with 'ways to evade and obfuscate' was simply to 'listen closely to the words that come from the mouths of the interviewee and chase up what they say'.

5. Cut to the chase. Interviewers are always working against the clock but especially so on TV and radio. But Paxman warned against conducting every interview at a gallop: 'An interview with the Archbishop of Canterbury on the morality of capitalism will be absurd if some idiot ends up asking him: "So, profit – in one word. Good or bad?"'

6. Keep it simple. Using an interview to show off your knowledge and expertise is, in Paxman's words, 'worse than useless'. You have to remember you're there to make it understandable to your audience.

7. Try to get to the human being behind the make-up. Paxman summed it up as 'trying to discover what sort of person [your interviewee is] and the depth of their convictions as much as anything they promise to do'.

8. Listen. This is the best piece of advice for any interviewer. Sticking religiously to your questions guarantees that you will miss what your interviewee is actually saying and totally removes

INTERVIEWS AND THE ART OF WAR

any chance of uncovering something surprising. 'One remarkable answer,' Paxman wrote, 'is worth torrents of blather.'

It's debatable whether Paxman put those principles into practice himself. He was certainly well prepared and tended to cut to the chase, but many of his victims would argue he wasn't particularly interested in politicians' humanity. He's not alone in offering insight into this trade, either. Interviewing the interviewers reveals how they see their job, and how the role of the interviewer has adapted to the change in the perception of interviews and the purpose they serve. I talked to a senior broadcaster who has been interviewing politicians and public figures on television for years. They argued that the days of the 'Jeremy Paxman-style aggressive interview have largely gone, in part because of the real-time feedback you get from viewers and other interested parties [via social media].' They believe that you notice more these days if someone talks over their interviewee or constantly interrupts.

Hammering away at the same point over and over again can stretch the audience's patience as much as it can frustrate the interview subject. Another interviewer for one of the news channels told me: 'We've had times when the government would not put ministers up [for interview]. There's always an element of that but it wouldn't stop us from doing aggressive, adversarial interviews if there was a situation that merited it. But we *do* think about it. The idea that we'd be cowed by pressure from a political party's press office simply isn't true, though.'

Someone who regularly interviews politicians on TV told me that the complaint they most often receive is that they don't call out blatant lies. They countered, 'I would have thought it was obvious

BREAKING

from the questions that I asked but people often need me to say it and when I don't, it somehow nullifies or reduces the impact of the interview.' The culture of YouTube compilations of moments when interviewers and interviewees 'own' the other side has contributed to this sense of the exercise as a full-contact sport; there's an expectation that journalists should explicitly signpost when an interviewee lies – fact-checking in real time – rather than expecting a level of engagement and intelligence from their audience.

The fact that most people don't see the whole interview now but instead encounter clips on social media is another important factor. The build-up of questions and answers which produces an arc or through-line in an encounter is missing and means that lines can easily be taken out of context. That removal of context has also led to a greater suspicion of interviewers who are trying to come from a more neutral position. 'People are used to receiving a lot of their political coverage from naturally partisan sources which share their worldview,' is how one political interviewer from a more traditional outlet put it to me. In that climate, interlocutors who simply try to get answers from their guests – putting equal pressure regardless of political allegiance – can still end up perceived as tragically biased because a lot of viewers treat the process more like a football match. When their team isn't scoring, they'll shout at the interviewer as if they were a bad referee refusing to award what they see as an obvious penalty.

Outside of the TV studios, with their spotlights, worldly-wise interviewers and slippery interviewees, exists a very different type of interview, one of the worst kinds: the vox pop – seeking out people on the street to get their opinion on an issue of the day. It's a task that's often thrown at junior journalists as a test of

INTERVIEWS AND THE ART OF WAR

their mettle and one that most reporters absolutely despise, but it plays into a media landscape that caters for online audiences looking for short bursts of news.

Vox pops can give the impression of getting the word on the street while ensuring that you only hear the most reactionary positions possible. Time and location mean that vox pops are never representative. The most obvious locations for them – marketplaces, pubs, high streets – and the fact they're usually done in the middle of the day creates an impression of a nation without young people. The willingness to offer your opinion to a reporter with a microphone who approaches you in the street should probably disqualify you from offering one. The people most likely to stop and give you their view are people without busy schedules, children to wrangle or jobs to be getting on with. They're also likely to be those with the strongest views and the greatest fondness for fringe opinions. That it would look far too much like bullying and/or rule out the most entertaining answers means that reporters rarely, if ever, challenge some of the unhinged responses produced by vox pops.

But aside from the clear difference between the vox pop and the more traditional TV interview, they do share some features. Broadcast and recorded interviews are a different challenge from ones intended to be presented as text alone. For one, on camera, the interviewer has to be a performer too. Almost all of the interviews I have done myself have been for print or online outlets. I didn't have to worry about the length of my questions or what my face was doing when I asked them. It also meant I could use the tactical pause, where you wait a moment after an answer to see if the person you're talking to goes on and gives you something unexpected.

BREAKING

All journalists, print or broadcast, do have to learn to be tactical – I particularly had to take time to grasp the eighth Paxman Principle, 'listen'. When you start out as an interviewer, nerves tend to make you gabble and you're tempted to use your questions as a crutch. However, arriving prepared and confident that you can formulate questions on the fly leads to much better answers. Gareth McLean, a journalist who's had a long career as an interviewer for the *Scotsman*, *Guardian* and *Radio Times*, says, 'There's two kinds of interview – the profile that tries to do the definitive summing up of someone's career and the snapshot that says, "this is what it's like spending an hour with this person".' He points out that you can produce both varieties from the same interview and some of the best do just that.

There are some interviews which, even among the relentless churning of the modern media, stand out as defining moments in the political or cultural landscape. Emily Maitlis's October 2019 interview with Prince Andrew is one of the most striking encounters of the last decade, but there's an argument for seeing it as less of a triumph of interrogation and more like social suicide by microphone. The royal was so arrogant and convinced that he could control the conversation that he blundered around like Sideshow Bob in *The Simpsons*, stumbling into rake after rake. In many respects, Maitlis simply had to keep out of his way and allow him to keep talking – as suggested by one of the journalists above. In the documentary *Secrets of Prince Andrew*, she said she thought someone would get in trouble for the interview ('I didn't think it would be him') and stressed that her 'intention was not to ruin his life'.

INTERVIEWS AND THE ART OF WAR

Arguably, the real genius of that programme was the work done by the booker Sam McAlister and the rest of the production team to get Prince Andrew to agree to the *Newsnight* interview in the first place. This is not to dismiss Maitlis's role, as she asked strong questions and her research and preparation paid off, but, largely, she just had to let an idiot keep talking. The Prince was so out of his depth, as evidenced by how he responded when the cameras were shut off. He was delighted with the interview and invited the *Newsnight* team to stick around for a cinema night at Buckingham Palace. It was the media equivalent of the farmer's dog seeing the henhouse covered in blood and feathers and wondering if the fox fancied a cup of tea.

In an interview with *The Times*, McAlister said Prince Andrew was afflicted by 'the royal delusion' which is the result of 'being told you're amazing, incredible, brilliant' and that he was convinced the interview would show that.[109] While royals are an extreme example of someone living in that kind of bubble, and Prince Andrew is the apotheosis of that kind of arrogance, it's a kind of disconnection you'll encounter in some celebrities, business people, and politicians. When someone is that conceited, a skilled interviewer can lay out the rope and let them tie the knot themselves.

Even more rare are the interviews which have gained notoriety for the exact opposite reason: for the fact that they never took place. During the 2019 general election, there were a lot of ruffled feathers about Boris Johnson not putting himself up for a BBC interview with Andrew Neil, while Labour leader Jeremy Corbyn did. It was simple: the Tory election machine set up a simple bait

BREAKING

and switch. They spent weeks implying that Johnson would agree to a date for an interview with Neil and then, once Corbyn had subjected himself to a grilling, they didn't need to pretend any longer – Labour had walked into the trap.

On the night, Neil placed an empty chair in the studio to represent Johnson's absence and lectured the Prime Minister down the lens, telling him he'd 'have to stand up to President Trump, President Putin, [and] President Xi of China' but couldn't 'spend half an hour standing up to me'. This was reported in the press as Johnson's no-show backfiring on him, but this opinion reflected only the view of political obsessives. Most voters wouldn't have watched the interview but any gaffes from it would have been clipped and spread around social media, as well as being picked over by newspapers. Even if Johnson had somehow dominated Neil, the Tories would still have seen little or no benefit for all that risk.

When questioned about the decision in 2021, Dominic Cummings, Johnson's former chief advisor, tweeted, 'Why the fu*k would [we] put a gaffe machine clueless about policy and government up to be grilled for ages? [An] upside = 0 for what? This is not a hard decision . . . Pundits don't understand comms, power, or management. Tune out!'[110]

In his book on political interviewing, *Why Is This Lying Bastard Lying to Me?*, Rob Burley, the BBC's editor of live political programmes at the time of the Johnson-interview-that-never-was, wrote that Cummings had '[used] the assumption of decency that had held sway for decades to run down the clock'.[111] Journalists are cynical but Cummings was more cynical. Burley called the decision to duck the challenge a sign that the Tory

INTERVIEWS AND THE ART OF WAR

election strategists' 'contempt for the voters and democratic accountability [was] unapologetic' – but really it was contempt for the BBC and for Neil. If the rules are unwritten and a matter of precedent, someone can always choose to entirely ignore them. The Johnson administration, with Cummings as its guiding intelligence, had already illegally prorogued Parliament in defiance of long-established norms – why would they worry about Andrew Neil? He might see himself as a well-varnished and integral part of the constitutional furniture, but the Conservatives clearly did not agree.

A previous interview with Johnson, conducted when he was still Mayor of London, was a stark example of what a determined interviewer can achieve and why subjecting themselves to interrogation is a high-risk proposition for politicians. In 2013, Eddie Mair, guest hosting *The Andrew Marr Show*, pressed Johnson repeatedly on a history of blatant lies and lying by omission. After opening with polite greetings, some expected back and forth on immigration policy and the future of the Olympic stadium, Mair moved onto questions about Johnson's character and past behaviour, using a recent documentary by the filmmaker Michael Cockerell as a hook. Examining the transcript of the encounter shows how Mair countered Johnson's use of the most common tactics for avoiding answering the question:

Mair: . . . *The Times* let you go after you made up a quote. Why did you make up a quote?
Johnson: Well. This . . . again, you know, these are, these are big terms for what happened. Well, I can tell you the whole thing, I think . . . you know . . . Are you sure our

BREAKING

viewers wouldn't want to hear more about housing in London...

Mair: [over] Well, alright. If you don't want to talk about it, if you don't want to talk about the made-up quote, let me talk about something...

Johnson: [over] But I will tell you. It was a long and lamentable story...

Mair: OK. But you made a quote up.

Johnson: Well, what happened was that... I ascribed events that were supposed to have taken place before the death of Piers Gaveston to events that actually took place after the death of Piers Gaveston...

Mair: [over] Yes, you made something up. Let me ask about another little, er...

Johnson: [over] Well, I mean, I mildly sandpapered something somebody said, and yes, it's very embarrassing and I'm very sorry about it.

Johnson first tried to reject the question as unimportant. Notice how he implies that the audience – which he called, with quiet arrogance, 'our viewers' – wasn't interested in the topic. Mair knocked that back by suggesting Johnson was afraid to answer the question, playing on his ego to keep him on the subject. By acting as though he'll move on to another issue due to Johnson's discomfort, Mair forced the Mayor to keep talking about it.

When Johnson then tried to make things sound more complicated, footling around historical details, Mair went back to the simplest form of the question – whether he'd made a quote up. That persistence paid off. While Johnson found a different form

INTERVIEWS AND THE ART OF WAR

of words to make the concession ('I mildly sandpapered something somebody said') it was a concession nonetheless – he made up the quote. This incident from his past was pertinent years later because the action and Johnson's explanation provided insight into his character.

Mair structured his questions to increase the intensity of the accusations against Johnson as he went on. He next questioned the Mayor about a 'barefaced lie' he told when, as a member of Michael Howard's shadow cabinet, he denied having an affair and was sacked. This rattled Johnson, who again attempted to reject the question ('I don't propose to go into all that again') and change the topic ('Why don't we talk about something else?'). Mair was ready with that something else:

Mair: [Cockerell's documentary] includes your reaction as you listen to a phone call in which your friend, Darius Guppy, asks you to supply the address of a journalist . . .
Johnson: Yes.
Mair: . . . so that he can have him physically assaulted. The words 'beaten up' and 'broken ribs' are said to you . . .
Johnson: Yes.
Mair: . . . and you, having heard that, you tell your friend, Darius Guppy, you will supply the address. What does that say about you, Boris Johnson?
Johnson: [over] Well, I . . .
Mair: Aren't you, in fact, making up quotes, lying to your party leader, wanting to be part of someone being physically assaulted? You're a nasty piece of work, aren't you?

BREAKING

Johnson: Well, Eddie, I think of all three things, I would dispute . . .
Mair: You don't factually dispute them?
Johnson: Well, I do. And I can, you know, if we had a long time, which we don't. I could explain that I think all three interpretations you're putting on this thing aren't wholly fair. And certainly, the final thing which you raise, which is the case of my old friend Darius, yes, it was certainly true that he was in a bit of a state and I did humour him in a long phone conversation, from which absolutely nothing eventuated and . . . you know, there you go. But I think if any of us had our phone conversations bugged, they might, you know, people say all sorts of fantastical things whilst they're talking to their friends.

That section of the interview shows Johnson using one of his most common techniques when interviewers put him under pressure: fast-paced, word-drenched gabbling; the rhetorical equivalent of fighter planes releasing silver foil chaff to confuse radar. Mair's choice to suggest to Johnson that he was 'a nasty piece of work' was subject to a lot of criticism at the time and the BBC received 600 complaints about the interview. But Mair had laid out evidence for the statement and it was one that a reasonable audience member could be asking themselves. Later in the conversation, Mair said Johnson chose to 'obfuscate' whenever he was asked a straight question – in that case, whether he wanted to be prime minister (a question to which we now know the answer) – and was treated to obfuscation in return:

INTERVIEWS AND THE ART OF WAR

Mair: What should the viewers make of your inability to give a straight answer to a straight question?
Johnson: I think people would rightly conclude that I don't want to talk about this subject because I want to talk about what I think should happen, which is the government deserves to win the next election and, indeed, I think it's a measure of the triviality of politics that I thought I was coming on to talk about the budget and housing in London, and, you know, you've – I mean, I don't mind all these questions about this other stuff, but I think it is more important that we look at the things that are happening now in the economy and we look at what the government is doing to help. And, by the way, the reason I want David Cameron to win and the reason I don't want Ed Miliband to win is because I'm genuinely alarmed by some of the things that the Labour Party is saying ...

In that avalanche of verbiage from Johnson, you get questioning the question, an attack on the interviewer, an attempt to change the subject and a political point all in one go. The interview is so worth watching because it shows all those familiar tactics for not answering the question coming up against a host who is not willing to acquiesce to them.

Twelve years on, the most obvious criticism of Mair's approach is along the lines of Peter Cook's quip – that his satire club The Establishment was modelled 'on those wonderful Berlin cabarets ... which did so much to stop the rise of Hitler and prevent the outbreak of the Second World War'. (For the benefit of any hard-of-thinking *Daily Mail* or *Daily Telegraph* journalists who might read this paragraph, I'm not comparing Boris Johnson to Hitler.) But had more interviewers been willing to interview Johnson as vigorously, his path to Number 10 might not have been so smooth.

Arguably, the greatest profile of all time – Gay Talese's 'Frank Sinatra Has a Cold' – was in fact the product of not getting the key interview. In November 1965, *Esquire* editor Harold Haye sent Talese to write about the singer as he approached his fiftieth birthday. However, Talese found himself with a problem: the protagonist of his profile was under the weather and under no obligation to talk to him. It's a mistake to think of the piece as about the absence of an interview, though; it is about Talese observing Sinatra with a gumshoe's determination, but it's also an example of using *other* interviews to build the picture. Unable to get Sinatra himself, Talese estimated that he spoke to more than 100 people in Old Blue Eyes' orbit, including 'the little grey-haired lady' who allegedly earned $400 a week for carrying his wigs around in a satchel. Talese turned Sinatra's cold into both an angle and a metaphor: 'Sinatra with a cold is Picasso without paint, Ferrari without fuel.' He was helped by events because the singer's voice returned in time for Talese to witness him putting it to good effect in the studio.

The technique of turning out a story when your subject has been uncooperative or simply didn't give good quotes is known as a 'write around' – you're literally writing around the obstacle of a lack of obvious material. But despite Talese's phenomenal talent, he had a lot of advantages over a modern interviewer trying to do the same. He had about ten weeks to report out the piece, filed a 50-page

INTERVIEWS AND THE ART OF WAR

draft and accumulated expenses of almost $5,000 (the equivalent of roughly $50,000 or £40,000 today). Such largesse doesn't exist in today's more parsimonious media environment. In the introduction to the Taschen edition of *Frank Sinatra Has a Cold*, Talese railed against 'computerised, bottom line, impersonalised workmanship' and argued against reporters carrying digital recorders, a suggestion that would give most media lawyers the heebie-jeebies.

While incredible interviews and artful write arounds are thinner on the ground today – driven to near extinction by sparse budgets and iron-fisted PR reps – there are still some practitioners. One of the most prominent of them is Taffy Brodesser-Akner, a *New York Times Magazine* staff writer and the author/screenwriter of *Fleishman Is in Trouble*. Her October 2023 profile of Taylor Swift, 'My Delirious Trip to the Heart of Swiftiedom', was very much in the lineage of 'Frank Sinatra Has a Cold', defining the singer through her songs and her audience's response.

In an interview with *The New York Times*, Brodesser-Akner said the key to her approach is '[finding] the essential question of someone's life' and that 'you can usually determine the person's answer over the course of an interview'. [112] Though she says that subjects sometimes want to stay in touch with her, she appears very comfortable with the fact that the interview process – more specifically its outcome – can be deeply uncomfortable. In another *New York Times* interview, she explained, 'If I do a good job and tell the intimate story that I, as a reader want to read, then probably that person I wrote about never wants to be in a room with me again.'[113]

Over the course of this chapter, names like Brodesser-Akner demonstrate the talent in this pool of journalists who have contributed to this specific brand of journalism. Historically, this area might have been considered a domineering and particularly male space, with names like Day, Mair and Paxman known for their firm and combative style of interviewing. As the journalist and co-founder of the Women's Equality Party Catherine Mayer told me 'interviewing is created in a very male image'. However, crucially, this is no longer solely the case. As Mayer went on to emphasise, while she accepts there is a time for aggressive interviewing – and that women can be as capable of using those techniques as their male colleagues – 'There's also a place for having a conversation and with some of the populist figures now you won't get a useful answer either way. Going in with the intention of having a dialogue is one of the joys of interviewing.' When the culture of interviewing is dominated by a small number of big beasts, the tactics they favour tend to be copied by everyone. When a wider range of voices is given the opportunity to ask the questions, the means of getting answers expands in turn.

Whether you approach interviewing as a conversation or combat, the non-negotiable element is that it has to be interesting. If the observer – whether they're reading your transcription of events, listening to them unfold or watching them live on a screen – does not come to the end having learned something they didn't know before, the interview is a failure. Politicians who think they have come out unscathed by saying nothing are kidding themselves too. If there is only heat and no light, viewers and voters get burned out and stop listening. The game shouldn't only be engaging for the interviewer and the interviewee. Once everyone knows the cheat codes, the rules have to be reset.

9.

Ethics Isn't a County in England

On the Morals and Ethics of Journalism

Journalism without a moral position is impossible. Every journalist is a moralist.'

– Marguerite Duras, *Outside, papiers d'un jour* (1984)

In February 2024, David Marchese, a *New York Times* columnist and feature writer, interviewed Patric Gagne, the author of a memoir called *Sociopath*.[114] When Gagne turned the questions around on him – 'Do you manipulate people in order to execute your job?' – he found himself thinking aloud and saying, ' . . . there are times when I've wondered if the skills that I've learned from doing my job over the years are basically just forms of interpersonal manipulation.' It was a level of honesty and self-reflection that I've found to be quite rare in journalism, where many unbelievable and often unforgivable types of behaviour are often dismissed as 'just how it's done'.

BREAKING

While academics often pick at the scab of journalistic ethics, the culture of newsrooms – a mixture of dark humour, frequent deadlines and deliberate emotional distance – contains very little space for their discussion. Immediacy trumps reflection. There is no journalistic equivalent of the Hippocratic Oath ('First do no harm, etc.'). The more common concern is to not cause problems for your bosses or harm to the company. Beneath it all, like a persistent drone, is the mantra, 'Do not get us sued, do not get us sued, do not get us sued.' Everything else is usually up for grabs, with the level of amorality that's accepted in pursuit of a story varying wildly from workplace to workplace. The journalist and screenwriter Gareth McLean, who spent nine years on staff at the *Guardian*, put it to me this way:

> I find reporters absolutely terrifying sometimes. They can be like sharks – there's a bit of empathy missing. Journalists are the most socially awkward people in some situations but they get to the heart of other people's emotions brilliantly. They become a conduit to tell other people's stories, but they don't understand the emotions of the story at all.

In her essay 'Slouching Toward Bethlehem' – a recounting of what she witnessed in San Francisco's Haight-Ashbury district at the height of hippiedom – Joan Didion writes about seeing a five-year-old tripping on acid. Almost 50 years later, her nephew Griffin Dunne asked her what she was thinking in that moment for his documentary, *Joan Didion: The Center Will Not Hold*. Her response was striking: 'Let me tell you, it was gold.

ETHICS ISN'T A COUNTY IN ENGLAND

That's the long and the short of it. You live for moments like that if you're doing a piece.' There, in that moment, journalism's most mercenary instinct is presented unvarnished and unmediated; the fragile-looking Didion – who featured in an ad campaign for the fashion brand Céline in her eighties – was not a songbird perched high in the branches but a hawk-eyed predator ready to snatch up experiences. Later in the documentary, Dunne asks Didion about a piece she wrote about being in Hawaii with her husband and fellow writer John Gregory Dunne 'in lieu of filing for divorce'. He wonders if his aunt and uncle had 'an agreement' about what parts of their life could be mined for writing. Again, Didion replies with an icy clarity: 'We didn't have an agreement . . . We thought generally that you used your material. You wrote what you had and that was what I happened to have at that moment.'

Nora Ephron, another writer for whom the personal was always fodder for the professional, summed it up more concisely by repeating advice her mother, also a writer, gave to her and her three sisters: 'Everything is copy.' In a 2015 HBO documentary, which took the aphorism as its title, she expanded on the idea: 'You'd come home with something that you thought was the tragedy of your life – someone hadn't asked you to dance, or the hem had fallen out of your dress, or whatever you thought was the worst thing that could ever happen to a human being – and my mother would say, "Everything is copy".'

In a way, this stubborn optimism is admirable, and Ephron's writing certainly demonstrates the merits of this way of thinking. But the biggest issue with 'everything is copy' comes when journalists descend to report on someone else's *real* tragedy. I've

BREAKING

spoken to a range of current and former reporters about covering stories of personal trauma and grief. One reporter explained the thinking that goes on in a newsroom: 'You'll often hear "it's what people want to read", because it's never been easier to look at the analytics and see exactly how much interest there is in something. And I know from experience that there's nothing like a heartbreaking quote from a grieving parent when it comes to writing an emotive, attention-grabbing headline.' However, their experience of seeing how audience interest can be used to excuse intense and sometimes very intrusive coverage has left them questioning the ethics: 'Saying, "our instincts tell us this is a big story that looks great on the page and lots of people are reading and sharing it" can't be the be-all and end-all.'

John D. Lewis, a former chief reporter and news editor at local newspapers including Brighton's *Evening Argus* and the *Derby Evening Telegraph*, and latterly of *The Times*, gave me some historical perspective:

> I started in journalism in 1975. Back then, I dreaded being sent to get a "pick-up picture" of a road accident victim. I hated the intrusiveness of it then and I hate it now. When I rose to the news desk on large regional papers, I would always counsel my reporters and editors that we'd get one or maybe two shots at the background information on victims of a tragedy and then we're gone. It's now descended into a feeding frenzy which serves no one except voyeurs.

ETHICS ISN'T A COUNTY IN ENGLAND

This practice of being sent to the scene was always rather mucky – as shown by John's experience of having to obtain a photo of the deceased from their family's collection to be used in the media – but the 'frenzy' in today's reporting is a product of a 24-hour news environment where competition is fierce and resources are stretched. A bereaved family can find themselves being treated like a resource to be tapped.

Others give a more complicated response to the question of the ethics of newsgathering following traumatic events, focusing particularly on the ritual of the death knock – the practise of knocking on the doors of victims' families in the attempt to get an interview and, with any luck, a heartbreaking family photo of the deceased. A broadcast reporter with extensive experience explained to me:

> I've been sent out on loads of death knocks by many editors and hated it, but had no choice. I've been physically attacked – once – on these sorts of jobs, or just told to fuck off. But I've also done quite a few stories where families wanted the press coverage of their loved ones and where I feel it helped them grieve in a small way and was in the public interest.

The first writer I spoke to echoed that perspective to an extent:

> If there's something political to be done that could stop something like, for example, the Grenfell fire happening again, or in cases like the murder of Olivia Pratt-Korbel, where initially we were hammering the people who were

BREAKING

shielding her killer, I think papers have a role and a duty and can do some good. But kids falling through ice and drowning feels like something where there's not really any more to say.

One broadcaster with a national news station I spoke to told me: 'My experience of arriving for stories like that is generally people appreciate and want to contribute to our presence. I've got Christmas cards to write to people I met on big stories years back that I've kept in touch with.'

The range of experiences from these different voices shows how complex it is to report on tragic events and the high levels of care required to prevent the very presence of the media from making things much worse. Whatever the intentions of individual journalists to interview and write sensitively about an event, the reality is that when a big story happens and many print reporters and broadcasters descend on a small place at the centre of a tragedy, it can become chaotic.

On 27 January 2023, Nicola Bulley disappeared while walking her dog in the village of St Michael's on Wyre, Lancashire. Despite Lancashire Constabulary quickly stating that its working hypothesis was that Bulley had fallen into the river and it did not suspect suspicious activity or third-party involvement, a true crime-obsessed public spurred on by the press and wider media detected the seeds of a mystery. The eventual inquest, which concluded in June 2023, showed there was no mystery: Nicola Bulley's cause of death was determined as accidental drowning. But in the three weeks before Nicola's body was found in the

ETHICS ISN'T A COUNTY IN ENGLAND

river one mile from the spot where she disappeared, the media and social media siege of the village was intense. To understand it, we have to begin at the end.

In a statement read during a police press conference after Nicola was found, her family said: '. . . it saddens us to think that one day we will have to explain to [Nicola's children] that the press and members of the public accused their dad of wrongdoing, misquoted and vilified friends and family. This is absolutely appalling; they have to be held accountable. This cannot happen to another family.' They went on to criticise two news outlets particularly for hounding them in the hours after Nicola's death was confirmed:

> We tried last night to take in what we had been told in the day, only to have Sky News and ITV making contact with us directly when we expressly asked for privacy. They again have taken it upon themselves to run stories about us to sell papers and increase their own profiles. It is shameful they have acted in this way. Leave us alone now. Do the press and other media channels and so-called professionals not know when to stop? These are our lives and our children's lives.

The next day, Nicola Bulley appeared on every national newspaper front page, but her family's words were absent from all except the *i* paper and the *Guardian*. And even then, the *i*'s headline was careful to remove any reference to newspapers ('Nicola Bulley's family accuse "shameful" TV crews and social media'[115]). Likewise, the *Guardian*'s report talked in broad terms

BREAKING

about the press and wider media but omitted the quote about newspapers. The broadcast news bulletins, including those from ITV News and Sky News, aired the family's statement, including the line criticising the behaviour of their correspondents and journalists.

Perhaps Sky News had had a moment of clarity or perhaps not. Either way, their involvement in the preceding clamour around the case was clear. On the morning before the press conference, Sky News's Kay Burley presented her show from the village graveyard, having previously traced the route of Nicola's final walk live on air with the channel's North of England correspondent, Inzamam Rashid. The walk-and-talk was a breathless dissection of the minutiae of Nicola's final morning, coming off like an improv troop presenting a true crime podcast in real time.

When Sky News posted a clip of the footage on YouTube, monetisation was switched on. I watched it after a chirpy clip advertising Uber Eats. As Rashid and Burley sauntered along, a dog walker attempted to pass them and asked with acid humour, 'Do you live here?' He was immediately buttonholed for an interview about his thoughts on the case. While he kept trying to walk away, Burley and Rashid questioned him, at no point mentioning to him that he was *live* on Sky News.

On the day that Nicola's body was found, but before she had been formally identified, quotes from her partner, Paul Ansell, were carried across the media. They were attributed to Sky News from a text message sent to the reporter but not intended for broadcast that was then quoted by Rashid on air. A report from the broadcaster boasted that Rashid had 'been in contact with the family throughout the three-week search'. A banner at the top of

ETHICS ISN'T A COUNTY IN ENGLAND

the same story prompted readers to find out why they could trust Sky News and linked to a policies and standards document.

Elsewhere, Newsquest, a UK subsidiary of the US media conglomerate Gannet, which owns 165 newspapers and 40 magazine titles, instructed its publications and individual journalists to use the police press conference on Nicola's case to promote the company's new true crime YouTube channel, which gleefully promised details on 'the most shocking cases across Britain' and to 'investigate some of the UK's biggest crimes'. In the three weeks before Nicola was found, Newsquest hosted seven live streams about the story. A tragic and, at the time, ongoing missing persons case was boiled down to cheap entertainment. The *Lancashire Telegraph*, one of the closest Newsquest titles to Nicola's home in St Michael's on Wyre, published numerous sensational pieces on the case.

That's not to say that everyone was on board with this line – lone journalists waded against the tide and tried to highlight the extreme lack of moral judgement. Joshi Herrmann, founder of rival independent publication *Manchester Mill*, wrote that Newsquest's biggest competitor, Reach, was also pumping out clickbait about Nicola: '[Their] big sites – *MEN* [*Manchester Evening News*], *Echo* etc. – have stories about a statement from [independent forensic search expert] Peter Faulding. The *Echo* tweeted it 6x. But there's no statement – it's a single line on social media. Pure clickbait trash, exploiting public interest in a woman's disappearance to drive traffic.'[116] He went on: 'Reach told the BBC recently that it doesn't publish clickbait. The *Echo's* editor said the same to a Commons inquiry. Stories like this are the definition of clickbait – they're purely about tricking readers. Reach staff who keep defending the

BREAKING

company are beclowning themselves.' When there's a tragedy, the British press sends in the beclowners.

Reach defended itself in a statement to local website Prolific North, claiming its coverage had 'been extensive' and simply involved reporting on 'newsworthy information'.[117] It was a sly response to criticism of the method and weight of its coverage. Here are some examples of *Manchester Evening News* headlines published during the search for Nicola:

'Pale-faced man's first words to police after discovering body in search for Nicola Bulley'[118]

'Exhausted and in the eye of a storm, St Michael's on Wyre waits after the news no one wanted'[119]

'In pictures: Scene in St Michael's on Wyre after body found in search for Nicola Bulley'[120]

'Ex-detective from Channel 4 show *Hunted* labels Nicola Bulley police "utterly ludicrous"'[121]

'Seven key bombshells from Nicola Bulley's partner Paul Ansell as he speaks out on missing mum'[122]

These stories represent neither proportional nor reasonable coverage of a story where reporters *knew* the police did not suspect foul play. Several of those headlines use the 'curiosity gap' style that tempts a reader with the promise of the answer to an implied mystery. It was a collision between newspapers' thirst for traffic and the misuse of the idea of public interest.

The use of the 'ex-detective', as seen in this above list, was not a tactic unique to this outlet. Other newspapers also turned to a familiar cast list of retired cops willing to pontificate and prognosticate on the case for a fee. Ex-Met police commander John O'Connor – a regular rent-a-quote for national news-

ETHICS ISN'T A COUNTY IN ENGLAND

papers – told the *Sun*: 'These search teams couldn't find a currant in a rice pudding. I find it pathetic that a body has been found a mile from where she went missing.'[123]

O'Connor, who once wrote for the *Guardian* decrying the 'cosy relationship' between the Met and the Murdoch press, is now quoted by News UK titles with depressing regularity.[124] Even more indefensibly, the *Sun*[125] and *The Times*[126] published stories amplifying the claims of a self-described 'spiritual medium' who was among the people who discovered Nicola's body. The *Daily Mail* jumped on the 'psychic' story on the same day that it exempted itself from the family's criticism: 'Nicola Bulley's relatives fire broadside at sections of the media and people speculating on social media'.[127] On the day Nicola was found, the *Mail on Sunday* contained a spread headlined 'Nikki is NOT an Unfit Mum'.[128] Why was the question even being debated in the pages of a national newspaper? Misogyny is the short answer. Misogyny and a prurient entertainment value is the slightly longer one.

In the age before social media and the true crime trend, Nicola's disappearance would likely have remained a local story. The newspapers and broadcasters didn't need to descend on the small village or barrage Nicola's family with questions. It was a choice and one driven by harnessing nosiness rather than sensing newsworthiness.

Journalists do have a choice of how to deal with tragic stories; they don't have to revert to the default approach. When a gunman shot and killed five people and injured two others before shooting himself in Plymouth in August 2021, the national media littered

BREAKING

its coverage with images of the killer and focused on the most shocking details. The local newspaper and news websites declined to picture the gunman and focused their coverage on the victims and the wider community. They also chose not to take part in the grim journalistic ritual of 'the death knock', nor did they go door knocking at houses near where the event took place.

At the time, Edd Moore, then digital editor of *PlymouthLive*, told the *Press Gazette* that the story was 'a tragic reminder that we're custodians of the city but we're all linked – this is our friends, our neighbours, our relatives that we're reporting on.'[129] One of the victims, Lee Martin, who was killed with his three-year-old daughter Sophie, was the cousin of Moore's colleague, Jess Morcom. Moore explained the decision not to door knock as a simple matter of empathy: 'We know people who are affected by this. So as far as the decision-making goes, it didn't feel like a decision to us – it's about doing the right thing.'

PlymouthLive's crime reporter, Carl Eve, tweeted in the aftermath of the shootings that he and his colleagues were 'not door-knocking residents' because they recognised that people needed 'time and space to process [the events]'.[130] He encouraged residents to process what had happened, telling them they could come and speak to journalists later ('We'll be here to listen to you'). It was a respectful decision but not one that was mirrored by reporters from national newspapers and broadcasters, who descended on Plymouth with vulturous intent. Jess Morcom, grieving the loss of her family members, wrote about her distress at the scenes: '. . . as someone who works in the industry myself, a large number of the national "journalists" need to be retrained with how to handle intrusion into grief. Turning up at family homes

ETHICS ISN'T A COUNTY IN ENGLAND

trying to hound is unforgivable. I appreciate the sensitivity shown by local colleagues.'[131]

While the *Press Gazette* gave *PlymouthLive* journalists space to talk about their approach, the trade title's UK editor Freddy Mayhew defended the death knock in an edition of its daily newsletter as:

> . . . one of the less savoury aspects of journalism [but] nonetheless important. It helps to reveal the truth when gossip might be spreading falsehoods and alarm. Not contacting people also assumes they do not want to speak. This is not necessarily true. Coming together to talk about an issue, whether intended for publication or not, helps us all to process tragedies.

It's a familiar argument. I've heard it countless times over the years from people at all levels of journalism and I find it a fundamentally self-serving one. If families want to speak to newspapers or broadcasters, it's not difficult for them to get in touch or to have that facilitated by the police or other authorities. The notion that unsolicited approaches at family homes usually do anything beyond adding to the stress to already traumatised people is fanciful. The true impetus behind most death knocks is not to provide catharsis or counteract falsehoods but to get emotional 'colour' and detail that your rivals don't have. It's why newspapers have been known to chase 'exclusive' access to victims' families and, at times, to pay for it.

Mayhew's right that 'coming together to talk about an issue' *can* 'help us process tragedies', but reporter after reporter

BREAKING

knocking on your door or leaning on the bell hunting for a quote, a heartbreaking home video or a candid photograph of your loved one is not 'coming together'. It is being hunted. And in the social media age, the 'death knock' has expanded to scraping through posts to steal images from better times and to drag previous messages out of context. Memories of loved ones can be easily lifted and put on a front page, changed forever in the white heat of the media's attention.

This most macabre side of the trade is so grim that it's almost beyond parody. Almost, but not quite ... Dan Hett, whose brother Martyn Hett was killed in the Manchester Arena bombing, made an online game to illustrate what it's like receiving the death knock experience, with reporters contacting you online and off. 'Sorry to Bother You' tasked players with trying to separate veiled requests from journalists from genuine expressions of condolence ('"like" the real messages and "trash" the journalist ones'). Hett told BuzzFeed News that he understood that 'we're news-hungry people' but that 'the aim of the game [was] to show the way in which it's done during unfolding events is not OK.'[132]

In the hours after the bombing, Hett tweeted an image of a journalist's business card and the message: 'I have dealt with 50+ journos online today. Two found my mobile number. This cunt found my house. I still don't know if my brother is alive.'[133] That is the reality of the death knock at its most brutal: vultures perched on telephone lines. While Hett later said he regretted the tweet, he was right to feel so angry at being asked for comment even as he waited for news of his brother. What was he expected to say and why was he expected to fill the silence with *his* words?

One former local news journalist that I know explained: 'At a

ETHICS ISN'T A COUNTY IN ENGLAND

local level, the police usually ask the family if they want to talk to the press before releasing identification. So death knocks were often either, "We're doing this before official ID" or "They've said they don't want to talk but it's a big story for us so we're doing it anyway." In truth, a lot of the time death knocking was driven not so much by the 'need to reveal the whole truth', but the 'need not to be embarrassed by a rival local paper, the BBC or – worse still – an agency that might punt the story and pics to the nationals'.

A 2017 article from the *Independent*, which discussed the Hett family's experience among others, takes the more familiar line that journalists *have* to do death knocks. The writer, David Barnett, another ex-local newspaper journalist, claimed that the process is 'not quite as grim as it sounds' and that because most local newspapers on any given week contain stories generated from death knocks, they are justified.[134] After all, the families and loved ones cooperated. But again, this is an argument which can easily be dismissed by taking basic human nature into consideration – many people who find themselves confronted by a journalist on their doorstep feel a pressure to answer. There's also the worry that if they don't, their dead loved one might be misrepresented. This is an implication that the more unscrupulous members of the profession lean on implicitly and sometimes state outright.

Barnett quoted the press regulator IPSO's guidelines in his article ('In cases involving personal grief or shock, enquiries and approaches must be made with sympathy and discretion . . .') but when a hack pack descends on the scene of a horrific event that rule goes out of the window. If dozens of reporters bombard you with requests, ringing your phone into near meltdown, it doesn't help if – and it's a huge Hollywood sign-sized 'if' – each

BREAKING

and every one of them is empathetic and kind: the cumulative effect cannot help but increase the stress and trauma. IPSO's guidelines on harassment ('[You] must not persist in questioning, telephoning, pursuing or photographing individuals once asked to desist') lose their weight when multiple news organisations and agencies are pursuing details about your family. It's worth noting too that IPSO only suggests that journalists have to identify themselves 'if requested', leaving plenty of space for deception. In today's world, with its increased awareness of the need for strict safeguarding, it is incredible that the regulator leaves room for deliberate ambiguity.

Barnett's personal example of a death knock is when, as a young reporter (only 19 himself), he was sent to cover the story of a man in his early twenties who had died of a brain haemorrhage. He ended up knocking three times, being asked to come back later twice by the man's mother as his father wasn't home. On the third visit, he writes that he was asked inside and spent time talking about the young man with his parents. The story appeared on the front page the next day and Barnett recalls '[receiving] the profuse thanks of the family, who had felt that seeing their son's life celebrated in their local newspaper had helped them to cope in some way'. But there's a clear difference between someone who dies of an illness and the sudden and shocking death of someone killed in a violent act or horrendous accident.

In 2014, *The Irish Times* published a more honest piece about death knocks – predominantly because it was written anonymously. It called the practice 'the dark side of journalism' and its author wrote of being sent to knock on a grieving mother's door just two hours after the news of her son's death had been

ETHICS ISN'T A COUNTY IN ENGLAND

broken to her: 'And here I was, knocking at her door, notebook in my pocket, smartphone in hand, to record her every word. I had left my shame at the kerb.'[135] Later in the piece, the journalist discusses the mechanics of the process, 'the pressure on reporters from radio and TV stations to talk to the family' and the collusion from authorities in handing over a victim's address or giving background information. The pitch-dark humour and attitude of some newsrooms is summed up in a line: 'I have heard, on multiple occasions, news editors cheering at the news of a tragedy involving an attractive woman.'

Unlike Freddy Mayhew's high-handed vision of the value of the death knock, *The Irish Times* contributor wrote about the gulf between the squeaky-clean theory presented in journalism courses and the reality in newsrooms: 'Some journalism courses include ethics modules, in which lecturers who may not have seen a newsroom since the 1970s expound upon Aristotle and Kant, Christ and Marx, for thousands in fees. Graduates will tell you that it's only upon entering an actual newsroom that you begin to see how little relation it all has to practice.' The writer recalls being sent to the funeral of a young sportsman and, having got quotes from the family, then being 'ordered to pressure the dead man's parents to leave their only son's funeral, walk to the local pitch, and stand in the goalmouth holding his picture'.

It's jackal behaviour and the notion that it is done to give families peace or to commemorate the dead is ludicrous. It's about competition. Every industry has practices that old hands will justify with the dread phrases 'we've always done it this way' and 'this is just how it's done', but it's not how it *has* to be done. There are many ways to tell stories, even in the most harrowing

BREAKING

of circumstances. *PlymouthLive*'s response to the shooting on its patch illustrated that. The trouble is that there's an ersatz toughness peddled by a certain strain of hack that they are desperate to retain, a belief that death knocks are the making of a young journalist. It's the same mentality that I encountered when reporting on the terror attack on the Bataclan in Paris, when an ITN producer approached the distraught man who was telling me what had happened and told him to be quiet because they were live. To a lot of the news crews there it was 'the scene'; to him, it was where he had been out celebrating with his brothers and friends before terrorists gunned them down.

What tragedies become major news and how they are covered is a complicated question. There is always a grim calculus at work whenever news value is measured. When four boys died in the icy water of Babbs Mill Lake near Solihull in December 2022, it was news. Had one child fallen into the lake and died, it would most likely have been a local story, the preserve of regional papers and news bulletins. The scale of the loss, the attendant shock and the proximity to Christmas made the Babbs Mill Lake deaths a national story and even led to international coverage. But is families' grief and the grief of the wider community a story in itself? When the facts are not disputed and the immediate incident is over, what justifies the continued presence of news crews and reporters?

ITV News interviewed a 13-year-old girl who tried to rescue the boys. A Facebook post by one of the boy's aunts was mined for stories with Facebook photos illustrating them. Peering into private grief is defended as being in the public interest because the public is interested. Again, we return to the tired refrain 'it's

ETHICS ISN'T A COUNTY IN ENGLAND

what people want to read' but this is just lazy journalism. There's clearly an argument for producing public information journalism in the wake of a tragedy like the events at Babbs Mill Lake – informing your audience about what to do when someone falls into icy water is the very definition of public interest journalism and could save lives. Standing in front of a pile of floral tributes and repeating lines about a community's understandable and visceral grief does nothing, particularly on day two or three of a story.

What the press and wider media consider 'reflecting' the response to a traumatic event can exacerbate that trauma, becoming a kind of emotional vampirism. The distinction between what reporters *can* do and *should* do is often lost in the scramble for details and 'colour' in the aftermath of an horrific event. That a 13-year-old girl and her family agreed for her to be interviewed on television after witnessing an event that led to the deaths of four children does not mean that broadcasters should have put her on TV. Experts agree that this type of coverage has no place in current media practice. As Professor Lucy Easthope, an expert in disaster recovery, tweeted: 'Sitting with a young girl and discussing how she feels she did not do enough to help should not be happening on a national news item. This is a huge issue in post-trauma and survivor guilt and is not to be trifled with by a reporter.'[136] Additionally, Sophie Michell, an historian of death and crime, pointed out that drownings were 'more common in the nineteenth century and [were] reported in the same kind of almost lascivious tone', but she noted that 'television media has made it more profoundly distasteful ... Attempts to create rolling news from grief and horror are deeply voyeuristic.'[137] That hungry voyeurism has been there since the start of TV news –

BREAKING

the media coverage of the Aberfan disaster in 1966, when a primary school in the Welsh village was crushed following the catastrophic collapse of a colliery spoil tip, killing 116 children and 28 adults, was extremely intrusive. The disaster was one of the first to be covered by national television. Gwynn Llewelyn, one of the first reporters on the scene, told *Wales Online* in 2006, that 'it turned out to be something of a broadcasting "circus" and naturally local people reacted angrily to this'. He remembered: 'There was a wedding in Aberfan that weekend and one TV programme film crew approached the family to ask whether they could film [it] in order to highlight the contrast between the happy event and the tragedy all around it. This kind of unethical behaviour was unforgivable.'[138]

After the murder of Sarah Everard by a serving police officer, the *Sun* printed a front page that featured a large picture of her beneath the headline 'Sarah Suspect Linked to Sex Offence ... Did Cops Fail to Act?'[139] The 65-word story that went with it avoided hyperbole, speculation or a surfeit of tabloidese. You could have even called the coverage respectful and restrained, save for the unnecessary image of the killer set into the copy. It was a straight news report on misogyny and violence in the police. Then, two pages later, on page three, which the *Sun* uses as a daily slot for a spurious story with a woman in lingerie or swimwear, it slobbered over a picture of Bryana Holly, an American model whose partner is the British actor, Nicholas Hoult, under the headline 'Holly-Day in the Sun'.[140] Quite the pairing.

In 2015, the *Sun* and its parent company, News UK, got a lot of coverage for 'scrapping' the topless pictures that had been

ETHICS ISN'T A COUNTY IN ENGLAND

printed on page three of the paper since 1969, when Murdoch turned the title tabloid. But Page 3 was not scrapped; it simply put its top on. On days when actual news needs to be spread across pages two and three, the nearly-nude 'news' story merely shimmies down the flat plan to page six or seven. In the same edition as the Everard front page and the Bryana Holly puff piece, Priti Patel, then Home Secretary, contributed an opportunistic op-ed[141] ('I'll do what I can to protect women and girls') which shared a spread with a story about Nicole Scherzinger wearing a dress. The latter 'report' was just one of many such 'woman wears clothes' or 'woman goes outside in possession of a physical body' stories that the *Sun* publishes on a daily basis. A few pages later, a 'story' on the singer and actress Alexandra Burke – comprised of two paparazzi pictures of her exercising in the park – was given ample space ('Alexandra Burke looks perky in pink as she heads to the park for a work-out'). Over at MailOnline, these 'woman simply exists' stories make up a huge proportion of the website's total output.

It's easy to dismiss that kind of story as harmless, or to linger on the fact that some of the photos are the product of direct cooperation with PR people, but what does day after day of that kind of 'news' contribute to society? In the *Sun*, women are still predominantly there to be leered over and judged on the basis of their looks. It remains fair game to have photographers follow a famous woman and take pictures of her going about her daily life – it's stalking with a contract – and the *Sun* is the official paper of men who shout things like, 'Cheer up, love, it might never happen.'

The *Daily Mail* and the aforementioned MailOnline have huge

BREAKING

female readerships but are no better. The *Mail* dedicates swathes of each edition to making women feel insecure and unhappy about their bodies, relationships and personal choices, particularly if they're a mother or, even worse, have chosen not to be one. Femail, its supplement dedicated to 'women's issues', is at times so unhinged it feels like it's been edited and approved by a panel of men's rights activists – which, given the editorial leadership of the *Mail*, in some senses it has. Overall, the *Mail* talks out of both sides of its mouth when it comes to issues like sexual assault, street harassment, domestic violence and workplace harassment.

Day in, day out, the *Sun*, *Daily Mail*, and the other tabloids use women as fodder – objectifying, observing and undermining – even as they purport to be pushing 'empowering' stories of female success. Speaking ahead of a documentary about the death of her daughter, the TV host Caroline Flack, who was hounded by the tabloids, her mother Christine Flack said she hoped 'the newspapers who wrote all the horrible things about [her] will take away that before they print anything, at least find out if it's true ... I don't think they've learned yet.'[142]

This exploitation of gender when combined with the grizzly fascination with murder creates a pretty ugly cocktail. Picture this *Daily Telegraph* front page: a tightly cropped picture of a teenage girl, her eyes dark with mascara, her lips shiny with gloss; she is smiling at the camera. It's an image that's almost crushing in its ordinariness. There are hundreds of millions of photos like that one on Instagram, tacked to pin boards and nestled in family photo albums. The headline beside it changes the context from ordinary to grotesque: 'Teenager's Lust for Fame Led to Murder of Brianna'.[143]

ETHICS ISN'T A COUNTY IN ENGLAND

I doubt that the *Telegraph* editors who nodded through that splash spent more than a moment contemplating the grim irony of opting for a smiling, polished shot of the 16-year-old killer rather than the girl whose life she took – Brianna Ghey. The judge's decision to name the girl and boy who planned and committed Ghey's murder – chivvied and cheered on by the press – enabled the very 'fame' that the paper said the killer lusted after. But the *Telegraph* could have chosen one of the stark images of the killers in police custody rather than a picture of how the girl chose to present herself.

In the hours after the murderers were named, the *Sun* published six stories on the case, only one of which focused on Brianna and her family rather than her killers. Peter Spooner, Brianna's father, told Sky News that he'd initially been in favour of naming the killers but that he had changed his mind: 'Now I think their names are always going to be tied to Brianna's . . . I think they should just be forgotten about, locked up and not spoken about again.'[144] That's the reason I won't name them in this chapter. Their names don't matter.

While the news media is well aware of how killers seek and thrive on notoriety, it plays the same game every time, led by its grimmest instinct and most prurient desires. Grizzled hacks – and those who like to cosplay as grizzled – sneer once again that it's simply how things work and, furthermore, it's what the public wants. Certainly, since the very first newspapers hit the streets, stories of murder have sold copies, but the ink-stained habitués of the early Grub Street spent far less time congratulating themselves on serving an honourable social purpose.

Even as reports detail the killers' fantasies, they reinforce them.

BREAKING

The *Sun*'s story on the convictions breathlessly explained that the girl 'had started fantasising about death and murder since she was 14' and had sought out videos of 'real-life torture and killing videos [on the dark web]'.¹⁴⁵ The killers' fantasies about red rooms and dark websites streaming live videos of death and torture were presented as an uncomplicated reality in the papers. The *Daily Telegraph*, without caveats, claimed that the girl used 'a "dark web" internet browser app to watch videos of the torture and murder of real people in "red rooms".'¹⁴⁶ Meanwhile, the *Mail* found an expert willing to imply that 'red rooms' exist but added that 'red rooms – underground internet sites where people are physically abused to draw blood and even killed – [are] difficult to find'.¹⁴⁷ They're 'difficult to find' because they . . . don't exist. While there are extremely violent videos on the dark web, it's not technically possible to livestream videos there. The many adverts for red rooms are usually scams. Brianna's killer may have believed she saw true horrors but a national newspaper reporting on a murder case should restrict itself to the realms of reality.

Even when the facts are largely adhered to, the language leaves something to be desired. The *Sun*'s subhead read 'Chilling messages revealed bloodlust' and the copy talked of Brianna being 'slaughtered' while detailing her fatal injuries in excruciating detail. A picture gallery – all the better for upping click rates – included an image of the murder weapon. Chasing the search-engine traffic after the judge's verdict, the paper fell back on its usual argot: Brianna was reduced to 'tragic Brianna', her life framed as an inevitable march to her violent death, while her murderers were 'the sadistic pair', 'the vile pair' and 'the twisted teens'. The plain truth of gruesome events is never

ETHICS ISN'T A COUNTY IN ENGLAND

enough for the tabloids; they always have to garnish them with horror movie language.

The same newspapers that write with justified horror about the killers seeking out violent videos, hungrily and hurriedly pointed their readers to clips from the day Brianna died and to the moment her killers were arrested. See the killers! See the weapon! See the victim in her last moments! See the police interviews! All of it became 'content', presented in the most cold and calculated manner possible.

The *Daily Mail*, which has created a ruthlessly efficient true crime production line, now turned ongoing murder trials, including that of Ghey's killers, into podcasts. After Ghey's murderers were named, it rushed out a YouTube 'documentary' on the case and promoted it in every story it published. Presented by *Mail* journalist Tom Rawstorne, who narrated in portentous tones over dramatic music, *Killer Kids Intent on Murder – Brianna Ghey: Teen Murderers Unmasked*, a title stuffed with search terms, was trash. For all the hushed voices, grim faces, and claims to be attempting to understand the killers' motivations, it was filth for *Mail* readers to roll around in as the publisher attempted to boost its lacklustre YouTube following.

An episode of the *Mail*'s podcast *The Trial*, which focused on Ghey's murder, began with a perky voiceover brightly noting that it was 'seriously popular', which was immediately followed by a horribly ironic advert for the TV series, *True Detective*. The podcast's producers and presenters turn real suffering into entertainment, bringing the 'true crime' trend to its most exploitative logical conclusion. The *Mail*'s podcast operation leaves barely any delay between events in court and their repackaging as something to listen to while walking the dogs or doing the washing up. This is not news coverage, it's attention mining.

What baffled the *Mail* about the murder of Brianna Ghey was that her killers were relatively well-off and, crucially, white, so its YouTube documentary, podcasts and features flailed around seeking reasons that could serve as excuses. In an article accompanying the YouTube production, Rawstorne wrote: '... what makes [the female killer's] story so hard to fathom is that, unlike so many other child murderers brought up in broken dysfunctional families, she had a start in life that many would envy.'[148] His 'investigation' boiled down to asking around in the local area about her family and picking over the girl's social media posts. Such efforts tend to turn unremarkable details into portents. That the girl killer liked a rather silly goth band called She Wants Revenge and their song 'Tear You Apart' became a sign of what was to come, as did the fact that she liked gothic architecture. Decades after moral panics over heavy metal and horror movies, newspapers like the *Mail* still delight in the notion that a taste for the macabre is an indicator of future murderous intent. If liking heavy metal, horror movies or dressing like a goth were any such thing, the streets of Britain would be piled high with bodies.

Mail on Sunday columnist Sarah Vine centred herself, her feelings and a bizarre daydream about her own children turning out to be killers:

> In some photos, [the girl] even reminded me of my own daughter at that age, a terrifying notion that I immediately pushed to the back of my mind. But it made

ETHICS ISN'T A COUNTY IN ENGLAND

me think: What if that were my child? What if I'd been responsible for bringing this killer into the world? What if that evil had been germinating in my house, without me even knowing?'[149]

I happen to think writing a column for the *Mail* is itself a form of germinating evil, but Vine's came from the same place as many of the other features and news reports – these killers came from 'nice' families and not the sort we usually demonise and they're *white* so we can't reach for our usual explanations. Vine dismissed transphobic motives for Brianna's murder ('That she was trans was also a factor, but it does not seem to have been the prime motivator'), which was handy as the *Mail* titles publish reams of negative stories about trans people daily. She looked instead to the hardy perennials 'violence and murder . . . legitimised and normalised by the films they watched and the games they played'.

The *Daily Telegraph* took a similar line and reported that '[The female offender] was . . . in the words of the judge who sentenced her to life in prison . . . the driving force behind the "sadistic and transphobic" killing of Brianna.' In the month leading up to the murderers being named, the *Telegraph* published 31 news stories and columns about trans people, every one of them negative. In common with most other British newspapers, it printed a victim impact statement from Brianna's mother, in which she wrote: ' . . . their premeditated and vicious attack, which was carried out not because Brianna had done anything wrong, but just because one hated trans people and the other thought it would be fun.'

BREAKING

Columnists default to those familiar warnings about films and games because moral panics provide an easy answer to the terrifying question: why do 'normal' people commit such horrific crimes? This avoids having to question wider society, the education system, the destruction of social services and safety nets, and, crucially, the influence of the media itself in how minorities are perceived and treated. Those issues are all a bit too complicated to be boiled down into an easily emotive column or strident editorial.

The death of a tabloid 'legend' provided an apposite example of how the British media can exercise severe double standards when a story involves one of its own. When the reporter John Kay died aged 77, on 7 May 2021, the *Sun*, where he'd worked for 41 years, gave him the newspaper equivalent of a Viking funeral – a double-page spread dedicated to his obituary[150] and a leader column singing his praises. It called him 'the greatest journalist of his generation' and 'Fleet Street's finest'. It didn't mention Harue, his first wife, who he killed in 1977. There was no space for that when *Sun* editor Victoria Newton was hailing the man 'who inspired generation after generation of young reporters'. We have no idea who Harue might have inspired or what she might have achieved because she never got the chance to show us. She was 27 when she died and lives on only in old newspaper cuttings and a brief reference on Kay's Wikipedia page.

John Kay's photograph is in the National Portrait Gallery. One picture of Harue Nonaka, a reproduction of one of her wedding photos with Kay, was published to accompany a report on his trial published by the paper where he got his first job, the

ETHICS ISN'T A COUNTY IN ENGLAND

Newcastle Journal. That news story opened with a gut-wrenchingly exculpatory line in Kay's favour: 'Top Fleet Street report John Kay was "a soul in torment" when he drowned the Japanese wife he loved as they took a bath together.'

The *Sun* obit detailed in glowing terms how Kay cared for his second wife, Mercedes, when she was dying of cancer. But Harue's death was erased in print with a reference to the case only added to the online version later after pressure from domestic violence charities. Her killing was treated like an unfortunate 'blip' in the life of an otherwise 'good' man. That News UK, which took Kay back after his time in a secure hospital following his conviction for manslaughter, was not willing to face up to the full history of one of its star journalists isn't surprising. *The Times,* not yet owned by Rupert Murdoch, reported on the case in a news in brief story on 12 September 1977, noting only that a *Sun* reporter was set to stand trial for the murder of his wife. It wasn't covered again.

The *Guardian* published the only significant report on the trial on 13 December 1977, under the headline 'Torment of Reporter Who Killed Wife'. It noted that Daniel Hollis QC, the prosecution barrister, told the court that 'Mr Kay was cracking up at the prospect of taking over as the *Sun*'s industrial editor – a job he did not feel able to hold down.'[151] Kay himself was quoted saying he was 'taken over by voices' and 'seemed possessed' before the report detailed how he killed Harue and listed his repeated attempts to take his own life (six in all). Kay was found by the police covered in blood after deliberately crashing his car.

In their unflinching history of the tabloid, *Stick It Up Your Punter! The Uncut Story of the Sun Newspaper,* Chris Horrie and

BREAKING

Peter Chippindale give the context of how Kay was welcomed back into the newsroom. They describe him as 'an ex-minor-public school boy . . . who was very keen and always seemed to be on top of things'. His party piece in the *Sun* office was reading out broadsheet stories and rewriting them in the tabloid's style on the spot but 'his manner was all a front'. Horrie and Chippindale recount that Kay's father blamed the *Sun* for his son's actions and the paper's then-editor Larry Lamb – later Sir Albert Lamb – agreed. The *Sun* paid for Kay's legal defence and Lamb sent a letter of mitigation to the court saying the newspaper would take him back when he was fit enough.

Kay, aged 33, pleaded not guilty to murder but admitted the lesser charge of manslaughter on the grounds of diminished responsibility. The court accepted his plea and he was sentenced to treatment in a psychiatric hospital. He received regular visits from *Sun* colleagues and Lamb kept his promise on Kay's release. As the years ticked up, Kay rose through the ranks, becoming chief reporter in 1990. He was twice named Reporter of the Year at the British Press Awards and, in 2005, the industry title *Press Gazette* ranked him as the sixteenth most influential British reporter of the post-war age. The events of September 1977 went unmentioned, officially taboo both in the office and the industry in general.

In February 2012, Kay found himself in the headlines again. He was named as one of eight people arrested as part of Operation Elveden, an investigation into alleged illegal payments to serving police officers and civil servants. In a trial at the Old Bailey that ended in March 2015, Kay was cleared of responsibility for payments totalling £100,000 made to a member of staff at the

ETHICS ISN'T A COUNTY IN ENGLAND

Ministry of Defence for stories on the British Army over the space of a decade. The *Sun* did pay the money to Bettina Jordan-Barber, Kay's source, and she was jailed for 12 months, found guilty of misconduct in a public office. Kay, who was already far beyond retirement age, was given an 'honourable' discharge from the *Sun* and left later the same year.

The issue with Kay's case is not that he was given a second chance or that he went on to have a long career. It's about the howling hypocrisy of his particular employer – which rarely offers empathy and leniency to ex-offenders – and the affronted response from some journalists when the uncomplicated memorialising for Kay was criticised. When the *Sun* revealed that *EastEnders* actor Leslie Grantham served prison time for a murder he committed aged 19, mocked Frank Bruno's mental health struggles and wrote fire and brimstone copy about the new identity given to one of the child murderers of the toddler James Bulger, John Kay was on the byline. His own experiences did not soften him or his paper to the crimes and misfortunes of others.

Ethics play a major part in every kind of journalism education, but the principles exposed in textbooks often fail to survive contact with the reality of a newsroom. Journalists tend to defend practices like death knocks and doorstepping until they are the ones with the voice recorders and camera lenses pointed towards them. There's a reason why Paul Dacre of the *Daily Mail* is so reticent to offer himself for interview and Rupert Murdoch rarely talks to outlets other than his own. Examples like that of Plymouth's local journalists when tragedy came to their community show us that it is possible to report on horror without contributing to it. The problem is that editors often lean

BREAKING

on the excuse that they have always done things in a particular way. When the story matters more than anything else, humanity can be swept to one side.

Where ethics are most absent, we find the seven deadly sins of modern journalism: pride from an overblown belief in journalism as a means of 'speaking truth to power'; greed from overpaid columnists and executives whose pay packets swell as their reporters' salaries are cut; lust over celebrity 'curves' and for prurient, privacy-destroying stories; envy provoked by gaudy rich-lists and supplements targeting bankers called 'Luxury' and 'How to Spend It'; gluttony expressed in freebie chasing; wrath at the impertinence of 'civilians' who question what the trade produces; and sloth when it comes cleaning up its own mess.

There are plenty of ethical journalists out there and they're the ones who worry whether they are. The hacks we should be most concerned about don't think about it at all.

10.
The Cock-up/Conspiracy Interface

Now Serving: A Potent Cocktail of Intrigue and Incompetence

'By means of an artificial system of hidden piping all the lavatories of London empty their physical filth into the Thames. In the same way, the world capital daily spews all of its social filth through a system of goose-quills into one central paper sewer – the Daily Telegraph.*'*
– Karl Marx, *Herr Vogt* (1860)

There's a human tendency to seek order in chaos. When that's applied to the world of news stories, events that were the result of error, arse-covering, self-interest or simple incompetence can be piled up and presented as conscious conspiracies – deliberate plans to conceal the real reasons for an event. In truth, cock-ups are far more common than conscious conspiracies because people, even very powerful people, are just not that organised or able to keep their mouths shut. So why do we expect journalists to winkle out conspiracies and how often are they caught up in the avalanche of cock-ups themselves?

I wanted to start this chapter by speculating on some hypothetical imbroglio featuring a politician flouting the countryside code and inadvertently flooding the roads with cattle, leading to Gategate and killing off the -gate suffix as the naming convention for scandals for good. Then I remembered that Plebgate – the 2012 row sparked by false claims that the Tory MP Andrew Mitchell had called a police officer at the entrance to Downing Street 'a pleb' – was called Gategate by *The Week* magazine, prompting *Business Insider* to comment that use of -gate had reached 'a new height of absurdity' and come to 'its logical conclusion'.[152]

Appending -gate to the name of unrelated scandals became a thing before the original Watergate affair had even concluded. A year before Nixon's eventual resignation, in August 1973, the American satirical magazine *National Lampoon* imagined Volgagate, a Soviet conspiracy with officials 'removing bugs from telephones, mixing actual letters and telegrams from Soviet citizens in with the usual phoney ones, telling the truth to foreign newsmen' and declining to lie at their trials. The first non-fictional use of -gate arrived the following month when a French wine industry source bizarrely told *Newsweek* that a scam to fob people off with cheap wine under the guise of expensive Bordeaux was 'our wine*gate*'.[153]

Of all the '-gates', the Watergate scandal remains influential for two reasons: one, it's the only time (so far) that a US president has been forced to resign, and two, the journalism spearheaded by Bob Woodward and Carl Bernstein – along with other

THE COCK-UP/CONSPIRACY INTERFACE

journalists at the *Washington Post* – has the best press of any investigation in journalistic history. Woodward and Bernstein smartly got their behind-the-scenes book, *All the President's Men*, out fast and the movie that followed it cast two incredibly charismatic performers as the protagonists. It's not hard to burnish the heroic journalist myth when you have Robert Redford and Dustin Hoffman on the case. But, as Professor W. Joseph Campbell writes in his book, *Getting It Wrong: Debunking the Greatest Myths in American Journalism*,[154] while Woodward and Bernstein's reporting was important and dogged, the media myth that they toppled the president smooths away the complexities of the scandal and the role of crucial investigative work by special prosecutors, federal judges, the FBI and committees of both houses of Congress and the Supreme Court. The fact that Woodward's secret source, 'Deep Throat', did not reveal himself as former senior FBI official Mark Felt until 2005, when he was 91, added to the glamour and mystery.

Even Woodward himself said the mythologising of the role he and Bernstein played in Watergate had 'gone to the point of absurdity' in a 1996 interview with PBS's *Frontline*. He explained that the *Washington Post* stories played 'some part in a chain of events' but 'were part of a very long and complicated process over many years'. Similarly, the *Washington Post*'s publisher at the time of Watergate, Katharine Graham, and its top editor, Ben Bradlee, both damped down hyperbole about the paper's reporting. In 1997, Graham told C-Span: 'Sometimes people accuse us of bringing down a president, which of course we didn't do. The processes that caused [Nixon's] resignation were constitutional.' The same year, Bradlee bluntly told *Meet the Press* that 'Nixon got Nixon.

BREAKING

The *Post* didn't get Nixon.' It was tapes of Nixon recorded at Nixon's behest which convicted him. By 2004, Woodward had grown even more frustrated with the mythology, telling the *American Journalism Review* that '[saying] the press brought down Nixon' was 'horseshit'.[155] He went on to say that while it always plays a role – either by being passive or aggressive – it's a mistake to overemphasise the influence of media coverage.

But the fact that the central players in the *Washington Post*'s Pulitzer Prize-winning investigation have tried to dispel the mythology around the reporting doesn't matter. The line from James Warner Bellah and Willis Goldbeck's screenplay for John Ford's *The Man Who Shot Liberty Valance* – 'When the legend becomes fact, print the legend' – is a popular one in journalism. The movie version of Woodward and Bernstein has inspired many people since to become journalists, so the legend beats the ornery reality. Journalists often complain about movie and TV representations of reporters because screenplays strip out the staring into space, waiting around, tedious phone calls, countless emails and total dead ends that are generally a feature of investigative reporting, but we also *love* when hacks are the heroes.

Identifying what's true is one of the hardest tasks in journalism. It goes beyond identifying outright lies and questionable statements. What is omitted from a story is often as important as what's stated. How we see the world depends on how aware we are of the forces that shape it. One of the most common kinds of conspiracy is conspiracy of silence: keeping information away from public view so that it's not possible to get a real sense of the truth because puzzle pieces are missing and the picture on

THE COCK-UP/CONSPIRACY INTERFACE

the box doesn't even show them. The history of British public life is littered with examples of these missing details.

MI5, more properly known as the Security Service, wasn't officially recognised in law until 1989. It took until 1994 – 32 years after the first official James Bond film – for the British state to confirm that MI6 (the Secret Intelligence Service) was more than a fictional conceit, and the signals intelligence organisation GCHQ was officially revealed in the same year. But the conspiracy of silence around the spy agencies had first been broken in 1976 when *Time Out* published 'The Eavesdroppers' by Duncan Campbell and Mark Hosenball, which publicly named GCHQ. The revelations resulted in Hosenball, who is an American citizen, being deported back to the US, where he continues to work as a reporter. Campbell was placed under surveillance by MI5 and later tried for a breach of the Official Secrets Act after being arrested for interviewing a former signals intelligence officer. He was found guilty but the judge imposed no punishment. He's continued to break stories about the secret state, including exposing the huge Anglo-American and European Echelon satellite surveillance programme. In a 2017 interview with the *Bristol Cable*, Campbell said he and Hosenball had not been secretive about their investigation: 'Early on I rang GCHQ and said, "Can I speak to your press officer, and get some basic information?" The switchboard was completely baffled because they thought they were completely secret.'[156] Media collusion with the government in keeping the existence of the intelligence services hidden in plain sight was astonishing. MI5 vetted job applicants at the BBC from 1933 right through to the

BREAKING

1990s, even after a story published by the *Observer* in August 1985 revealed the existence of the programme.

Despite so much light being thrown on secret worlds – the existence of the secret services, the extent of dirty tricks sanctioned, funded and undertaken by the British state across the world, including at home in Northern Ireland, among many other things – it's still common for those who question the narrative provided by governments to be framed as conspiratorial. It's almost as though Establishment figures are saying, 'Yes, yes, all of that happened but that was in the past and we don't get up to that sort of thing anymore.' Tell that to the victims of the 'Spy Cops' scandal, where undercover officers married and even had children with members of peaceful polities groups they were infiltrating. That was only revealed in 2010. Or go back just a little further to the notion that Saddam Hussein was working with Al Qaeda, a conspiracy theory propagated by the British and American governments and accepted by large parts of the media, which is rarely seen as such.

The British state has a very cosy and terribly polite system for policing the media's respect for secrecy. The Defence and Security Media Advisory Committee (DSMA) – colloquially known as the D-notice committee – is run by the Ministry of Defence and meets every six months to discuss how well-behaved or otherwise the British media is being. Its stated purpose is to 'prevent inadvertent public disclosure of information that would compromise UK military and intelligence operations'. It attempts to achieve that by issuing DSMA notices to the media, encouraging outlets not to publish information it classes as potentially dangerous. The DSMA committee itself is made up

THE COCK-UP/CONSPIRACY INTERFACE

of 19 representatives from the media – who currently include senior executives from the BBC, ITV and Sky News, as well as the editor of the *Mail on Sunday*, the associate editor of the *Sunday Times* and the editor of the *Press Association* – and five representatives of the UK government (two from the MoD and one each from the Cabinet Office, the Foreign Office and the Home Office).

There are five DSMA notice categories: military operations, plans and capabilities; nuclear and non-nuclear weapons systems and equipment; military counter-terrorist forces, special forces and intelligence agency operations, activities, communication methods and techniques; physical property and assets; and personnel who work in sensitive positions and their families. The breadth of issues covered effectively means that the DSMA Committee could find a reason to suggest that almost any detail of a military or intelligence operation shouldn't be published. These notices are, as the name suggests, advisory and therefore heeding them is supposedly voluntary. The current secretary of the DSMA Committee, Brigadier (Ret.) Geoffrey Dodds, a former Royal Engineer, explained to *Computer Weekly* in 2023: 'Journalists can report what they want: as an example, I advise that sensitive personal information of a certain person should not be broadcast or published. If a journalist wants to do that, for whatever reason – and some do – then they go ahead . . . If I had any form of sanction, then no member of the media would speak to me.'

But that impression of good chaps persuading other good chaps to do the right thing as any jolly good bloke would is deceptive. After the *Guardian* published details from a massive leak of

BREAKING

secret US government documents supplied by National Security Agency (NSA) contractor Edward Snowden in June 2013, the subsequent minutes of the DSMA committee called the events 'very concerning' because the paper didn't talk to the committee before publishing its first story.

The day after the *Guardian* published the first of the Snowden stories, a DSMA notice was issued to editors at all major UK publications urging them to refrain from publishing information that might 'jeopardise both national security and possibly UK personnel'. The communication was marked 'private and confidential: not for publication, broadcast or use on social media'. Not only did the committee want the papers to shut up, it wanted them to shut up about being asked to shut up. However, the notice quickly became public after it was sent to the Guido Fawkes blog and published there.

In Parliament, then Prime Minister David Cameron warned that he didn't 'want to have to use injunctions or D-notices, or other tougher measures' but would if the newspapers didn't show 'some social responsibility'. The implicit threat worked – the *Financial Times* and *The Times* did not report on the initial revelations; the BBC largely ignored the story and the *Daily Telegraph* only published a very short report. The *Independent* followed up the story. Meanwhile, the *Daily Mail*, through its columnist Stephen Glover, used a full page to attack the *Guardian*: 'Whatever [it], with its head in the clouds, may believe, the British government has an obligation to protect this country's strategic and economic interests in a world in which foreign governments are ruth-lessly pursuing theirs.'[157] *Press Gazette* editor Dominic Ponsford questioned the patriotism

THE COCK-UP/CONSPIRACY INTERFACE

of the *Guardian*'s editors: '. . . perhaps it is worth pondering the fact that with two-thirds of *Guardian* online readers now abroad, notions of serving the UK national interest may become more complicated.'[158]

The tougher measures that Cameron promised arrived in the shape of representatives from GCHQ overseeing *Guardian* staff taking drills and angle grinders to their computers to destroy their copies of the Snowden files before the pieces were passed through a 'degausser' – which permanently erases data – supplied by the spy agency. The process, which the paper recorded and published on its website, followed what *Guardian* correspondent Luke Harding described in his book, *The Snowden Files*, as 'tense meetings' between editor Alan Rusbridger and Cabinet Secretary Jeremy Heywood.[159] The civil servant told the journalist that they could 'do this nicely or [they could] go to law' before adding that 'a lot of people in government [thought the *Guardian*] should be closed down'.

The *Guardian*, in the shape of its deputy editor Paul Johnson, claimed that the destruction of the hard drive was 'purely a symbolic act'[160] because the government and GCHQ knew that the leaked material was also in the possession of *The New York Times* and the revelations would continue. He wrote that 'the episode hadn't changed anything'. But it had. There had been a show of strength and it was followed by the DSMA Committee appearing to hug the *Guardian* close. By May 2014, Johnson had been invited to join it and had attended his first meeting. He remained a member until October 2018.

The appointment of Katharine Viner as the *Guardian*'s new editor in March 2015 seemed to usher in an era of even closer collaboration between the paper and the security services. In November 2016, the paper trumpeted an exclusive with the head of MI5, Andrew Parker, which it said was 'the first newspaper interview given by an incumbent MI5 chief in the service's 107-year history'.[161] Johnson shared the byline with the paper's then defence correspondent, Ewen MacAskill. Four months later, the *Guardian* was given another spooky exclusive – the first national newspaper interview with the chief of MI6, Alex Younger.[162]

Over the past five years, as Mark Curtis of Declassified, an investigative website that covers UK military and foreign policy, has highlighted, the *Guardian* has published a significant number of overwhelmingly positive pieces about GCHQ,[163] the organisation that encouraged it to batter its own computers in the basement. As well as favourably covering the agency's festive PR stunt puzzles for children as other papers do, *Guardian* headlines have included 'Neurodivergent Women Sought for Jobs at GCHQ and BAE Systems'[164] and 'GCHQ Seeks to Increase Number of Female Coders to Tackle Threats'.[165] But the most striking and supine of the bunch was a May 2022 feature ostensibly about the benefits of job-sharing, which has the headline '"Huge Sense of Pride": The mothers who job-share counter-terrorism at GCHQ[166] and opened with the line: 'It sounds like an idyllic job-share for two mums...'

You don't need to be conspiratorially minded to observe that in less than a decade, the *Guardian* went from a thorn in the security state's side to the place where its most senior officers give exclusives and participate in promo pieces that read like something from an internal newsletter. But I don't think that's

THE COCK-UP/CONSPIRACY INTERFACE

a conspiracy. I think it's what happens when an organisation tries to correct its course and protect itself. The *Guardian* still publishes critical coverage on GCHQ but it's blunted by the soft stuff.

*

Newsrooms are chaotic and journalists are loose-lipped and typically very undisciplined. Most conspiracy theories rely on the notion of a cabal of people keeping secrets close. Any complex conspiracy that relied upon the discretion of journalists would collapse almost immediately, especially if confronted with the promise of some free drinks and a half-decent selection of canapés to enjoy while blabbing all about it.

Despite the tilt of prominent fact-checking efforts in the British media to focus on what they deem to be the far right and the far left, smack bang in the centre is home to just as many wild notions. When Boris Johnson used his Resignation Honours list to give his former advisor, the then 30-year-old Charlotte Owen, a peerage, rumours immediately started rattling around social media that she was his secret daughter and that there was a secret super-injunction preventing the press from mentioning it. The more obvious explanation – that Johnson valued her loyalty and wanted to put an ally in the House of Lords for a very, very long time – wasn't remotely as appealing. Owen's ennoblement stank but no more pungently than Johnson putting another of his advisors, 32-year-old former News UK journalist Ross Kempsel, in the upper chamber.

Owen got more heat because she's a woman and she shares a surname with Boris Johnson's first wife, Allegra Mostyn-Owen,

BREAKING

who is not the mother of any of his many children. Centrist types on Twitter and elsewhere, who'd rail against conspiracy theories from the left and right, gleefully seized on the ludicrous idea that Owen was Johnson's love child. It followed similar obsessions with pinpointing Russia as the main source of all of Britain's woes and the idea that Donald Trump would be felled by an explosive dossier any day now. The question that people taken with the 'Johnson's secret daughter' theory seemed incapable of answering was why he would keep her hidden for so long and then . . . put her in the House of Lords. The fact this theory got so much airtime is symbolic of the widespread mistrust which is endemic at this level. Members of the public felt there had to be something going on here that they weren't being told about.

The super-injunction scandal of 2011, which began with the *Sun* publishing stories that omitted details it was legally prohibited from including, played a big part in creating this culture of mistrust. Online guessing games about the identity of a footballer concealing details of an affair – later confirmed in the US and on Twitter as Ryan Giggs – spiralled into questions about more than 30 super-injunctions that had been granted over the previous year. The story left many people feeling that the media was always hiding something and, specifically, that the courts were regularly being used by household names, including journalists, to keep things out of the press.

In April 2011, *Private Eye* launched a legal challenge against one of the injunctions and, the following week, the man who'd sought the injunction named himself: it was BBC journalist and political correspondent Andrew Marr. He told the *Daily Mail*

THE COCK-UP/CONSPIRACY INTERFACE

that he'd sought the injunction in 2008 to prevent reporting on an extramarital affair and said he was embarrassed by it because he didn't 'come into journalism to go around gagging journalists'.[167] *Private Eye*'s editor, Ian Hislop, said it 'was pretty rank of [Marr] to have an injunction while working as an active journalist'.[168] It was almost understandable that actors, who joyfully lie for a living, would seek injunctions to hide parts of their private lives, but for a journalist to do so while demanding the truth from others was a very different matter.

Around the same time as the storm around injunctions, another smaller weather system was forming around the *Independent*, leading to a hard rain for one of its star columnists. Johann Hari had been named joint winner of *The Times*' Student News Journalist of the Year award in 2000 for work published in one of Cambridge University's two student newspapers, *Varsity*. The prize fuelled a rapid rise; Hari was hired by the *New Statesman* before being snapped up to write two weekly columns for the *Independent*. His first book, *God Save the Queen?*, was published in 2002. The following year, he was named Young Journalist of the Year at the *Press Gazette* Awards. His work was syndicated across the world; he joined the panel on BBC 2's *Review Show* and the US politics site *Slate* as its book critic. Soon, he was so ubiquitous that even the *Daily Telegraph* was recognising him as one of 'the most influential left-wingers in Britain'. In 2008, Hari won the Orwell Prize for Political Writing. The pieces that secured him the award included features on France's secret war in the Central African Republic, the US right-wing, and an exploration of multiculturalism and women. Having been given free rein by his editors at the *Independent*, Hari had gained the status many columnists grab for themselves – he was now an expert in almost everything.

When the crash came, it was spectacular. In 2011, accusations that Hari was guilty of plagiarism exploded across blogs and social media. A group calling itself the Deterritorial Support Group, along with a journalist called Brian Whelan, showed that many of the interviews Hari had filed as original were actually based on material taken from previously published conversations with and books by the subjects.[169] Hari defended himself at first, denying he'd done anything wrong and saying that the unattributed quotes were merely more polished versions of what interviewees had said to him and that he hadn't passed off anyone else's work as his own.

Following the plagiarism revelations, Hari was suspended from the *Independent* for two months. The council that administers the Orwell Prize conducted an investigation and ruled that Hari should return the prize. He offered to repay the £2,000 but *Political Quarterly*, the award's sponsor, requested he donate it to the writers' human rights charity, English PEN. It was to have been paid back in instalments once Hari returned to the *Independent*. In parallel to the plagiarism scandal, it emerged that Hari had used a pseudonym – David Rose – to systematically smear people he considered 'enemies' through Wikipedia edits.[170] It also just so happened that the fictional Rose was an enormous fan of the very real Johann Hari, diminishing his rivals and foes while giving the impression that there was no greater columnist in history and no more essential commentator on modern times.

In September 2011, Hari apologised for both the plagiarism

THE COCK-UP/CONSPIRACY INTERFACE

and the waspish Wikipedia edits in an *Independent* column. It was an instant classic of self-justification:

> When I recorded and typed up any conversation, I found something odd: Points that sounded perfectly clear when you heard them being spoken often don't translate to the page ... When this happened, if the interviewee had made a similar point in their writing ... I would use those words instead ... I was wrong. An interview isn't an x-ray of a person's finest thoughts. It's a report of an encounter. If you want to add material from elsewhere, there are conventions that let you do that ... If I had asked the many experienced colleagues that I have here at the *Independent* ... they would have told me that ...'[171]

This was playing cute in the worst sort of way. If Hari truly didn't understand the basic principles of interviewing, he shouldn't have been anywhere near a national newspaper in the first place.

He then disappeared to the US for 'retraining' while one of the *Independent*'s co-founders, the former editor Andreas Whittam Smith, conducted an inquiry – the findings from which were never made public. The paper had intended to take Hari back, but he decided to resign instead, announcing he was going to write a book.

Hari reappeared in 2015 with *Chasing the Scream: The First and Last Days of the War on Drugs*. Soon after, he became part of the TED Talk industrial complex with a presentation called 'Everything You Know about Addiction Is Wrong'. But, spoiler: everything that Hari thought you knew about addiction

BREAKING

being wrong was . . . largely wrong. That was demonstrated by many experts when he turned the talk into his next book, *Lost Connections: Uncovering the Real Causes of Depression – and the Unexpected Solutions* (2018). Hari argued that addictions are a response to experiences and a lack of positive, supportive relationships, rather than a result of any sort of biological need or neurological imbalance. It's a dangerous concept that could easily have encouraged people who are on medication to drop it on the say-so of Mr Johann Hari, not M.D. His pitch about depression was like Lyle Lanley in *The Simpsons* grifting the people of Springfield with a malfunctioning monorail, only with this crash, it would be people with serious mental health issues experiencing the impact.

The neuroscientist Dean Burnett calmly summed up the fundamental problem with Hari's book in a review for the *Observer*: 'Logically, someone with a reputation for making false claims should be the last person making high-profile, controversial, sweeping statements about something as sensitive as mental health. And yet, here we are.'[172] But Hari had something more powerful than facts on his side. He had celebrity. In the years since his departure from the *Independent*, he'd become fast friends with Elton John and a then still largely mainstream Russell Brand. Hillary Clinton was among the people who blurbed his books and, having previously engaged in a performative feud with Noam Chomsky, Hari had now got him on board too.

I'm not implying there was a conspiracy to make Hari a star at the *Independent* but there was a series of catastrophic cock-ups driven by editorial laziness and the desire to let a columnist that had found fame fast keep going. There's no secret to how Hari

THE COCK-UP/CONSPIRACY INTERFACE

has resurrected his career either. He writes books that seem to offer novel prescriptions about modern life – his latest is about the weight loss drug Ozempic – and those messages fit neatly into promo pieces that sit perfectly in newspapers' glossy weekend supplements. The media and the publishing industry tend to value commercial opportunity over doggedly sticking to the truth.

*

One of the most common phrases you'll see when people are looking for a conspiracy between the British press and politicians is 'that's a dead cat'. However, the 'dead cat strategy' is one of the most misunderstood concepts in political communications. Brought into the public consciousness by Tory election guru and second most malign Australian in British politics Lynton Crosby, it means introducing a shocking or sensational topic into a debate to distract from something that's more substantive and damaging to your candidate.

Crosby advised the Conservative Party on and off for years and was Boris Johnson's campaign manager during his successful 2008 and 2012 London mayoral campaigns. Just after his second term as Mayor began in 2013, a puffed-up Johnson explained Crosby's advice in his *Telegraph* column:

> Let us suppose you are losing an argument. The facts are overwhelmingly against you and the more people focus on the reality, the worse it is for you and your case. Your best bet in these circumstances is to perform a manoeuvre that a great campaigner describes as "throwing a dead cat on the table, mate". There is one thing that is absolutely certain about throwing a dead cat on the dining room table

and I don't mean that people will be outraged, alarmed, and disgusted. That is true, but irrelevant. The key point, says my Australian friend, is that everyone will shout, "Jeez, mate, there's a dead cat on the table!" In other words, they will be talking about the dead cat – the thing you want them to talk about – and they will not be talking about the issues that have been causing you so much grief.[173]

Since then, practically every story in British politics, especially those even tangentially related to Johnson, instantly draws crowds of people who confidently assert that a dead cat has landed on the table. Whether it was Johnson buying a dog that humped everything it saw – a bit too spot on as a metaphor – or comparing Theresa May's Brexit deal to a 'suicide vest', every word was seen as part of a coherent strategy rather than the actions of a chaotic character who his former advisor Dominic Cummings compared to a 'shopping trolley smashing from one side of the aisle to the other'.[174]

While it was obvious that Johnson was taken with dead-catting as a strategy – adding a digression about Peppa Pig World into a major speech or claiming his favourite hobby was making model buses, for example – which fitted well with the bumbling persona he has wrapped around his scheming core, not everything stinks of fatally wounded feline. Sometimes politicians are just crap or scrabbling for a lie to cover up a cock-up or catastrophe. David Cameron was the essay crisis prime minister who came up with rushed solutions at the last minute; Theresa May turned in too much homework and Boris Johnson was the leader who claimed he'd read the books then made up his own story. His time

THE COCK-UP/CONSPIRACY INTERFACE

in office shifted the cock-up versus conspiracy balance firmly to the latter in many people's minds because fundamentally, people prefer to think there's a scheme at work rather than chaos. That Johnson was buoyed up by the majority of the media for so long contributed to that sense.

The problem with having so many people rush to shout 'dead cat' when a political story breaks is that it obscures the actual mechanisms that are at work. Similarly, if anyone critical of the status quo can be dressed up in a tinfoil hat and categorised as a basement-dwelling obsessive, the reality of how politics and the media interact can be denied, with any suggestions of conspiracy or collusion waved away as pure fantasy. Sometimes, things really are being concealed.

Conspiracy is a strong word and that makes it easy to dismiss but, at the risk of leaving space for an obvious joke, British politics and media interactions are dominated by other c-words. At the mildest end, there is cooperation, an inevitable consequence of reporters needing to cultivate sources and find out information, but there is also cosiness, cronyism and client journalism (coverage that bolsters those in power rather than challenging them). When the last three are dominant and combined, the result is as close to conspiracy as you can get without dead drops and lurking around multi-storey car parks in the dead of night.

The space between cock-up and conspiracy is where most of the British media exists on any given day. It's a place of convenience, where access can be secured by asking questions (but not too many questions), where keeping some things you know in your peripheral vision is useful. There needn't be a devilishly complicated

BREAKING

plot at work when opportunism and convenience tend to produce the same result.

Beyond conspiracies of silence and convenience, some people with major platforms in the British media are engaged in the production of straight-up conspiracy theories. I want to conclude this chapter by looking at just two examples – the *Daily Telegraph*'s Allison Pearson and GB News host, Neil Oliver.

Pearson got her start as a purveyor of the paranoid while she was still a columnist at the *Evening Standard*, amplifying the moral panic around the MMR vaccine, but in her current berth, she's descended to new depths. One of the most notorious examples of Allison's alternative facts took place during the 2019 general election. A picture of a child sleeping on the floor at Leeds General Infirmary had become a flash point during the campaign as a symbol of an NHS in crisis, but Pearson claimed that she had been contacted by a Great Ormond Street nurse who had told her that the image was not real.

On 9 December 2019, Pearson posted on Twitter that she had a 'detailed explanation from paediatric nurses explaining why photo of child on the floor [sic] is "100% faked"' and promised she would publish it in her *Telegraph* column the following week.[175] She raged: 'Stage a photo. Cause outrage. Castigate people who doubt it for showing insufficient compassion. Jesus.' I don't think Jesus had anything to do with it. When Pearson's regular column appeared, the promised revelations were nowhere to be seen. Instead, she attacked the BBC for covering the 'gotcha! story' in its news bulletins and dismissed the whole thing as 'spite masquerading as compassion'.[176] Almost six years later, the evidence for her fake photo theory has still not seen the light of day, but then it

THE COCK-UP/CONSPIRACY INTERFACE

didn't need to – the story had already served its purpose of further muddying the waters during an election campaign.

Since then, Pearson has spread doubt about the existence of the Covid-19 pandemic – though simultaneously admitted that everyone in her family had caught the virus – and positioned herself as a leading voice in the 'vaccine sceptic' movement as the presenter of the *Telegraph* podcast, the unintentionally ironically named Planet Normal. She's also echoed the Great Replacement Theory – a piece of white nationalist propaganda that claims white European populations are being actively and deliberately 'replaced' – in columns that decry 'the multicultural monster'[177] and quote a range of outraged readers and senior sources who, curiously, always seem to sound exactly like Allison Pearson.

Over at GB News, Neil Oliver, who was once a rather placid chap who presented BBC documentaries about the heritage of the British coastline, has become a one-man disinformation vector. He told his viewers that there had been a 'silent war' for generations as politicians tried to impose 'a one-world government'; compared opposing Covid vaccines to fighting Nazi Germany; accused the BBC of fearmongering over climate change and suggested that the coronavirus vaccine was causing 'turbo cancer' in children. He told viewers: 'I don't know about you, but until just a few months ago, I'd never heard of turbo cancer.' That's because it doesn't exist. But still, Ofcom responded to complaints by clearing Oliver, concluding that 'the brief comments were the presenter's personal view and did not materially mislead the audience.'

We've gone from Watergate to a media environment where regulators aren't even willing to close the gate after the horse has

BREAKING

bolted. The coming man among British media proprietors is Paul Marshall, the founder of *UnHerd* and major investor in GB News, who subsequently acquired the *Spectator*. When *The News Agents* podcast and Hope Not Hate – an anti-racism advocacy group – highlighted likes and retweets from Marshall's locked Twitter/X account that amplified Islamophobic, anti-refugee and anti-LGBTQ+ rhetoric and policies, they asked whether Marshall was a 'fit and proper person' to own the *Daily Telegraph*, for which he was then in the running as a buyer. A representative for Marshall said the posts flagged up by the Hope Not Hate investigation were 'a small and unrepresentative sample'. But looking at the views already published on a daily basis by that paper, it seemed to me that if those tweets were representative of Marshall's worldview, it was a perfect fit. It's more than a cock-up when conspiracists control major media properties.

In the absence of agreed truth, conspiracies rush in to fill the vacuum – conspiracies of silence, conspiracy theories that serve those in power, conspiracy theories that favour those who seek power, and, crucially, conspiracy theories from those who seek to explain how power acts upon them. The online world allows anyone to present themselves as a truthteller and that's why it's so crucial that truth plays a more fundamental role in the media landscape. Journalism has a higher bar to reach when lies have become the coin of the realm.

11.

When You Become The Story

In The Eye of The Storm

'The press is so powerful in its image-making role, it can make the criminal look like he's the victim and make the victim look like he's the criminal.'

– Malcolm X in a speech at Audubon Ballroom, Harlem,
13 December 1964

Christopher Jefferies was a bookish 65-year-old retired teacher who didn't own a TV – he preferred the radio – and didn't regularly buy newspapers. It's not surprising, then, that it came as a shock to him when the police arrived at his door early on the morning of 30 December 2010 and arrested him for the murder of his tenant, Joanna Yeates. He had not been aware of the progress of the investigation into the young woman's murder – she had been reported missing on 19 December 2010 and found dead on Christmas Day at the edge of a quarry three miles from her home in Bristol. After giving the police two voluntary statements, he had thought his role in it was over.

Jefferies hadn't murdered Yeates or had any involvement in her death, but after his arrest, the British press moved quickly to suggest he was unquestionably guilty. The media engaged, to quote Jefferies' own words from one of his statements to the Leveson Inquiry, in 'a frenzied campaign' to blacken his character 'by publishing a series of very serious allegations ... which were completely untrue, allegations which were a mixture of smear, innuendo and complete fiction'.

Over the three days that Jefferies was in custody, the papers painted him as a pervert, a voyeur, a malign influence on his pupils, most probably a paedophile and perhaps the perpetrator of an unsolved murder from 1974. It began on the day of his arrest, with the *Daily Mail* running his photo on its front page alongside the headline 'Could This Man Hold the Key to Joanna's Murder?'.[178] Since he was her landlord and *literally* had keys to the basement flat she shared with her boyfriend, Greg Reardon, it was a heavy-handed hint.

By Friday, the front pages were ablaze with accusations and wild claims. The *Sun*'s headline – 'The Strange Mr Jefferies' – was the most memorable. Its front page set a small photograph of Joanna Yeates next to a cropped section from a school photo from 30 years earlier showing Jefferies with blue hair grinning at the camera. It was a classic case of an image stripped of context and furnished with new meaning by a tabloid. Inside the paper, a range of quotes from mostly unnamed sources was offered to support a caricature of Jefferies as an angry, violent and scary teacher who was a dirty, unkempt loner. The page four story encouraged the

WHEN YOU BECOME THE STORY

reader to focus on four words in bold, each accompanied by a phrase designed to justify it: '**WEIRD**: Strange talk, strange walk; **POSH**: Loved culture, poetry; **LEWD**: Made sexual remarks; **CREEPY**: Loner with blue rinse hair'. The main copy began: 'Joanna Yeates murder suspect Chris Jefferies was last night branded a creepy oddball by ex-pupils, a teaching colleague and neighbours.'

Let's look at those four pillars of 'guilt' offered by the *Sun*'s story. Putting aside the baseless accusations of making lewd and sexual remarks – which would be a crime if it were true – the other three were nothing more than the snarls of a school bully. He likes books! He looked different! We thought his voice and walk were weird! When a paper wants to frame you in a particular way, no aspect of your physicality or personality is safe from being forced through the prism of suspicion and scorn. As the journalist and media critic Brian Cathcart wrote for the *Financial Times*:

> It would have been possible to flip the picture entirely. This man had taught for 34 years in a well-known local independent school, Clifton College, leaving without a blemish on his record. He was involved in Neighbourhood Watch, the Liberal Democrat Party and a number of conservation campaigns. He had a large circle of friends, owned a handful of properties and was studying for a degree in French at the University of the West of England.[179]

In fact, the teaching colleague quoted in the *Sun*'s story, Richard Bland, had called Jefferies a 'loner' and mentioned his blue hair but he'd also said he was a dedicated and successful teacher. That part of his quote was given far less prominence because it did not fit with the picture the paper wanted to present. Others who spoke to the press about Jefferies – a former tenant, a friend, his ex-boss and one of his neighbours – described him as dedicated, responsible and an active member of the community, but each time these comments appeared towards the end of articles, buried beneath the avalanche of innuendo.

The *Daily Mirror* used its front page to claim 'Jo Suspect is Peeping Tom'. The *Daily Mail*, in a story headlined 'The Teacher They Called Mr Strange', used Jefferies' enjoyment of the Romantic writer Christina Rossetti to howl that he idolised a mentally ill poet who 'often wrote about death' and was 'prone to apocalyptic visions'. The *Daily Star* exclaimed, 'Jo landlord a creep who freaked out schoolgirls and called him an 'angry weirdo'. That's just a small portion of the headlines the day after Jefferies' arrest – the sheer weight of invective led his solicitor to write to editors warning them to stop publishing defamatory claims about his client. The letters were ignored. Even more outrageously, a public reminder to editors from Attorney General Dominic Grieve about publishing material that could prejudice the view of a future jury was swept aside.

The following day, a Saturday, the *Sun*'s front page screamed that Jeffries was 'Obsessed by death' and claimed 'Jo suspect scared kids'. The justification for these claims was that he had shown some students Alain Resnais' Holocaust documentary, *Night and Fog* (1955), and taught the spooky Victorian novel, *The Moonstone*, during his teaching career. The *Mirror* used its front page to speculate 'Was killer waiting in Jo's flat?' and continued to focus on Jefferies. Meanwhile, the *Star* also picked up the angle about the teacher's clearly unacceptable love for Rossetti.

WHEN YOU BECOME THE STORY

That evening, Jefferies was released without charge. At roughly the same time, Joanna Yeates' boyfriend, Greg Reardon, issued a statement paying tribute to his partner. It also included a passage about the press: 'Jo's life was cut short tragically but the finger-pointing and character assassination by social and news media of as yet innocent men has been shameful. It has made me lose a lot of faith in the morality of the British press and those that spend their time fixed to the internet in this modern age.'

Inevitably, the criticism of social media was more to the papers' taste than the stinging criticism of their own behaviour. The *Mail on Sunday* and *Sunday Express* both reported the statement leaving the comments about newspaper character assassinations out entirely, while the *Sunday Mirror* told its readers that Reardon had 'attacked internet ghouls who have posted hurtful and lurid speculation'. Ghouls with expense accounts and access to newspaper bylines were fine.

Jefferies went on to sue eight newspapers – the *Daily Express*, *Daily Mail*, *Daily Mirror*, *Daily Record*, *Daily Star*, *Sun*, *Sunday Mirror* and the *Scotsman* – and, on 29 July 2011, the news organisations apologised to him in court and paid damages said to be in the region of £500,000 in total. It was some measure of justice, but Jefferies explained at the conclusion of one of his written statements to the Leveson Inquiry that 'the incalculable effects of what was written about me by these highly influential tabloid newspapers is something from which it will be difficult to ever escape.'

In a 2021 article – 'Chris's Ordeal: Who Is Christopher Jefferies and Where Is He Now?' – written to capitalise on search engine traffic around that year's ITV drama about the case

BREAKING

(*The Lost Honour of Christopher Jefferies*), the *Sun* wrote: '. . . he later won a libel case for defamatory media coverage of his arrest, with convicted murderer Vincent Tabak trying to implicate Mr Jefferies on a number of occasions after seeing him in the news.'[180] Oh, so it was Tabak who was running news conferences at eight different national newspapers and writing countless stories smearing an innocent man. If anything, the *Sun* was a victim, right?

After the Leveson Inquiry Report recommendation that newspapers do not name suspects before charge and a more binding Supreme Court decision in 2022 that individuals under criminal investigation are entitled to 'a reasonable expectation of privacy', the experience Jefferies went through is unlikely to be replicated. But the press and wider media's approach to how people in the news are treated is still hugely bruising.

Catherine Mayer, a journalist who has also experienced being inside new stories about friends and relatives, explained it to me like this: 'All journalism has an element of dissociation to it. Some of that is good because balanced reporting requires you to keep a distance even in intimate circumstances, but it becomes a problem when dissociation is valorised and turns into not caring and dehumanisation.' Mayer wishes 'journalists had a better understanding of how their stories impact people'. She draws the important gap between public interest journalism and things that simply interest the public. The person at the heart of the story is not the only one affected: 'What does it mean for their family and friends?' She thinks 'journalism training should give you some experience of what it's like to ride out human events in the public eye. Being humane is not the same as being soft.'

Mayer and her late husband, Gang of Four songwriter and

WHEN YOU BECOME THE STORY

guitarist Andy Gill, were close friends with the TV presenter Paula Yates and her partner, INXS frontman Michael Hutchence. She says, 'The stuff with Michael and Paula was the worst I'd ever seen until [Paula's daughter with Bob Geldof] Peaches died. How was it that the children were fair game? There were photographers hiding in the hedges outside their schools.'

The chase for stories about Yates included trying to orchestrate images that fitted with the editorial line. Mayer recounts that 'after Paula had been in rehab, they tried to get pictures of her looking drunk and a photographer pushed her to the ground and took photos'. For people at the heart of stories, it's apparent that coverage of even the most horrific events does not reflect what actually happened. Mayer recalls: 'When Paula died, I read so many different accounts of the funeral. They were so full of mistakes. The tabloids led the way and the broadsheets repeated them.'

For people of a certain age, the former cabinet minister David Mellor is synonymous with having sex in a Chelsea kit. It never happened but it has been repeated as fact so often that it feels more real than reality. It's a relic of the era when John Major's dying Tory government seemed to be drowning under the toxic sludge of sex and corruption that the tabloids subbed 'sleaze'. Another false memory from the period is that it was Major's October 1993 'Back to Basics' speech, calling for a return to 'the old values', that acted as the starting gun for the tabloid rush to find racier and racier stories about more and more MPs, but again, it's not the case.

The Mellor story was published by the *Sun* a year before 'Back to Basics'. His extramarital affair with the actress Antonia de Sancha was significantly 'spiced up' by the publicist Max Clifford, who was later jailed for a series of historical sexual assaults and died in prison in 2017. Clifford told the *Sun* that Mellor had sucked de Sancha's toes in bed and worn a Chelsea shirt during sex. Both claims were later revealed as total fabrications by de Sancha herself in a 2002 interview with the *Guardian*.[181] She said she'd been persuaded by Clifford to go along with the *Sun*'s claims as 'a strategy of damage limitation' after the affair was first revealed by *The People*. She posed in football kits and catsuits, making around £35,000 in the process, but her acting career was over.

At the Leveson Inquiry, Mellor said that the Chelsea shirt story was 'cooked up between [Clifford] and the deputy editor of the *Sun*, [Stuart] Higgins' and that he 'had it on very good authority from someone who was a very senior person there at the time... [that] it was a bidding game. "If she says this, what will you pay? If she says that, what will you pay?"' In his own Leveson Inquiry statement, Higgins said he 'never published a story against the specific advice of [the *Sun*'s] legal department but there were some very tough discussions which, in all candour, turned on the desire to achieve the maximum "edge" to the story... In other words, the question was: "How far can we go without risking a writ?"'

Mellor was and is no saint – unless the Vatican is looking for a patron of free lunches – but there was plenty for the papers to go on without inventing whole cloth (and half kit) dubious detail about his sex life. The affair was news – evidence of hypocrisy from a minister in a government that liked to make statements about morality – but the details were just dirty lies generated to satisfy dirty minds.

While people remember the Chelsea shirt, they forget that Mellor remained in office for two months after the affair story

WHEN YOU BECOME THE STORY

broke, finally forced to resign as a minister over a free holiday he accepted from the daughter of a senior member of the Palestine Liberation Organisation (PLO). The sex scandal is simple and salacious, so it remains in our collective memory, but the financial shenanigans faded fast; they're too complicated and detailed to stick. As Catherine Mayer puts it: 'These things aren't true but they become more true than the truth.'

The 'Chelsea kit' lie wasn't even the most outrageous one trafficked onto the *Sun*'s front page by Clifford. That dubious honour belongs to 'Freddie Starr Ate My Hamster'. That headline ran on 13 March 1986 above a story that claimed Starr, a stand-up comedian with a forthcoming tour that was selling slowly, had put a pet hamster between two slices of bread and proceeded to eat it when his friend's girlfriend refused to make him a sandwich.

Starr wrote in his 2001 autobiography, *Unwrapped*, that he hadn't stayed at the friend in question's house since 1979 and that even then, he'd 'never eaten or even nibbled a live hamster, gerbil, guinea pig, mouse, shrew, vole, or any other small mammal.'[182] The girlfriend, stage name Lea La Salle, real name Louise Fox, was quoted in the *Sun* story as saying she was 'sickened and horrified' by the event and would 'never forget' it. In 2019, after Starr's death, she remembered that it actually never happened and told the *Daily Mirror* that the story was an exaggeration of something that happened five years before the *Sun*'s front page: 'He did bite into the bread, but not the hamster. I was upset because the hamster was covered in butter which took two days for it to lick off.'[183]

At the Leveson Inquiry, Clifford justified the story because of the need to sell tickets for Starr's British tour: 'Kelvin MacKenzie, editor of the *Sun*, called me and said, "We've got this great story on Freddie Starr"... I phoned Freddie and he denied it... My decision was to say to Kelvin, "Freddie denies eating a hamster, but I'm more than happy for the story to go in because... I think it would be great publicity for him."'

In the modern era, a very different kind of comedian, the satirist and stand-up Nish Kumar, found himself in the middle of a storm whipped up by the right-wing newspapers about *The Mash Report*, the BBC political comedy series that he co-wrote and co-presented. When the show was first broadcast in the summer of 2017, there was what Kumar described to me as 'a warning shot' – a critical double-page spread in the *Daily Mail*. 'I remember sitting on a train and somebody opening the paper,' he told me. 'There was a huge picture of me. I remember thinking, "That seems odd".' He went on to describe *The Mash Report* as 'the only thing in my life and career that became more of a problem as it became more successful.'

The right-wing criticism of *The Mash Report* was even more frustrating for Kumar because it frequently contradicted itself:

> The problem that I had was the dissonance at the heart of what was being said: they were simultaneously trying to get across the point that the show was both not being watched and completely irrelevant, while it was also a threat to the moral and social fabric of the country. It was one of the first times I saw in action something we'd already slowly realised: there's no point in pointing out conservative hypocrisy. Observing hypocrisy only really counts for something if

the instigators of that hypocrisy have a sense of shame. If they don't, they don't really care.

The following year, when the second batch of *Mash Report* episodes was broadcast, the *Mail* titles ramped up the rhetoric. In the *Mail on Sunday*, Charlotte Gill declared herself 'appalled by the Corporation's Tory-bashing satire'.[184] Months of right-wing columnists using Kumar as the physical manifestation of all they felt was wrong with the BBC, comedy and Britain in general built up to a massive monstering surrounding two events that took place in the space of a month, either side of the 2019 general election: Kumar being jeered and having a bread roll thrown at him during a charity gig where he joked about Brexit, and a confected uproar after he introduced an old *Horrible Histories* sketch that joked about British customs with foreign origins.

There were 44 articles published in the British press in the 24 hours after Kumar's appearance at the charity lunch. The fact that a comedian's jokes had gone down badly with a few attendees at an event where he was appearing for free was covered as if it were a major sporting upset or the outbreak of a small war. The tone of much of the coverage was jubilant, as though the papers in question had won a great victory over a historic enemy. 'Brexit Stage Right' chortled the *Sun*.[185] 'A moment's silence for the stage death of Nish Kumar,' chuckled the wags over at Westminster gossip blog, Guido Fawkes.[186]

In the storm around the *Horrible Histories* video, Piers Morgan, who *The Mash Report* had previously criticised, howled that Kumar was a 'horrible piece of work'[187] and the *Mail on Sunday* condemned him for 'trashing Britain',[188] while Andrew Neil dismissed it as 'anti-British drivel'.[189] When Kumar made a joke about the irony of the *Mail* sponsoring Index on Censorship's Freedom of Expression Awards, which he was compering, at the same time as it was demanding he be taken off air, Matthew Parris wrote in *The Times* that he had wanted to 'heckle, storm the stage, disrupt'.[190] At least it allowed Kumar to joke that he had been deemed 'too offensive' for the Freedom of Expression awards.

Like a lot of people under sustained media bombardment, Kumar struggled to ignore what was being said about him. 'I think probably the biggest mistake I made was that I read everything,' he says. 'I felt I should be aware of what was being written about me. That's probably a combination of self-obsession, narcissism and some element of self-preservation.' That feeling was exacerbated, of course, by the fact that he was writing and performing jokes about the news: 'It sort of feels like the job of a topical comedian is to be outside of something you're commenting on, but obviously, when you become the story that's very strange.'

The effect of all the invective directed towards Kumar was to generate social media bile, which in turn led to further coverage piggybacking on the attention, creating a decidedly vicious circle. Kumar explains: 'If you're willing to say something that could be placed politically anywhere to the left of, at best, Tony Blair but really David Cameron, the opinion pages of the *Telegraph*, *The Times*, the *Mail* and the *Express* will rain shit down on you. I draw a clear line between what they wrote and fanning the flames of internet nutcases who then send you death threats.'

Kumar rightly identifies the effect the lack of balance in the British press has when you suddenly find yourself under its Sauron Eye: 'The way that print media in the UK is weighted, if you

WHEN YOU BECOME THE STORY

upset the left, you might get an op-ed in the *Guardian* and a lot of tweets. But if you upset conservatives, you will get op-ed after op-ed written about you. And that's when stuff gets wrenched out of context and you don't recognise the things you're supposed to have said.'

While Kumar knows that if you're in the public eye people are going to write about you and scrutinise what you say, the level of incoming fire he faced was simply not normal. It went way beyond what you might expect from press coverage of a comedy show. He told me, 'When you become a character in the news, people stop seeing you as a human being. That's a real problem. It's when things start to feel very, very serious.' Kumar also recognises that he at least had the advantage of a supportive partner, friends who understood the situation, an agent who recognised the press's playbook and the resources to be able to afford professional help. In his stand-up show, *Your Power, Your Control*, he discussed being at the heart of the media storm and concluded by asking the audience to think about what happens when people without those resources are subject to that kind of unrelenting attention.

While celebrity increases the chances of you finding yourself at the centre of a news story, Christopher Jefferies' experience illustrates just one of the ways you can be drawn to the media's attention without having any desire to be in the spotlight. Misery loves company and tragedy draws journalists. In the previous chapter on ethics, we looked at how journalists behave and how they should behave, but what does it feel like to be at the centre of that attention? One person I spoke to told me, 'When I was in sixth form, a major car accident killed a 14-year-old at my school.

BREAKING

The day her life support was switched off, we, the older students, were briefed that we might have to protect younger students from predatory journalists at our school gates trying to interview them.'

Another interviewee experienced that unwanted attention: 'When my friend was murdered when I was 16, me and my friends visited the place he was killed. A journalist asked me if I wanted to give a quote about him and I said no. The journalist then got arsey with me, saying they thought it might be nice to share my memories of him. It stuck with me.'

That same pressure was applied on another person I spoke to, who remembers: 'When two girls from my high school drowned during a trip, the media pitched up at the gates to get pictures of crying kids on their way in. Many of us didn't find out what had happened until morning assembly. Awful ghouls. It killed my desire to become a journalist stone dead at 13.' What journalism thinks it needs and what's best for human beings who are suffering are often in conflict.

A report published in 2021 by the campaign group Survivors Against Terror (SAT)[191] working with the polling firm Kantar talked to 116 people who had been involved in terror attacks in the UK and abroad about their experiences with the media. The most common form of intrusion reported by survey respondents and interviewees was pestering and pressure to talk. As with the Hett family after the Manchester Arena bombing, survivors who were hoping desperately for a call from a missing loved one found their phones deluged with calls from reporters demanding information, and the same experience was replicated across email and social media. Some who did agree to interviews found themselves subject to misrepresentation. A survivor of the 7/7 attacks on London said that after agreeing to an interview, they were told they were being driven to find a good place to talk but instead they were taken to Edgware Road Station to have their reaction filmed as they walked up to it. The survivor hadn't been there since the attack and recalled that they felt 'extremely vulnerable and [taken advantage of] to get a good story'.

Invasion of privacy was another common complaint as survivors who had never wanted any kind of notoriety were turned into public figures. Others faced journalists breaking the news of their loved one's deaths before they were given any official confirmation and experienced long-term effects of the specific trauma caused by media interest. SAT chose not to link specific news organisations with particular events, but it detailed those organisations that were named by more than one survivor. That list included the BBC, ITV, Channel 4 News, Sky News, the *Sun*, the *Mirror*, *Mail*, *Daily Express*, *The Times*, Reuters, the Press Association and representatives of local radio and local newspapers, as well as freelancers and journalists from the foreign media.

SAT noted that regulators have guidance on how to cover terror attacks but that they are seriously flawed. It raised the example of IPSO, which has published guidelines on 'Reporting major incidents' but offers no solutions to the question of intrusion other than woolly entreaties to 'take care' and 'be sympathetic'. That document also notes that survivors and their family members will feel bombarded by requests but gives no suggestions on how to avoid that. The regulator's ten pages of guidance for those caught up in a major incident, which is already highly unlikely to be read by people in that situation, waits until page seven to suggest changing your voicemail message to say you don't want to speak to journalists. It's very much 'if you don't have a fire-retardant suit, try wrapping yourself in chocolate to walk through the inferno'-style advice.

Over half of survivors (52 per cent) said they had some positive experiences working with journalists. SAT recognised that 'journalists have a responsibility to report' but it concluded that media intrusion into the grief and lives of the injured and bereaved is 'endemic across the media'.

In the years that have followed its recommendations, very little has changed. Politicians and the royal family benefit from a system where getting pool clips – a single interview shared among all broadcasters – is common, but when it comes to traumatic events, there's still a thirsty rush to secure an exclusive on the most extreme and upsetting material.

The UK charity Disaster Action developed guidelines for reporters after working with families who'd been caught up in 30 different natural and human-created disasters. Based on that feedback, they created a list of six key factors that made working with the media more positive: honesty, acknowledgement, consent, control and compassion. Its guidelines say journalists should be transparent when approaching someone, explain the type of questions they might ask, how they might fit into the broader story and why they're interested in that particular interviewee's experience. What they shouldn't do is claim they 'know' what someone is going through. Elana Newman, research director of the Dart Center for Journalism and Trauma, told *Nieman Reports* that it was better to say 'I'm sorry that happened to you.'[192]

In the same article, Melissa Stranger, a social worker, psychotherapist and former journalist, said that reporters need to 'speak to their interviewee and see a person there, not just a source of information'. This is where the language of journalism is a problem. The habit of calling people you interview 'sources' is a product and cause of the disassociation Catherine Mayer spoke about. Journalists who live in a particular place and are part of a particular community which form their subject are less likely to see the people they talk to as 'sources'. When you arrive on a scene, dispatched by a national news organisation, it's a lot easier to lose sight of humanity, in part as a way of protecting yourself from the pain. Ed Yong, a staff writer at *The Atlantic*, put it well: 'If you respect the sources as people, then you can avoid the trap of treating them as these macabre circus acts for people to gawk at. I don't want people to gawk at them. I want readers to empathise with them.'

A more holistic approach to reporting on tragic events known as trauma-informed journalism has been discussed a lot in recent years but has yet to make significant inroads into the newsrooms of the UK. Tamara Cherry, author of *The Trauma Beat: Victims, Survivors and the Journalists Who Tell their Stories*, defines trauma-informed journalism as 'understanding what a trauma survivor is experiencing before you show up at their door and understanding how your actions will impact them after you pack up and leave.'[193] It's a form of journalism that sees reporting as a process that does not simply end when the story is filed but realises that the impact ripples on. Cherry continued: 'It's about forgetting all the rules that we usually abide by when we're interviewing . . . officials and politicians, and recognising that when it comes to trauma.'

When the tennis player Naomi Osaka announced in 2021

BREAKING

that she would not be attending press conferences at the French Open, it provoked indignant responses from large swathes of the press. Osaka wrote: 'I've often felt that people have no regard for athletes' mental health and this rings true whenever I see a press conference or partake in one. We're often sat there and asked questions that we've been asked multiple times before or asked questions that bring doubt into our minds and I'm just not going to subject myself to people that doubt me.' The most obvious attack offered by the most obvious people, like the relentless self-promoting contrarian Piers Morgan, was to call Osaka 'a brat' who was 'ducking media scrutiny'. The question of how much 'media scrutiny' a tennis player needs to subject themselves to hung in the air and the fact that Osaka has commercial sponsorships was the focus of a great deal of ire. But its another prominent example of the entitlement journalists can feel towards other people's experiences and emotions.

When you become the story, it's difficult to avoid also becoming something less than human: a character, a source or just a stereotype. Now more than ever, the media has access to resources and research that can help them put the wellbeing of the people they cover at the heart of their reporting. There are plenty of journalists who don't lose sight of the humanity of the people they deal with when covering tragic events but there are far too many that do. Whether that's down to self-preservation, pressure to get the scoop or a simple lack of care, the result can end up the same: a traumatic event can be made worse or that encounter with a member of the media can be the source of trauma itself.

12.

The Future of The News

Don't Shoot the Fortune Teller

'The only thing that makes life impossible is permanent, intolerable uncertainty; not knowing what comes next.'
– Ursula K. Le Guin, *The Left Hand of Darkness* (1969)

Making predictions about the future of the media is a brilliant way to guarantee you'll look stupid in a year's time, let alone five or ten. As I was researching this chapter, I came across a BBC News feature from 2005 with a headline that asked 'What Will Newspapers Look Like in 20 Years?'.[194] The news hook was the *Guardian*'s switch to a new format (the Berliner size, which was taller than a tabloid and narrower than a broadsheet), which required an £80 million investment in new presses and was presented as a game changer. In 2017, the *Guardian* left the Berliner behind, going tabloid so it could be printed on presses owned by Trinity Mirror, saving itself millions of pounds a year.

The prognostications in the BBC News piece sound quaint

BREAKING

now. One academic speculated that 'you could imagine newspapers existing as data which can be sent to many kinds of electronic screens' and that 'newspapers [might be] delivered to public screens in stations'. Meanwhile, a media commentator suggested the print newspaper would prevail because it's 'terribly convenient: how many newspaper-buyers read them on the loo?' Both were making their guesses two years before the iPhone turned the stumbling smartphone race into a sprint.

To get to the latest vision of the future, I want to take you back to what the future looked like at the start of the 2010s. In the 2011 documentary, *Page One: A Year Inside the New York Times*, the paper's then-media reporter – the late, legendary David Carr – clashed with Shane Smith, one of the founders of Vice, in a discussion about the latter's documentary on Liberia. Smith implied that Vice got far closer to the truth than the more venerable publication, albeit in a fractured, explosive and typically Vice-like manner:

> **CARR:** If you're a CNN viewer [watching the *Vice* documentary], and you go, 'Hmmm, I'm looking at some human shit on the beach ...'
> **SMITH:** Well, I've got to tell you one thing: I'm a regular guy and I got to these places and I go, 'OK, everyone talked to me about cannibalism, right? Everybody talked about cannibalism.' Now I'm getting a lot of shit for talking about cannibalism. Whatever. Everyone talked to me about cannibalism! ... That's fucking crazy! So the actual – our audience goes, 'That's fucking insane, like, that's nuts!' And *The New York Times*, meanwhile, is writing about

THE FUTURE OF THE NEWS

surfing and I'm sitting there going like, 'You know what? I'm not going to talk about surfing. I'm going to talk about cannibalism, because that fucks me up.'
CARR: Just a sec, time out. Before you ever went there, we've had reporters there reporting on genocide after genocide. Just because you put on a fucking safari helmet and looked at some poop doesn't give you the right to insult what we do. So continue . . .

The scene became a totemic example of the conflict between 'traditional' media and an insurgent new generation of online publishers that were in their pomp through the 2000s and 2010s. But it bears dissection and further scrutiny, especially from the vantage point of 2025, where Vice is bankrupted, hollowed out and under the control of private equity vultures, while *The New York Times* appears to be an ongoing success story.

Carr, who died in 2015, aged 58, was a reporter of the old school who approached his drug addiction and recovery memoir *The Night of the Gun* as though he were writing a profile of someone else, interviewing 60 people from his past to construct the narrative. But he wasn't a fusty old coot; as a media reporter, he took then-nascent organisations like BuzzFeed seriously. Asked in 2014 if BuzzFeed's initial forays into investigative journalism, which eventually led to the website winning a Pulitzer Prize, could be taken seriously, his unhesitating answer was, 'Of course they can be!'[195] Smith's snide comment about the *NYT* reporting on surfing in Liberia ignored a key bit of context: it had published a single piece on the phenomenon but it was written by a Liberian-American, Helene Cooper, who was born in the country's capital, Monrovia.[196] At the same time, the paper was reporting on Liberia's drug trade[197] and the hunt for millions of dollars in state assets pilfered by the country's deposed president, the war criminal Charles Taylor.[198]

When Carr's interview with Smith and other Vice executives appeared in *The New York Times*, there was no hint of the argument that was captured on film.[199] He later wrote that he didn't think it was relevant. Carr's verdict in print was that Vice's Liberia documentary was 'pretty rugged, pretty wonderful' and he summed up the company's overall aesthetic as 'nifty and naughty'. By 2014, undoubtedly softened further by the fact his daughter Erin Lee Carr now worked at Vice, Carr reflected on his earlier scepticism in a column headlined, 'Its Edge Intact, Vice Is Chasing Hard News': 'Being the crusty old-media scold felt good at the time, but recent events suggest that Vice is deadly serious about doing real news that people, yes, even young people, will actually watch.'[200]

He was equally bullish about the other new media companies that dominated coverage in those years, predicting that same year that BuzzFeed, Gawker, the Huffington Post, Vice and Vox, which had 'huge traffic but [were] still relatively small in terms of profit' would 'eventually mature into the legacy media of tomorrow'.[201] It was not a wild bet to make. The portents seemed positive for the companies he listed, but each in turn has crashed, burned or been brought to heel by the coldest of commercial realities. The dream of the millennial media companies was fuelled by a rush brought on by the drug of social traffic but, like any dealer, Facebook first got media companies into the product for free then jacked up the price once they were hooked.

THE FUTURE OF THE NEWS

The history of online media can be divided into BZ and AZ – Before Zuckerberg and After Zuckerberg. In the BZ era, which didn't end with the emergence of Facebook in 2005 but rather with its IPO and acquisition of Instagram in 2012, traffic was more like magic than a drug. Editors spent an inordinate amount of time trying to get their content shared on big link exchanges like Reddit, Digg and StumbleUpon, while hard news outlets, especially on the right, hoped they might catch the eye of Matt Drudge, whose site, The Drudge Report, could bring a deluge of visitors. Meanwhile, the largely snake-oil shifting industry of search engine optimisation promised to make sites irresistible to Google, with extremely variable levels of success.

On the financial side, Vice, BuzzFeed et al. gorged on cheap money, thanks to low interest rates, and were courted by legacy media vultures, private equity and venture capitalists. But big investments came with big expectations for growth and profitability. That rush to expand made them like exotic plants filling a small room, snuffing out the light from a single window with their foliage.

The greed of its founders (Shane Smith sold more than $100 million in shares just after Vice secured $500 million in investment in 2014) and the hunger of its investors for returns (in 2023, a source told the *FT* that the private equity firm TPG was 'choking the company to death'[202]) killed Vice. BuzzFeed is limping on as a producer of a listicles but it shuttered its award-winning news operation in 2023. Founder and CEO Jonah Peretti claimed he hadn't 'focused enough on profitability'.[203] Shareholders demanded BuzzFeed News' closure because awards did not translate into financial returns. For *The Atlantic*, former BuzzFeed staffer

BREAKING

Charlie Warzel wrote bluntly: 'The business of news gathering – not content creation – is expensive, and it does not scale.'[204]

In 2009, *The Atlantic* was one of many who made grim predictions about the death of the established media brands. The TV producer and *Atlantic* contributing editor Michael Hirschorn speculated about the imminent demise of *The New York Times* and suggested that a best-case scenario might be that it recast itself as 'a bigger, better, and less partisan version of the *Huffington Post*'.[205] It's cruel to carp over bad predictions, hindsight is 20:20 and you don't have to pay a fortune at the opticians to get it, but the idea that news brands with decades of heritage would be swept away in a tsunami of online innovation now looks more than a little myopic.

Instead of going from disaster and decline to rack and ruin, *The New York Times* has transformed its business over the past 15 years. It began in 2010 with the announcement that it would introduce a paywall, giving readers 20 free articles a month, after which they would have to stump up to read more. The media commentator Jeff Jarvis called it 'cockeyed economics' and argued that the *NYT* had abandoned the chance 'to become the preeminent news brand on earth' in favour of '[ducking] into its shell'.[206] Other critics decried the decision as 'doomed to fail'[207] and listed 'five reasons . . . why it's really dumb'.[208] At the end of the paywall's first year, the *NYT*'s digital subscriber base had grown to 390,000. Fast forward 12 years to December 2023 and that number was 10.36 million.

The *NYT* made its paywall more dynamic and sophisticated over the years, but it also fundamentally changed the nature of its business. It's no longer a traditional media company but an

THE FUTURE OF THE NEWS

entertainment company that does news. It's turned its constantly growing library of recipes and popular puzzles section, including its famous crossword, into standalone products as well as bundled with its news output. It acquired the product review site, Wirecutter, in 2016 and the sports site, The Athletic, in 2022 to expand both its content production and audience. Audio and video also play a huge part in its success, along with a selection of subscriber-only email newsletters. Throw in events and you realise that the *NYT* wants to be (and is) a lifestyle brand influencing every aspect of its subscribers' lives.

So is the future of the news making sure that you own and run a world-famous title founded in the nineteenth century and produce a lot of other attention-grabbing content that isn't actually news at all? Well ... a bit. Print as a mainstream proposition will inevitably die. Those daily newspapers still clinging to printing presses and a presence on shelves in newsagents and supermarkets will be gone within ten years. Even those titles with a long and illustrious history will not be able to make the economics of daily production work.

But one of the biggest mistakes that people make when predicting the future is to assume that new technology inevitably displaces the old. Video *still* hasn't killed the radio star but year after year, we're treated to predictions that suggest that the latest version of the screen will wipe out all the others. One reason that VR, putting aside many other issues with it, hasn't killed off movies or television is that entertainment that encourages you to sit back serves an entirely different purpose to immersive experiences.

The printed book is an even more resilient form of technology: you can take a book practically anywhere, it's tough and it never needs to be recharged. But books are designed to have a longer life than newspapers and the daily newspaper no longer makes economic sense. In the UK, newspapers now make most of their sales at the weekend – they've become a slow luxury rather than the means of getting a quick information hit. Leaning into that sense of indulgence is the future of news in print.

The future of the news business overall is probably a mix of the very big and the very small: legacy brands consolidating into big players in a diminished news market and niche outfits that survive by creating strong connections with smaller but more committed audiences. We're deep into an era of individual reporters becoming independent stars with their own brands but, in part as a reaction to that, we're also seeing news executives seeking increased profits by sweeping away as many human staff as possible in favour of automated options.

You should ask two questions about artificial intelligence (AI) and journalism any time some puffy-vest-wearing venture capitalist or startup douchebag suggests the future of news inevitably means surrendering further to the vagaries of an algorithm: why do you want to eradicate what humanity remains in journalism? And how do you think you're going to do that? While a large language model can be trained on millions upon millions of words of reporting and can regurgitate a passable impression of a news report, it cannot go out and investigate a story. In its current state, AI is not creative, it is imitative. To be a like-for-like replacement for a *good* human journalist, the AI would need to have a general intelligence, capable of independent and creative reasoning, something that many experts believe will *never* happen. However, it's necessary

THE FUTURE OF THE NEWS

to look at the ways in which it *is* impacting the way journalism works to understand the threat it poses.

AI has been infiltrating the journalism industry for some time. The appeal of automation and cost-cutting is as strong (or even stronger) for media executives as it is to bosses in any other industry. Since 2015, the Associated Press has been using AI to automatically write thousands upon thousands of earnings reports. The news agency proudly called itself 'one of the first news organizations to leverage artificial intelligence' and said in 2019 that it had gone from producing 300 articles based on companies' earnings reports every quarter to 3,700.[209]

It's appropriate that finance reporting has been at the forefront of using AI in journalism because the industry it covers has been harnessing machine learning for some time to get a further edge in the quick-twitch world of trading. AP's rivals at Bloomberg and Reuters both use AI to generate reports. All three justify their use of AI as a means of 'freeing up' journalists and other staff to work on more interesting jobs rather than being tied up writing tedious data stories that bots can produce faster and with fewer errors.

Using AI to summarise articles written by human journalists is already becoming common too. Several Nordic newspapers, including *Verdens Gang* (Norway), *Aftonbladet* (Sweden) and *Helsingen Sanomat* (Finland), have started using generative AI to add bullet points to the top of their articles. The summaries – known as Snabbversions ('quick versions') – increased the time the audience of the *Aftonbladet* website spent reading articles compared to those without them. The newspaper's editor, Martin Schori, told *Press Gazette* that the newsroom was surprised by the findings and initially thought they were a mistake.[210]

BREAKING

In both of these cases, the comforting fairytale that executives try to tell journalists is that AI will free them from boredom but won't take away their role in writing *real* reporting. It's as hard to believe as a woman emerging from a lake with a magic sword or a bunch of miniature miners living platonically in the woods with a princess. The creep of AI into areas where real reporting and expertise would once have been a prerequisite is speeding up all the time.

In January 2023, it emerged that the tech news company CNET had been publishing financial advice articles using what it called 'automation technology' – a clumsy euphemism for AI – but hid the bots building those articles behind a byline that read 'Written by CNET Money Staff'. CNET is owned by Red Ventures, a media conglomerate that makes most of its revenue from encouraging readers to click on affiliate links that guarantee it a small fee whenever someone buys a product or service. The automated CNET articles were choked with errors and littered with lies that large language models are so prone to creating and which people with a financial stake in their success have rebranded 'hallucinations', injecting an unwelcome sense of whimsy into something serious. CNET's AI models plagiarised from other sources extensively and after the project was revealed by a human journalist, Frank Landymore at *Futurism*,[211] it had to issue corrections on the majority of the articles produced by the project. *Futurism* found that a number of the AI pieces were identical to articles published by the publication's competitors. In the end, the content was thoroughly overhauled by humans whose names appeared in the bylines under the label 'our experts'. CNET is still using AI tools.

THE FUTURE OF THE NEWS

When *Sports Illustrated* pumped out a torrent of AI sludge, it went even further than CNET. It published 'articles' supplied by a third-party company that were bylined to non-existent writers whose profile pictures were AI-generated headshots purchased from stock image marketplaces. Once again, it was *Futurism* who broke the news of the AI artifice, noticing that the articles were frequently reassigned to new bylines linked to different invented writers.[212] When it approached *Sports Illustrated* for comment, the articles were erased. It then spotted that The Street, another site owned by *Sports Illustrated*'s parent company, Arena Group, was playing the same game – generating stories attributed to totally fictional writers with AI-generated faces.

In November 2023, Reporters Sans Frontières and 16 partner organisations including the International Press Institute, the Pulitzer Centre and the Thomson Foundation launched the Paris Charter on AI and Journalism. Its ten principles are intended to offer a framework for the future use of AI in reporting and ... they'll be utterly ignored in the pursuit of cost savings and increased profits. The tenth principle in particular, which calls for 'formal agreements that ensure the sustainability of journalism and uphold the long-term shared interest of the media and journalists', is already being blown away by the greed and short-sightedness of media executives.

There are instances of suspicion, many news organisations have blocked AI platforms from accessing their content and *The New York Times* is currently suing OpenAI, the creators of ChatGPT, for copyright infringement – albeit after discussions about a licensing deal fell through. But in the majority of cases, publishers have begun to cosy up to the emerging AI platforms just as they previously did to the social media companies. In December 2023, Axel Springer – the parent company of the German newspapers *Bilt* and *Welt*, the Politico network of political sites and *Business Insider* – signed a deal with OpenAI worth more than $10 million a year to access both its historic data and its new content. The Associated Press signed a similar agreement to license its news archive. And in May 2024, Rupert Murdoch's News Corp signed a multi-year deal to let OpenAI use new and archived material from its publications in the US, UK and Australia. Effectively, OpenAI, with the help of its major investor, Microsoft, has been rewarded for years of scraping from news sites without permission.

Another reason for this acquiescence is the media's previous experiences with tech platforms: having effectively seen their traffic held hostage by Facebook with years of algorithm tweaks and changes in business focus, news publishers are frightened and about to fall into the same trap again. The COO of a leading UK news provider, quoted anonymously in the Reuters Institute for the Study of Journalism's 2024 trends report, predicted with almost tragic naivety: 'There's an opportunity for the industry to work with AI players to design a symbiotic ecosystem and that's an opportunity we must not squander.'

Too many media executives have allowed themselves to be taken in by tech industry propaganda, convinced that generative AI domination is inevitable and unstoppable. In June 2023, when Axel Springer announced a €100m programme of cuts with 200 redundancies at *Bild*, its memo to staff said that it would 'unfortunately be parting ways with colleagues who have tasks that in the digital world are performed by AI and/or automated processes'. The message went on to rub a further shaker of salt in

THE FUTURE OF THE NEWS

the wound by warning that further editorial cuts would come as a result of 'the opportunities of artificial intelligence'.

The Paris Charter also calls for media outlets to be transparent about how they use AI systems. That feels especially unlikely in the UK, where transparency doesn't sit well with publishers who are rarely comfortable letting their audiences see how the sausage is made and are deeply paranoid about their rivals getting wind of their particular recipe, even if most of the products taste very similar.

But beyond the further destruction of trust, media executives salivating at the thought of AI slashing newsroom costs and getting rid of most of those irritating human beings (who have an awful tendency to unionise) are making a fatal assumption that audiences will accept it. They won't. Presented with material that is utterly devoid of any human personality or connection, they'll just stop paying attention. The example of news websites strangled by ads and relying on lowest-common-denominator content already proves this. Cheap and sensational slop can draw people in for a while, but it never produces loyalty. When Hannah Arendt, the historian and philosopher, was interviewed by Roger Errera in 1974, she couldn't have imagined the amount of visual and textual sludge generative AI would pump into the world, but she left us a good summary of its effects: 'If everybody always lies to you, the consequence is not that you believe the lies, but rather that nobody believes anything any longer.'[213]

So while some welcome AI and others try and run from it, we can draw one ultimate conclusion on the future it will play in journalism: it is for us to decide. Despite AI already being used for taking over boring and repetitive tasks like compiling results from

BREAKING

the financial markets or synthesising large amounts of statistical data, that's not *reporting*. Reporting is a complicated process with lots of individual elements and it's expensive. That's why tech bros and media company executives are enamoured with the idea of AI replacing human journalists: the output would be much worse but it would also be much cheaper. For men in power, and it usually is men, the poisoning of the information environment, like the pumping of shit into rivers, is of little concern. They can afford bottled water and they're quite happy for other people to swim through the sewage. A world in which fact and fiction are swirled together works well for the ultra-rich, for whom a well-informed and engaged population have always been a threat. Very wealthy people prefer journalists to be flatterers and sycophants or simply not present at all. AI journalism will suit the uber-wealthy because it won't ask anything of them.

But journalism corrupted by AI is not inevitable. If we want, we can choose a future in which real reporting, imbued with decency, empathy and compassion, is valued. The argument that even bigger job cuts are inevitable due to AI is motivated reasoning. If audiences reject AI-generated content as crap and refuse to buy it then companies will soon go off the idea. AI should be treated as an existential threat to truth, a sewage pipe spewing crap into the waters of our public debate and civil society. Real people seeking out real stories and trying to offer their audience the truthful and the unexpected should be seen as the organic option versus AI's pesticide-laden, nutrient-deficient crop.

Looking to tech billionaires as the cavalry coming to save the media is a mistake. There are echoes of the nineteenth- and early

THE FUTURE OF THE NEWS

twentieth-century media barons this book started by considering. When *Time* magazine made Taylor Swift its Person of the Year in 2023, Marc Benioff, the founder of the software company Salesforce, who bought the struggling publication in 2018 with his wife Lynne, excitedly (and inaccurately) claimed it was 'the best-selling issue of all time!' A few weeks later, *Time*'s union said 15 per cent of the magazine's unionised editorial staff had been laid off.[214] The future of news is not the largesse of billionaires who buy titles as another kind of bauble to indicate how influential they are. The media has long been blighted with executives who have no idea of what it takes to produce good reporting. Mega-rich owners who made their money in other sectors often represent that problem amplified ten thousand-fold.

Amazon founder Jeff Bezos acquired the *Washington Post* for $250 million in 2013 and brought the mentality that he had used to run the 'everything store' to the world of editorial hires. Marty Baron, then executive editor of the *Post*, was told that he didn't need more editors to accomplish Bezos' plan to take the paper from a regional powerhouse to a global one. In a decidedly Amazon-esque flourish, reporters were classed as 'direct' employees and editors as 'indirect', with the instruction that the number of indirect staff should be kept down. In his memoir, *Collision of Power*, Baron explained the trick he devised to get the editors he needed: 'To avoid setting off alarms up the line, my deputies and I would strip the word "editor" from proposed new positions whenever possible. "Analyst" or "strategist" were among the limited set of workarounds.'[215]

While it's been said that Bezos sees the company as a legacy for his family, it appears he purchased the paper thinking his experience of dominating retail through technology would translate to the news business. It hasn't really. The media has structural issues that aren't easily fixed. Bezos has found that out, much like Laurene Powell Jobs who bought a controlling stake in *The Atlantic* for $160m; the biotech billionaire Patrick Soon-Shiong who paid an inflated $500m for the *Los Angeles Times* and the Benioffs, with their $190m spending spree for *Time*. And journalists who told themselves that this new class of press barons might be content to treat media acquisitions like expensive heirlooms are out of luck. The layoffs and restructurings continue in this new golden era, which now looks like it may be more gold-plated.

A future where news organisations are the playthings of billionaires is not a bright one. The problems of the old-school proprietors – interference and conflicts of interest – are heightened when the owner has only a partial interest in the press and is even more focused on prestige and influence. The level of wealth Bezos has makes Murdoch look almost quaint. While sources within the *Post*'s newsroom say that Bezos has never taken any steps to interfere with its editorial line or even shown an inclination to do so, it's not necessary. Reporters and editors there know that their ultimate boss has many commercial interests and it would be unwise to criticise them. No one needs to say it out loud.

In his open letter to employees upon acquiring the company, Bezos wrote: 'The values of the *Post* do not need changing. The paper's duty will remain to its readers and not to the private interests of its owners. We will continue to follow the truth wherever it leads.' It's fine rhetoric but any mogul making that purchase would have said the same; it's smart marketing

THE FUTURE OF THE NEWS

that has very little to do with reality. Rich people do not buy media organisations to see them attack their interests or humiliate their friends. They buy them to burnish their legacies and to extend their soft power. And while Bezos does not run Amazon day to day, it is the goose that lays his golden eggs and there is no chance that he will tolerate foxes from the fourth estate – especially foxes fed by his largesse – sneaking around the farm.

There is an argument, of course, that Bezos may have bought the *Post* because its ideological position was already pretty close to his own and so he simply hasn't needed to interfere with the editorial stance. Professor Robert W. McChesney, the American political economist and media critic, told *Colombia Journalism Review* that Bezos 'didn't need to make any changes; the *Post* had already adopted the establishment, pro-corporate view. Its editorial line was pretty compatible with his on the issues that mattered to him.'[216] Perhaps when you're that rich, it's easier to buy your preferred ideology right off the peg.

When Bezos tweeted to attack a post from President Biden's account about raising taxes on corporations in May 2022, the *Post* reported that 'the White House responded by pointing out that Bezos' attacks emerged days after Biden met in the Oval Office with labour leaders behind Amazon's unionization drive, which the company has vehemently opposed'.[217] So far, so good. But after Bezos fired another social media shot at the White House, *Post* opinion writer Catherine Rampell – who'd called for higher taxes for Bezos in a 2018 column – published a piece castigating the Democrats for their 'misguided economic policies',[218] taking a very similar line to the one put forward by the big boss. Bezos enthusiastically retweeted the column.

BREAKING

The influence of the owner on the *Washington Post* was made even more apparent in October 2024 when it announced that it would not be endorsing a presidential candidate less than two weeks before the election. The paper's editorial board had agreed to back Kamala Harris but was prevented from publishing the endorsement on the same day that executives from Bezos' space exploration firm, Blue Origin, met officials from Donald Trump's campaign.[219] After newsroom unrest – including the paper's cartoonist publishing a dark formless image skewering the paper's 'Democracy dies in darkness' slogan, criticism from former editors and reporters, resignations from the editorial board, and the loss of 250,000 subscribers in less than a week (approximately 10 per cent of its paid circulation) – Bezos defended the decision in the pages of the *Post*:

> What presidential endorsements actually do is create a perception of bias. A perception of non-independence. Ending them is a principled decision, and it's the right one. Eugene Meyer, publisher of the *Washington Post* from 1933 to 1946, thought the same, and he was right. By itself, declining to endorse presidential candidates is not enough to move us very far up the trust scale, but it's a meaningful step in the right direction. I wish we had made the change earlier than we did, in a moment further from the election and the emotions around it. That was inadequate planning, and not some intentional strategy.

The timing is precisely what made Bezos' explanation so unconvincing. As a move to gain greater trust from the *Washington*

THE FUTURE OF THE NEWS

Post's readers, it was a bust. And Bezos' decision to explain the move felt more than a little like a Wizard of Oz moment, the man behind the curtain demanding that the audience pay no attention to him or all those government contracts that Amazon and Blue Origin bid on every year. The latter's deal to build a lunar lander for NASA is worth $3.4 billion alone.

In a piece for *Jacobin*, Andrew Perez and David Sirota called Bezos' tweets 'a digital era version of *Citizen Kane* behaviour'.[220] In *Citizen Kane*, the titular character's legal guardian quizzes him on the wisdom of pouring money into a newspaper that is costing him a million dollars a year, only for Kane to reply that if the losses continue at that rate, he'll 'have to close this place in . . . 60 years.' Bezos is so rich that he could sustain the *Post*'s losses for as long as he wants. He has more wealth than any press baron in history – and that shouldn't be comforting to anyone in journalism. It should be terrifying. Bezos' supposed desire for a global *Post* only increases the likelihood that the future of news is dominated by a small number of huge outlets, controlled by a very narrow set of individuals.

Sir Max Hastings, the former editor of the *Daily Telegraph*, concluded in his memoir, *Editor*, that 'whatever the professed convictions of proprietors, most are moneylogues rather than ideologues' whose political convictions 'add up to an uncomplicated desire to make the world a safe place for rich men to live in'.[221] Surveying a landscape where the new breed of proprietors has even less emotional connection to news than the ones who came before them, Hastings' words only seem truer with each passing year.

*

BREAKING

So, with the rise of AI and the intrusion of the tech billionaire press barons, where does this leave us? A 2019 report from the Reuters Institute for the Study of Journalism outlined five things that its authors – the institute's director and a professor of political communication at Oxford University, Professor Rasmus Kleis Nelson, and its senior research associate, Meera Selva – said everybody needed to know about the future of journalism:

1. That media still creates the news agenda, but platform companies control access to audiences.
2. That 'automated serendipity and incidental exposure' pop filter bubbles and drive people to more and more diverse sources of information.
3. That journalism is often losing the battle for people's attention and the public's trust.
4. That the challenge to the business models that fund news is weakening professional journalism, leaving the media more vulnerable to commercial and political pressures.
5. That news is more diverse than ever and 'the best journalism is, in many cases, better than ever'.[222]

Let's take those statements in turn. The first, about the dominance of platform companies, carries with it an assumption that the FANG corporations – Facebook (Meta), Apple, Netflix and Google – are like great empires destined for many decades of power. But history offers plenty of examples where dominant companies fell into decline or were broken up by politicians or taken down by new challengers. As I write, the US government has besieged Apple with an anti-trust lawsuit, Netflix is struggling to make its

THE FUTURE OF THE NEWS

model financially sustainable in the long term, Meta is drifting, having haemorrhaged hundreds of millions of dollars on the dead end of Mark Zuckerberg's Metaverse dreams, and Google's core services are becoming less and less useable even as it embarrasses itself with its AI endeavours.

As for point two, the rhetoric of 'automated serendipity' – algorithms leading people to sources they'd otherwise not encounter – is wishful thinking dressed up as science. The tech companies' business models are built on keeping our attention and algorithms that deliver more of what they know we already like bolster that. The report puts great faith in the power of technology to push people out of their comfort zones and to encourage them to shatter the echo chambers that exist beyond our screens. The diversity of sources and the quality of those sources are not directly correlated.

Next, the third point suggests that journalism is losing the battle for people's attention and failing to maintain public trust. This is true and only getting worse. In part, that's because there are simply more demands for attention, but it's also because journalism has not worked nearly hard enough to change its approach to gaining it. Many hacks think they can arrive on a new platform and simply do what they have always done, certain that the authority bestowed upon them by their publication's relative fame will power them through.

Considering the fourth point, publishers spent years not valuing the work of their journalists and failing to invest in it. It's not surprising that audiences have come to expect journalism to be free and grew increasingly frustrated by the tidal wave of low-quality content pushed towards them. The way money is distributed in news media is also completely unbalanced, with executives still paying themselves huge salaries and bestowing lavish fees to a small group of stars while holding down the wages of the majority of staff who make their products.

And finally, the sheer volume of news produced may be higher but it's created the same discovery problem that bedevils streaming services. It's even harder to pick out good journalism from the vast amount of dreck out there than it is to find good songs or TV shows. For about a decade, social media served as a means of surfacing good content, but Elon Musk has made finding interesting things to read on the renamed X deliberately harder and Meta has decided, not without good reason, that prioritising news articles on Facebook kicked up too many political problems. If the best journalism is 'better than ever', it's becoming like truffles – expensive, hard to snuffle out and an acquired taste.

There's also still a place for instinct in predicting what comes next. I began this book by looking at the newspaper culture that Lord Northcliffe created and Rupert Murdoch redefined. Both men made mass-market products that made mass-market money. While Murdoch has not come up with some definitive solution to a media business where subscriptions haven't replaced the ad revenue lost to Google and Facebook, he did predict the direction of travel back in 2006. In a speech to The Stationers' Company, one of the City of London's professional guilds, he said that media would become like fast food: 'People will consume it on the go, watching news, sport and film clips as they travel to and from work on mobiles or handheld wireless devices.'[223] It was the year before the iPhone and he knew what was coming.

It's important that Murdoch used the phrase 'fast food'. It reflects a philosophy that says, give the people what they want.

THE FUTURE OF THE NEWS

If they want a burger, fries and a milkshake, that's what you should serve them. Even if that diet is bad for their health, they're free to make that choice. And if they don't want to eat fast food, you can always accuse them of being elitist. Fox News is fast food. The *Sun* is fast food. *The Times* and the *Wall Street Journal* are fast food marketed like Five Guys to persuade their consumers that despite all the fat, salt and sugar, this is a better class of fast food.

The common attack from traditional media is that YouTube has accelerated the culture of information as fast food and TikTok has sped things up even more. One reason that Establishment publishers are at war with those platforms while at the same time trying to master them is that they provide a much wider variety of attention-grabbing material, including plenty of gourmet options. There are thousands of people making a living on YouTube by creating work that looks an awful lot like journalism. A future for news as a niche product delivered by these new and trusted groups of independent journalists is already out there. The human instinct to be curious and to seek out the truth isn't reliant on nineteenth- and twentieth-century ideas of what a news organisation should be. That idea only serves those players clinging to relevance to pretend that it is.

Journalism can have a bright future even if the companies that have dominated it for the last 50 years do not. There are more ways of reporting on the world today than ever before and more means of getting paid for those stories. Yes, it's a challenge to do that without the resources of a big company behind you but, in recent years, new publications born out of carcasses of online outlets that couldn't survive have shown how independents can grow. There is scope for more collaboration, for cooperatives, for local news

BREAKING

organisations that return to the premise of serving a community and for specialists who turn their passion into reporting for which people will pay.

There is no inevitable future of the news, but we know that it doesn't need to be given wholesale to tech billionaires or surrendered to AI. It's easy to be cynical – in this book, I've shown that many times – but while we continue to ask questions about the people and world around us, journalism will have a future.

Epilogue

At the start of this book, I quoted a broadcaster who worried that people now think 'journalism is worthy of scorn and contempt'. For all the criticisms I've detailed in the previous pages, I don't believe that. We need good journalism. Without professional curiosity and fierce scrutiny, the world gets worse. We can all help foster good journalism by seeking it out and choosing to spend our time and, crucially, our money supporting it.

In return for that support, we should expect journalists to hold themselves accountable and be less quick to rally around when their profession falls short. We should read, listen and watch with an openness to new ideas but with scepticism as our constant companion. Most of all, we should reserve our contempt for those obviously out to muddy the waters, but we should match that with a willingness to change our minds through honest arguments.

The era of journalism that was defined by Northcliffe and refined by Murdoch is in its dying days. It's a slow decline and there's plenty of thrashing and wailing as the giants fall.

BREAKING

But we will always find new ways of telling stories and there will always be a desire to find out about the world around us. Some things have already got better: The naked tabloid cruelty of the 1980s and 1990s is no longer acceptable and many younger journalists simply won't tolerate newsrooms where cruelty trumps humanity.

It's easy to sink into despair thinking about the spread of disinformation and misinformation, the shadow of AI and the notion that future generations might not care about journalism at all. But this time of upheaval is also a time of great opportunity. Young people are as curious as they have ever been and there is greater access to the tools needed to report on the world around us and share those discoveries than ever before.

The solution to broken news isn't to give up completely but to keep feeding our instincts to seek out the truth. You need good journalism and good journalism needs you.

Acknowledgements

Writing a book that sets out to a critique a whole industry isn't a great way to make new friends. Thankfully, I'm lucky to have some good ones already.

Breaking would not have been possible without a lot of people who were willing to talk to me anonymously about how they do their jobs. You know who you are. I'm also enormously grateful to those who are quoted by name – Nesrine Malik, Stephen Bush, Nish Kumar, Catherine Mayer, John D. Lewis and Gareth McLean – and to Stephanie Hawthorne, Tom Dunmore, James Brown, John Doran, Rowan Pelling and Tom Mills, whose input contributed massively to how this book turned out.

I'd also like to thank the readers of my newsletter, 'Conquest of the Useless', for supporting me in writing media criticism on a weekly basis, the viewers of The Paper Thing, who made me laugh and think in equal measure, and the denizens of the Discord server, where a real community has grown and thrived. All of this would have felt very lonely without you.

BREAKING

My best friend John Lynch deserves special thanks for the support he's given me since we first met in a rehearsal room aged 11. I'm also thankful for all the conversations I've had about the media and so many other things with John Hill over the years and for all the help and friendship from Rob, DB, Mike, Julie and Tony, among many others.

I'd like to offer a mix of gratitude and apology to all my former colleagues and editors. I'm especially indebted to my editor, Ellie Carr, who brought order to the chaos and kept the faith whenever I was losing it, and to Liz Marvin for a superlative copy edit. Special thanks to Ian Winwood for helping to put me on the path to writing this book and to my agent, Cathryn Summerhayes, for having faith in my ideas.

My mum and dad have always said I had a book in me and, as always, they were right. I'm so very lucky to have had them behind me all the way. I'm also very grateful for all the love and wisdom that my gran has offered me over the years.

Most of all, I want to thank my wife, Kate, who is the love of my life, my first and best reader, and the person who has put up with the most as I worked to turn a pile of thoughts into something that made sense. I can't imagine doing any of this without her and my wonderful stepdaughter, Rosie.

Endnotes

1. BECOMING A JOURNALIST

1   H.R. Fox Bourne, *English Newspapers: Chapters in the History of Journalism*, Chatto & Windus, 1887.

2   F. Hunter, *Hacks and Dons: Teaching at the London University Journalism School, 1919–1939, Its Origins, Development and Influence*, Kultura, 2012.

3   T. Kessler, *Paper Cuts: How I Destroyed the British Music Press and Other Misadventures*, White Rabbit, 2022.

2. WHO OWNS THE NEWS?

4   E. Longford, *Wellington: Pillar of the State*, Panther, 1972.

5   Lord Beaverbrook, *Men and Power: 1917–1918*, Hutchinson, 1956.

6   T. Clarke, *My Northcliffe Diary*, V. Gollanz, 1931.

7   P. Brendon, *Eminent Edwardians*, Secker & Warburg, 1979.

8   S. Hewlett, 'Why Britain has reason to be grateful to Rupert Murdoch', *Guardian*, 28 Apr 2013.

9   W. Marsh, *Young Rupert: The Making of the Murdoch Empire*, Scribe, 2023.

10   J.W. Robertson Scott, *The Story of the 'Pall Mall Gazette', of Its First Editor Frederick Greenwood and of Its Founder George Murray Smith*, Oxford University Press, 1950.

11   'Memoirs: The Perils of Christine', *Time*, 10 Oct 1969.

12   Ibid.

13 M. Wolff, *The Man Who Owns the News: Inside the Secret World of Rupert Murdoch*, Bodley Head, 2008.

14 D. Frost, *An Autobiography: Part One – From Congregations to Audiences*, HarperCollins, 1993.

15 B. Grundy, 'The Press', *Spectator*, 26 Jul 1969.

16 P. Brogan, 'Citizen Murdoch', *The New Republic*, 11 Nov 1982.

17 P. Chippindale and C. Horrie, *Stick It Up Your Punter: The Rise and Fall of The Sun*, Faber & Faber, 2012.

18 B. Page, *The Murdoch Archipelago*, Simon & Schuster, 2011.

19 Ibid.

20 R. McGibbon, 'Old Mac Opens Up', *Press Gazette*, 2006.

21 T. Conlan, 'MacKenzie speaks out on Hillsborough comments', *Guardian*, 12 Jan 2007.

22 V. Lenin, 'Where to Begin', *Iskra*, May 1901.

23 N. Davies, *Hack Attack: How the Truth Caught Up with Rupert Murdoch*, Chatto & Windus, 2014.

24 M. Sweney, 'Sunday Express editor David Wooding departs Reach amid further job cuts', *Guardian*, 16 Nov 2024.

3. WHAT'S THE STORY?

25 J. Galtung and M. Holmboe Ruge, 'The Structure of Foreign News', *Journal of Peace Research* vol. 2, no. 1, 1965.

26 H. Caple and M. Bednarek, 'Delving into the Discourse: Approaches to News Value in Journalism Studies and Beyond', Dec 2013.

27 U. Haagerup, 'Academic who defined news principles says journalists are too negative', *Guardian*, 18 Jan 2019.

28 For example: M. Hunt, 'I went from earning £17k at 18 to buying my first home by 21', *Daily Telegraph*, 14 Aug 2020.

29 D. O'Neill and T. Harcup, 'What is news? News values revisited (again)', *Journalism Studies*, Mar 2016.

30 L. Gerard, 'How Fleet Street missed the Post Office scandal', *New European*, 9 Jan 2024.

31 R. Snoddy, 'Delivering justice for the sub-postmasters', *InPublishing*, 14 Feb 2022.

ENDNOTES

32   'Post Office Scandal: Why has justice taken two decades?', *The News Agents*, 12 Jan 2024.

33   'Examining trends in editorial standards in coverage of transgender issues', IPSO, Nov 2020.

34   E. Folan, 'Transphobia is on the rise – and the press is to blame', *Pink News*, 9 Sept 2023.

35   https://x.com/PatrickStrud/status/1548288970198355969

36   M. Miner, 'Undercover Journalism's Last Call', *Chicago Reader*, 3 Oct 2002.

37   P. Mejia, 'How a Chicago Dive Bar Exposed Corruption and Changed Journalism', Atlas Obscura, 8 Mar 2019.

38   R. Lloyd Parry, 'Inside a Purpose-built Guerrilla Lair', *Independent*, 27 Nov 2001.

39   M. Forney, 'Inside the Tora Bora Caves,' *Time*, 11 Dec 2001.

40   M. Shaw, 'Bullies Film Fights by Phone', *Times Educational Supplement*, 21 Jan 2005.

41   A. Harrison, 'A Complete History of Happy Slapping', *Vice*, 26 Feb 2018.

42   'Mylene's Happy Slap Hell', *Daily Mirror*, 8 Dec 2005.

43   E. Behr, *Anyone Here Been Raped and Speaks English?: A Foreign Correspondent's Life Behind the Lines*, Viking Press, 1979.

44   Andrew Marr interview with Noam Chomsky, *The Big Idea*, BBC, Feb 1996.

45   F. Naqvi, 'Is Anyone Here a Muslim, With a Victim Anecdote for My Column?', The Wire, 30 Nov 2020.

4. AN ANATOMY OF THE NEWS

46   M. Seddon, 'Smaller Size, Higher Brow?', *New Statesman*, 21 Feb 2005.

47   I. Betteridge, 'TechCrunch: Irresponsible journalism', Technovia, 23 Feb 2009.

48   A. Withnall, 'Ed Miliband fails to look normal while eating a bacon sandwich ahead of campaign tour', *Independent*, 22 May 2014.

49   F. Graddon, '"We're doing for bums what we've done for boobs for years": M&S hails its new £15 knickers with built-in padding to give backsides oomph and create an ample-bottomed curvey silhouette', *Daily Mail*, 13 Mar 2024.

50   A. Razazi, 'To Tie For: *Griselda* star Sofia Vergara, 51, shows off incredible figure in lace-up swimsuit', *Sun*, 14 Jun 2024.

BREAKING

51   S. Lyall, 'In Trumpworld, the Grown-Ups in the Room All Left, and Got Book Deals', *The New York Times*, 1 Aug 2020.

52   'Uranium shipped to UK on passenger jet originated from Pakistan', Sky News, 11 Jan 2023.

53   S. Wooler, 'Warning over risk to pets from human painkillers', *Daily Mail*, 13 Mar 2024.

54   X. Leatham, 'A canine companion can result in fewer dog days', *Daily Mail*, 13 Mar 2024.

5. A MATTER OF OPINIONS

55   C. L. Edson, *The Gentle Art of Columning*, Brentano, 1920.

56   W. Turvill, 'Marina Hyde on the Art of Writing a Column: "It's a trade. You just have to fill the space"', Press Gazette, 5 Oct 2022.

57   J. Moir, 'A Strange, Lonely and Troubling Death…', *Daily Mail*, 16 Oct 2009.

58   C. Brooker, 'Why There Was Nothing "Human" about Jan Moir's Column on the Death of Stephen Gately', *Guardian*, 16 Oct 2009.

59   J. Moir, 'The Truth about My Views on the Tragic Death of Stephen Gately', *Daily Mail*, 23 Oct 2009.

60   R. Liddle, 'A Teenage Girl, a Maths Teacher and a Righteous Tabloid Fury', *Spectator*, 29 Sept 2012.

61   S. Hattenstone, 'Rod Liddle Interview: "I'm not a bigot"', *Guardian*, 13 Jun 2014.

62   G. Coren, 'Poor Elon Hates His Job as Much as I Hate Mine', *The Times*, 16 Jul 2021.

63   G. Coren, 'Did You Really Expect to Turn over a New Page?', *The Times*, 17 Aug 2021.

64   M. Dowd, 'Liberties; The Slander Strategy', *The New York Times*, 28 Jan 1998.

65   M. Dowd, 'Liberties; The Price Of His Pleasure', *The New York Times*, 8 Feb 1998.

66   M. Dowd, 'Liberties; President Irresistible', *The New York Times*, 18 Feb 1998.

67   M. Dowd, 'Liberties; Monica's Frowny Face', *The New York Times*, 31 May 1998.

68   M. Dowd, 'Liberties; Feathered and Tarred', *The New York Times*, 10 Jun 1998.

69   M. Dowd, 'Liberties; Monica And Me', *The New York Times*, 17 Jun 1998.

70   M. Dowd, 'Liberties; Monica Gets Her Man', *The New York Times*, 23 Aug 1998.

ENDNOTES

71   M. Dowd, 'Liberties; Maladroit Du Seigneur', *The New York Times*, 30 Sept 1998.

72   M. Dowd, 'What's Up, Slut?', *The New York Times*, 15 Jul 2006.

73   M. Dowd, 'Burning the Beret', *The New York Times*, 6 May 2014.

74   M.Tani, 'Maureen Dowd: The only thing I wish I could take back is a negative column I wrote about Seinfeld', *Business Insider*, 14 Sept 2016.

75   J. Samuel, 'Politicians should take a hint from the King', *The Times*, 3 May 2023.

76   'Elitist Britain 2019', The Sutton Trust and the Social Mobility Commission.

77   R. Groen, 'Salman Rushdie Gets Back to His Day Job', *Globe & Mail*, 1 Sept 2012.

6. POLITICAL THEATRE

78   R. Day, *Grand Inquisitor*, Pan Books, 1990.

79   I. Hargreaves, 'Kebabbed Pt.1', BBC News, 26 Mar 2000.

80   L. Barber, 'The Knight Historical', *Literary Review*, Mar 1993.

81   S. Hoggart, 'A Homage to Levin, Father of the Modern Sketch', *Guardian*, 22 Oct 2004.

82   J. Nott, 'Why I walked out on Robin Day', *Daily Telegraph*, 14 Mar 2002.

83   W. Turvill, 'Andrew Marr: Questioning from "tortured, angry" Jeremy Paxman no replacement for Cameron-Miliband debate', *Press Gazette*, 30 Mar 2015.

84   '"It was an absolute riot": nine *New Statesman* political editors reunite', *New Statesman*, 12 Apr 2023.

85   A. Marr, 'Andrew Marr webchat – your questions answered on Brexit, the BBC and the Beatles', *Guardian*, 12 Apr 2017.

7. THE IMPRACTICAL QUESTION OF IMPARTIALITY

86   E. Maitlis, 'When an agent of the Tory Party decides the BBC's "bias", it's a huge problem', *Guardian*, 25 Aug 2022.

87   A. Briggs, *The History of Broadcasting in The United Kingdom Vol.1: The Birth of Broadcasting*, Oxford University Press, 1961.

88   C. Higgins, 'What can the origins of the BBC tell us about its future?', *Guardian*, 15 Apr 2014.

BREAKING

89   Lord Reith, 'Forsan', *Parliamentary Affairs*, Volume XVII, Issue 1, Aug 1963, Pages 23–30.

90   G. Orwell, 'As I Please', *Tribune*, 21 Jan 1944.

91   A. Pearson, 'The BBC lost its way the minute Auntie turned into an aggravating know-it-all', *Daily Telegraph*, 19 Jan 2022.

92   Letters to the Editor, *Daily Telegraph*, 19 Jan 2022.

93   P. Beaumont, A. Barnett and G. Hinsliff, 'Iraqi mobile labs nothing to do with germ warfare, report finds', *Observer*, 15 Jun 2003.

94   K. Marsh, *Stumbling Over Truth: The Inside Story of the Sexed-up Dossier, Hutton and the BBC*, Biteback, 2012.

95   'What Andrew Gilligan said in the *Mail on Sunday*', *Guardian*, 22 Jul 2003.

96   L. Katz and M. Tempest, 'Kelly naming would "fuck Gilligan" – Campbell', 22 Sept 2003.

97   T. Mangold, 'Do you remember what happened to David Kelly?', *Open Democracy*, 30 Jan 2017.

98   A. Gilligan, 'I did not betray David Kelly or reveal him as my source', *Observer*, 29 Aug 2010.

99   'Iraq War TV coverage "sanitised"', BBC News, 6 Nov 2003.

100 P. Dacre, The Hugh Cudlipp Lecture, 22 Jan 2007.

101 C. Higgins, 'The BBC: there to inform, educate, provoke and enrage?', *Guardian*, 16 Apr 2014.

102 Tim Davie speaking to BBC Radio 4's *Today* programme, 14 Oct 2024.

103 R. Urwin, 'Sarah Sands on the *Today* programme and why she left the BBC', *The Times*, 6 Sept 2020.

8. INTERVIEWS AND THE ART OF WAR

104 P. Bull and K. Mayer, 'How Not to Answer Questions in Political Interviews', *Political Psychology*, vol. 14, no. 4, Dec 1993.

105 P. Bull, 'Equivocation and the Rhetoric of Modernization: An Analysis of Televised Interviews with Tony Blair in the 1997 British General Election', *Journal of Language and Social Psychology*, vol. 19, iss. 2, Jun 2000.

106 T. Blair and M. Sheen, '"I Tried to Give Britain a Different Narrative": Tony Blair and Michael Sheen in conversation', *New Statesman*, 23 Mar 2022.

ENDNOTES

107 R. Day, '... *But with Respect*', Weidenfeld & Nicolson, 1993.

108 J. Paxman, 'How Do You Get a Politician to Tell the Truth?', *The Times*, 4 Apr 2015.

109 M. Odell, 'How I Persuaded Prince Andrew to Do That Car-crash Interview', *The Times*, 5 Apr 2024.

110 https://x.com/Dominic2306/status/1405827979029237762

111 R. Burley, *Why Is This Lying Bastard Lying to Me?: Searching for the Truth on Political TV*, Mudlark, May 2023.

112 'Taffy Brodesser-Akner, Profile Writer, on Getting Inside Subjects' Heads', *The New York Times*, 2 Aug 2019.

113 'Talking to Taffy Is Low Tech. And Intense.', *The New York Times*, 20 Mar 2019.

9. ETHICS ISN'T A COUNTY IN ENGLAND

114 D. Marchese, 'What It's Like to Be a Sociopath', *The New York Times*, 23 Feb 2024.

115 J. Duggan and N. Duffy, 'Nicola Bulley's Family Accuse "Shameful" TV crews and social media', *i*, 20 Feb 2023.

116 https://x.com/joshi/status/1627668513862176771

117 C. Newbould, 'Manchester Mill founder criticises Reach sites' Nicola Bulley coverage as family condemns "shameful" media intrusion', Prolific North, 20 Feb 2023.

118 S. White, A. Chamberlain and P. Jobling, 'Pale-faced man's first words to police after discovering body in search for Nicola Bulley', *Manchester Evening News*, 20 Feb 2023.

119 J. Holt, 'Exhausted and in the eye of a storm, St Michael's on Wyre waits after the news no one wanted', *Manchester Evening News*, 19 Feb 2023.

120 N. Wootton-Cane, 'In pictures: Scene in St Michael's on Wyre after body found in search for Nicola Bulley', *Manchester Evening News*, 19 Feb 2023.

121 A. Kindred and M. Gibson, 'Ex-detective from Channel 4 show *Hunted* labels Nicola Bulley police "utterly ludicrous"', *Manchester Evening News*, 18 Feb 2023.

122 J. Roger and T. Molloy, 'Seven key bombshells from Nicola Bulley's partner Paul Ansell as he speaks out on missing mum', *Manchester Evening News*, 11 Feb 2023.

123 M. Sullivan, '24 DAYS OF PAIN: Inside Nicola Bulley's police search using drones & choppers which drew blank until dog walkers found a body', *Sun*, 19 Feb 2023.

BREAKING

124 J. O'Connor, 'The Met and Murdoch: A cosy relationship that began in Wapping', *Guardian*, 18 Jul 2011.

125 S. Grealish, 'GRIM FIND: "Psychic" Jason Rothwell claims he found body during Nicola Bulley search before helping cops to recover tragic find', *Sun*, 20 Feb 2023.

126 T. Ball and F. Hamilton, 'Police Focused Search Five Miles from Where Nicola Bulley Was Found', *The Times*, 20 Feb 2023.

127 R. Marsden, 'Nicola Bulley's Relatives Fire Broadside at Sections of the Media and People Speculating on Social Media', *Daily Mail*, 20 Feb 2023.

128 I. Gallagher and J. Taylor, 'Nikki Is NOT an Unfit Mum', *Daily Mail*, 18 Feb 2023.

129 C. Tobitt, '"This is more than a news story for us": Why local journalists in Plymouth won't doorknock or show gunman's face', *Press Gazette*, 16 Aug 2021.

130 https://x.com/CarlEveCrime/status/1426987382772011012

131 https://x.com/jessmorcom/status/1426620224686727169

132 P. Smith, 'This Game Shows What It's Like When Journalists Keep Contacting People Caught Up in Tragic Events', *BuzzFeed News*, 29 Oct 2018.

133 https://x.com/danhett/status/866960257150529536?lang=en-GB

134 D. Barnett, 'Inside the World of the "Death Knock"', *Independent*, 4 Jun 2017.

135 Anonymous, 'Death Knocks: The dark side of journalism', 30 Sept 2014.

136 The original tweet has now been deleted, but I referenced this in a piece written at the time: M. Wright, 'Thin Ice', Conquest of the Useless, 14 Dec 2022.

137 https://x.com/SophieMHistory/status/1602731854813069322

138 Unbylined, 'The saddest 24 hours I would ever know', *WalesOnline*, 20 Oct 2006.

139 M. Sullivan and D. Keane, 'Sarah Suspect Linked to Sex Offence . . . Did Cops Fail to Act?', *Sun*, 12 Mar 2021.

140 D. Howbrook, 'Holly-Day in the Sun', *Sun*, 12 Mar 2021.

141 P. Patel, 'Police Officers Are Sickened by this Abhorrent Crime – I'll do all I can to protect women and girls', *Sun*, 12 Mar 2021.

142 A. Bland, 'Media Failed to Learn from Caroline Flack's Death, Her Mother Warns', *Guardian*, 12 Mar 2021.

143 W. Bolton, 'Teenager's Lust for Fame Led to Murder of Brianna', *Daily Telegraph*, 2 Feb 2024.

ENDNOTES

144   G. Milam, 'Brianna Ghey: Murdered Teenager's Father Says Killers "Will Never Change" as he describes "complete horror" of her death', *Sky News*, 3 Feb 2024.

145   H. Cristodoulou and S. Ridley, 'Monsters Caged', *Sun*, 5 Feb 2024.

146   W. Bolton, 'Doodled Hearts and Lists of Killers: Inside the diaries of teenage murderer', *Daily Telegraph*, 2 Feb 2024.

147   L. Hull, 'How Brianna Ghey's Warped Killer Watched Torture and Death on the Dark Web', *Daily Mail*, 20 Dec 2023.

148   T. Rawstorne and L. Hull, 'Evil with a Pretty Face', *Daily Mail*, 3 Feb 2024.

149   S. Vine, 'Their Normality Made Me Think … What If that Evil Had Been Germinating in My Own House?', *Mail on Sunday*, 2 Feb 2024.

150   M. Ridley, 'KING OF SCOOPS RIP John Kay – The legendary *Sun* reporter who broke Fleet Street's biggest stories', 8 May 2021.

151   Unbylined, '"Torment" of reporter who killed wife', *Guardian*, 13 Dec 1977.

10. THE COCK-UP/CONSPIRACY INTERFACE

152   A. Taylor, 'The Latest Political Scandal in London Has The Best Name Yet', *Business Insider*, 24 Sept 2012.

153   D. Uberti, 'Gate-keepers', *Columbia Journalism Review*, 2 Mar 2015.

154   W. Joseph Campbell, *Getting It Wrong: Debunking the Greatest Myths in American Journalism*, University of California Press, 2016.

155   M. Feldstein, 'Watergate Revisited', *American Journalism Review*, Aug/Sept 2004.

156   L. Stephenson, 'Uncovering the Secret State', *Bristol Cable*, 21 Nov 2017.

157   S. Glover, 'Shock horror! Britain spies on other nations: The Guardian rightly attacks the hacking of private phones – but glories in betraying Britain by revealing our State secrets', *Daily Mail*, 17 Jun 2013.

158   D. Ponsford, 'Guardian Spying Revelations Were in Breach of DA-Notice Guidance', *Press Gazette*, 19 Jun 2013.

159   L. Harding, *The Snowden Files: The Inside Story of the World's Most Wanted Man*, Guardian Faber Publishing, 2014.

160   L. Harding, 'Footage Released of Guardian Editors Destroying Snowden Hard Drives', *Guardian*, 31 Jan 2014.

161   E. MacAskill and P. Johnson, 'MI5 Head: "Increasingly aggressive" Russia a growing threat to UK', *Guardian*, 1 Nov 2016.

BREAKING

162   N. Hopkins, 'MI6 Returns to "Tapping up" in Effort to Recruit Black and Asian officers', *Guardian*, 2 Mar 2017.

163   M. Curtis, 'Why Does the *Guardian* Write So Many Puff pieces about GCHQ?', Declassified, 8 Mar 2024.

164   J. Jolly, 'Neurodivergent Women Sought for Jobs at GCHQ and BAE Systems', *Guardian*, 16 Nov 2022.

165   R. Booth, 'GCHQ Seeks to Increase Number of Female Coders to Tackle Threats', *Guardian*, 29 Aug 2022.

166   A. Topping, '"Huge Sense of Pride": The mothers who job-share counter-terrorism at GCHQ', *Guardian*, 15 May 2022.

167   S. Greenhill, 'Gagging Orders Are Out of Control, Says Andrew Marr as He Abandons High Court Injunction Over HIS Extra-marital Affair', *Daily Mail*, 26 Apr 2011.

168   O. Bowcott, 'Andrew Marr Superinjunction Challenge Cost "Tens of Thousands", Says Ian Hislop', *Guardian*, 26 Apr 2011.

169   D. Sabbagh, 'Johann Hari Denies Accusations of Plagiarism', *Guardian*, 29 Jul 2011.

170   D. Allen Green, 'The Tale of Mr Hari and Dr Rose', *New Statesman*, 15 Sept 2011.

171   J. Hari, 'Johann Hari: A personal apology', *Independent*, 15 Sept 2011.

172   D. Burnett, 'Is Everything Johann Hari Knows about Depression Wrong?', *Observer*, 8 Jan 2018

173   B. Johnson, 'This Cap on Bankers' Bonuses Is Like a Dead Cat – Pure Distraction', *Daily Telegraph*, 3 Mar 2013.

174   H. Stewart and P. Walker, 'Dominic Cummings Says Boris Johnson "Unfit for Job" of PM amid Covid Crisis', *Guardian*, 26 May 2021.

175   J. Mitchinson, 'My Paper Reported the Story Of The Boy On A Hospital Floor. Then Online Lies Took Over', *Guardian*, 11 Dec 2019.

176   A. Pearson, 'At a Crucial Crossroads in Britain's History, the BBC Got It Wrong – Thank God the People Got It Right', *Daily Telegraph*, 17 Dec 2019.

177   A. Pearson, 'Politicians Have Created a Multicultural Monster Beyond Control. Who Gets the Blame? We Do', *Daily Telegraph*, 28 Nov 2023.

ENDNOTES

11. WHEN YOU BECOME THE STORY

178   L. Salkeld, A. Martin and R. Kisiel, 'Could This Man Hold the Key to Joanna's Murder?', *Daily Mail*, 30 Dec 2010.

179   B. Cathcart, 'The Ordeal of Christopher Jefferies', *Financial Times*, 8 Oct 2011.

180   A. Storer, 'Chris's Ordeal: Who Is Christopher Jefferies and Where Is He Now?', *Sun*, 9 Sept 2021.

181   E. Ferguson, 'He's Behind You . . .', *Guardian*, 3 Nov 2002.

182   F. Starr, *Unwrapped*, Virgin Books, 2001.

183   T. Pegden, 'Freddie Starr: Woman reveals what REALLY happened on day he "ate her hamster"', *Daily Mirror*, 10 May 2019.

184   C. Gill, 'The Primetime BBC "Comedy" That's Like a Party Political Broadcast for Jeremy Corbyn', *Mail on Sunday*, 16 Dec 2018.

185   J. Gamp, 'Brexit Stage Right', *Sun*, 3 Dec 2019.

186   'Nish Kumar Booed Off Stage', Guido Fawkes, 3 Dec 2019.

187   https://x.com/piersmorgan/status/1223540671484776449

188   J. Heale and C. Hastings, 'Outrage at BBC *Horrible Histories* Brexit Show for "Trashing Britain" with Song that Says "Your British Things Are from Abroad and Most Are Stolen" on Day UK Left EU"', *Mail on Sunday*, 1 Feb 2020.

189   https://x.com/afneil/status/1223324986724769792

190   M. Parris, 'Double Standards of the Smug Liberal Left', *The Times*, 6 Apr 2019.

191   https://survivorsagainstterror.org.uk/wp-content/uploads/2023/01/Media-Report-Oct-2021-A-Second-Trauma-5.pdf.

192   J. Craven, 'Why Some Journalists Are Centering Trauma-Informed Reporting', *Nieman Reports*, 24 Aug 2002.

193   N. S. Miller, 'Trauma-informed Journalism: What it is, why it's important and tips for practicing it', *The Journalist's Resource*, 13 Apr 2002.

12. THE FUTURE OF THE NEWS

194   'What Will Newspapers Look Like in 20 Years?', *BBC News Magazine*, 14 Sept 2005.

195   A. Jahnke, 'David Carr: Journalism Is Still Serious, Just Different,' *BU Today*, 6 Mar 2014.

196   H. Cooper, 'On Liberia's Shore, Catching a New Wave', *The New York Times*, 22 Jan 2010.

BREAKING

197 B. Weiser and W. K. Rasbaum, 'Liberia Aids U.S. in Drug Fight', *The New York Times*, 1 Jun 2010.

198 D. Carvajal, 'Hunting for Liberia's Missing Millions', *The New York Times*, 30 May 2010.

199 D. Carr, 'Inviting in a Brash Outsider', *The New York Times*, 14 Feb 2010.

200 D. Carr, 'Its Edge Intact, Vice Is Chasing Hard News', *The New York Times*, 24 Aug 2014.

201 D. Carr, 'Ezra Klein Is Joining Vox Media as Web Journalism Asserts Itself', *The New York Times*, 26 Jan 2014.

202 A. Nicolau and S. Indap, 'The Fall of Vice: Private equity's ill-fated bet on media's future', *Financial Times*, 25 May 2023.

203 A. Ross Sorkin, R. Mattu, S. Kessler et al., 'Why BuzzFeed Is Closing Its News Division', *The New York Times*, 21 Apr 2023.

204 C. Warzel, 'The Internet of the 2010s Ended Today', *Atlantic*, 20 Apr 2023.

205 M. Hirschorn, 'End Times', *Atlantic*, Jan/Feb 2009.

206 J. Jarvis, 'The Cockeyed Economics of Metering Reading', *BuzzMachine*, 17 Jan 2010.

207 B. Grasmayer, 'Why The NY Times Paywall Business Model Is Doomed to Fail (Numbers)', 22 Mar 2011.

208 G. Satell, '5 Reasons Why The New York Times Paywall Will Fail (And Why It's Really Dumb)', *Toronto Digital*, 23 Mar 2011.

209 J. Peiser, 'The Rise of the Robot Reporter', *The New York Times*, 5 Feb 2019.

210 A. Majid, 'Swedish Daily *Aftonbladet* Finds People Spend Longer on Articles with AI-generated Summaries', *Press Gazette*, 26 Jul 2023.

211 F. Landymore, 'CNET Is Quietly Publishing Entire Articles Generated by AI', *Futurism*, 15 Jan 2023.

212 M. H. Dupré, '*Sports Illustrated* Published Articles by Fake, AI-Generated Writers', *Futurism*, 27 Nov 2023.

213 H. Arendt, 'Hannah Arendt: From an Interview', *New York Review*, 26 Oct 1978.

214 L. Reilly, 'TIME Magazine Lays Off 15% of Unionized Editorial Staff, Becoming Latest News Outlet to Slash Workforce', *CNN*, 23 Jan 2024.

215 M. Baron, *Collison of Power: Trump, Bezos, and the Washington Post*, St Martin's Press, 2023.

ENDNOTES

216 D. Froomkin, 'The *Washington Post* Has a Bezos problem', *Columbia Journalism Review*, 27 Sept 2022.

217 J. Stein, 'Jeff Bezos Spars with Biden White House Over Inflation', *Washington Post*, 16 May 2022.

218 C. Rampell, 'Democrats Need More Tough Love on Their Misguided Economic Policies', *Washington Post*, 16 May 2022.

219 B. Mullin and K. Robertson, 'Inside the *Washington Post*'s Decision to Stop Presidential Endorsements', *The New York Times*, 27 Oct 2024.

220 A. Perez and D. Sirota, 'When Jeff Bezos Tweets, He Wants His Journalists and Joe Biden to Listen', *Jacobin*, 23 May 2022.

221 M. Hastings, *Editor: A Memoir*, Macmillan, 2014.

222 R.K. Nielsen and M. Selva, 'More Important, But Less Robust? Five Things Everybody Needs to Know about the Future of Journalism', Reuters Institute for the Study of Journalism, Jan 2019.

223 'Rupert Murdoch: "Newspapers Will Change, Not Die"', *Independent*, 20 Mar 2006.